THE COLLECTED PLAYS OF
JOHN WHITING

Volume One

In Volume Two

THE COLLECTED PLAYS

OF

JOHN WHITING

VOLUME ONE

Edited by

Ronald Hayman

HEINEMANN

LONDON

Heinemann Educational Books Ltd

LONDON   MELBOURNE   EDINBURGH
SINGAPORE   JOHANNESBURG
TORONTO   AUCKLAND
IBADAN   HONG KONG
NAIROBI

SBN 435 23400 5

Published by
Heinemann Educational Books Ltd
48 Charles Street, London WIX 8AH
Printed in Great Britain by
Morrison & Gibb Ltd, London and Edinburgh

CONTENTS

ACKNOWLEDGMENTS

I AM most grateful to Mrs Jackie Whiting who was extremely kind and helpful in giving me access to unpublished material and newspaper cuttings, and to Dr Gabriele Scott Robinson who allowed me to make use of the valuable Ph.D thesis she wrote for London University on Whiting's work. It was through this that I learned of the existence of *Noman* and *The Nomads* and of the unpublished novel *Not a Foot of Land*. I have also drawn on the exhaustive bibliographical work she did.

INTRODUCTION

JOHN WHITING was one of the unluckiest playwrights in the history of the theatre. In the early fifties, London audiences weren't ready to listen very hard to the words in a play or to adjust to such a violent departure from the diet they were used to—theatrical reproductions of their own drawing-rooms, not as they actually were but as they would have wished them to be. Whiting's way of looking at things was very different and as theatrical incarnations of his vision, his plays were far too accurate and uncompromising to succeed at the box-office. Despite their failure, though, *Saint's Day* and *Marching Song* made an impact which helped to prepare the ground for Beckett and Pinter, but the success of their plays did nothing to help Whiting's.

The moods and movements of theatrical fashion are hard to chart and harder to explain. When *The Birthday Party* flopped at the Lyric, Hammersmith, in 1958, nobody could have predicted that Pinter would become fashionable. His use of working-class characters was very different from that of playwrights like Osborne and Wesker, and his use of working-class speech was highly stylized, but at least he was using both at a time when both were becoming fashionable. Whiting was using neither.

The lecture he gave on 'The Art of the Dramatist' at the Old Vic in 1957 shows he was quite aware that the easiest way of communicating with an audience was in 'the direct unornamented speech of everyday life' and in an effort to show why, for him, it was insufficient, he invented a snatch of conversation such as you might pick up any day in the street.

> Now look here I said I'm not having this I said and so he says What and I says I'm not having it I'm telling you I says up and down the stairs you were four times this morning telling him I was up and down I says in your boots with little Else trying to sleep oh I told him.

Kenneth Tynan afterwards commented that this piece of invention proved Whiting was a born playwright while his rejection of it proved he was determined not to be a playwright at all. Today the passage would probably be called Pinteresque, though none of Pinter's plays had been staged in 1957. And when *Conditions of Agreement,* Whiting's first play, written in 1948-9, was finally produced in 1965, critics like Penelope Gilliatt commented on the strong foretaste of Pinter in it. So the questions we have to ask are why his development was so different from Pinter's and why demotic speech was no use to him.

Both playwrights were deeply influenced by T. S. Eliot, but while Pinter took his cue from *Sweeney Agonistes,* Whiting was more affected by *Murder in the Cathedral* and *The Family Reunion.* Stella's big speech in Act Two of *Saint's Day* is a direct parody of Eliot. But while critics in the late forties were counting on a renaissance of verse drama to let fresh air into our stale drawing-room naturalism, Whiting showed that a heightened prose dialogue was far more viable than verse. His plays are much more 'poetic' than *The Confidential Clerk* or *The Elder Statesman* but the poetry is in the pressure of the situation and in the atmosphere he conjures out of his locales. Whereas Eliot, even in his earlier plays, never makes his people as interesting as what they say, Whiting harnesses the dialogue fully to the characterization, creating people who are highly conscious, sensitive, sometimes pathetic, and above all capable of being altered profoundly by the situations they find themselves in.

The turning points in *Saint's Day, Marching Song, The Gates of Summer* and *The Devils* involve personality changes which are so basic it's no exaggeration to call them conversions. The characters fall in and out of love not with each other but with life and death. But these moments of conversion are not directly dramatized. We see the beginning of a process, we see the end result and we may see intermediate signs of what's happening but we don't know exactly when Procathren loses his faith in man or when Rupert Forster gets whatever it is he needs from Dido to make him decide to go on living or when he reverses his decision or when Grandier fixes on a course of self-destruction. But we do see how and we do see why these moments of conversion occur. To dramatize them too directly would be to write melodrama.

None of these conversions could possibly have been treated adequately in simple language and as Whiting's technique improved, he became not more but less explicit about them. Procathren's conversion is the one which suffers most from obscurity in the writing and his big speech in Act Three of *Saint's Day* is the hardest passage in the whole of Whiting's work for an audience to follow. When the play was in rehearsal at the Arts, both Alec Clunes (the artistic director) and Stephen Murray (the producer) urged him to make it more explicit. But the reason for the obscurity is that it's already too explanatory: Procathren is being made to explain things that he can't himself understand.

What he has discovered—both in himself and in the world outside —is the violence which is there all the time underneath the civilized surface. What he decides to do is to revenge himself with an act of violence, ordering Melrose and the other soldiers to kill Paul and Charles. The hardest point for the audience to follow is the connection between the discovery and the revenge. But there's no logic in this connection and Procathren can't possibly explain it. On the contrary, it's because he's so terrified at losing control, as he did when the pistol went off in his hands, that he's compulsively trying to regain control by a willed act of revenge. Against what? There's no reason for picking Paul and Charles as his victims but there was no reason for Stella's death either.

Tragedy always rests on the playwright's profound conviction that the universe is not and cannot be governed by reason. The gods are not just and no programme of political or economic changes can make them alter their ways. Tragedy is a resounding vote of no confidence not only in the powers that be but in the powers that could supplant them. This is why there can be no Christian tragedy and no Marxist tragedy. Tynan's argument that there can be no twentieth-century tragedy was worked out on roughly Marxist lines. 'There is today hardly an aspect of human suffering (outside the realm of medicine) for which politics, psychiatry and environmental psychology cannot offer at least a *tentative* solution.' And he concluded that tragedy had 'little to say to a rebellious generation obsessed by the danger of imminent mega-deaths'. For Whiting, the existence of the bomb made it all the more necessary to look closely at the forces operating inside human nature that had brought it into existence. Some of the phrases in Procathren's speech may, as Christopher Fry has said, allude directly to the bomb. What's more important though is the way his behaviour epitomizes the sub-animal capacity for destruction in human nature. And it's striking that before he carries out Procathren's instructions, Melrose is made to argue, just as the American pilots who dropped the bombs on Hiroshima and Nagasaki may have argued with themselves and just as the Nazi war criminals argued at Nuremberg, that they were only acting under orders.

Whiting's vision of life is essentially a tragic one. The whole of his work is characterized by its sensitivity to the violence of unreason and the impossibility of reasoning about violence. This is why soldiering features so prominently in his plays: the soldier embodies an attempt to synthesize discipline and killing, order and chaos. Even in *A Penny for a Song* and *The Gates of Summer,* where the attempts at military action are comic, tragedy is never very far from the surface. What Sir Timothy Bellboys and Lamprett do to defend their country against a Napoleonic invasion is ludicrous because they're so unaware of what warfare—and life—are really about. But the comedy never conceals Whiting's awareness of their fear of looking into the gulf and the brevity of the pleasure that the lovers snatch at. Predominantly the mood is a happy one here but his other comedy, *The Gates of Summer,* is bitter and nihilistic. It's comic only because John Hogarth, the hero, falls so short of the ideal he sets for himself. Rupert Forster emerges as a tragic hero because the play makes us believe in him as a man who'd prefer an honourable death to a messy life; John Hogarth aims consciously at heroism but he's too small a man to do anything but survive in a comic mess.

These characters couldn't have been created in demotic speech any more than *Murder in the Cathedral* could have been written in the language of *Sweeney*. A 'Pinteresque' tragedy is unthinkable because that kind of realism over speech-patterns tends to make the playwright detach himself from his characters and find comedy in the fact that that is the way they talk.

Altogether, our present cultural milieu is extremely inimical to tragedy. We may now have pop music, pop art and pop theatre but we'll never have pop tragedy because tragedy could never be made to appeal to a mass audience.

Already in 1957, when Whiting gave his Old Vic lecture, it was apparent that the mass media and the socialization of education would have an enormous effect on art. If the vast new audiences wanted art at all, they wouldn't want the same sort of art, and Whiting took a pessimistic view of the changes the arts would have to undergo if they were to survive. The individual voice, he said, would have to give way to the collective voice. To communicate with the new mass audience, the artist would need a public address system.

Tynan wrote a mocking review of the lecture:

It was an historic occasion. In the annals of the theatre it may indeed
come to be regarded as Romanticism's Last Stand, the ultimate cry of
the artist before being engulfed by the mass, the final protest of indi-
vidualism before being inhaled and consumed by the ogre of popular
culture. One pictured, as each phrase of Mr Whiting's elegant jeremiad
came winging out into the dark, some attenuated hermit saint bravely
keeping his chin up while being sucked through the revolving doors of
a holiday camp. Even before he began, I felt I was in the presence of a
condemned man. There was resignation in the very set of his gentle,
scolded face, and the expression in his large dark eyes seemed to anticipate, even to embrace, defeat. He stood before us like one lately
descended from an ivory tower, blinking in the glare and bustle of day.

But just over ten years later Tynan himself was hailing the Beatles'
Sergeant Pepper record as 'Britain's most important contribution to
the arts in 1967', and intellectuals galore, falling over each other in
their eagerness to commit the same *trahison des clercs*, are taking their
oaths of allegiance to pop music as 'the classics of today'.

Oddly enough, Tynan's accolade for the Beatles is based mainly
on the Lennon-McCartney words. It's quite fashionable now for
intellectuals to discuss these lyrics just as if they were poems, though
Paul McCartney has made no secret of his amusement at people who
interpret words like 'She was just seventeen' as meaning anything
more than that she was just seventeen. I don't know whether anyone
would argue that John Lennon must be a greater writer than John
Whiting because he reaches a greater audience or that he's more in
touch with the times. But no-one seemed to find it odd that *In his
Own Write* should find its way into the repertoire of our National
Theatre before any play of Whiting's.

The fact has to be faced though that, apart from *The Devils*,
Whiting's plays have not been successful with audiences, and the
question 'why?' has to be answered. With the very minor exception
of the silent and anonymous boy in *No Why*, Whiting fails to provide
a character for the audience to identify with. Paul is a brilliant and
forceful creation but hardly an attractive one, and English audiences
can't be expected to go beyond a certain point in sympathizing with
a German general who has shot a small boy through the head and
ordered his tanks to advance over the bodies of a crowd of children.
John Hogarth seems at first to be more attractive but he turns out to
be cynical and weak. Grandier certainly gets our sympathy at the end

of *The Devils* when he's a passive victim of his enemies, but he's bound to antagonize some of the audience when he turns out to be a profligate priest and most of the rest when he abandons the pregnant Phillipe, in spite of having joined himself to her in a secret wedding ceremony.

Whiting couldn't have been unaware of how much audiences like to identify with a character, so why did he make the same mistake again and again? If it was a mistake. I don't think it was a simple matter of forgetting or refusing to make his heroes likable. He was concerned very seriously with the questions of how an individual rose above the rest of humanity, and of whether he became less human in the process of doing so. Rupert's tragedy is that he does and finds out too late. Paul and Charles have, in effect, exiled themselves from humanity in retreating from society and Grandier is prevented by society from being fully a man.

The characters could all have been made more attractive easily enough if they had been seen less clear-sightedly or weighed less scrupulously in the moral balance. But like Beckett, Whiting had absolute integrity as a dramatist. He consistently used his talent and his technique to embody his vision as fully and as honestly as possible in dramatic form. The writer who goes all out to please his audiences, planning his play or his poem or his lyric in terms of the effects he wants it to make on them is an entertainer. Whiting was an artist.

This is not to say that he was unconcerned about the problems of communication. *Saint's Day* was written mainly as a technical exercise: at the time of writing it he thought it would never get a production. No doubt he'd have written it differently if he'd known it would. Certainly he wrote *Marching Song* very differently, taking great pains to make the meaning clear. The texture is very rich and the surface of the action very crowded, but the symbolism is fully integrated into the naturalistic structure and the play's statements are always perfectly lucid.

Unfortunately, the critics never forgave him for *Saint's Day* and many of them went on reviewing it when they were writing their notices of *Marching Song*. Some of the notices it got are quite inexplicable except in the rather dim light of press reactions to the earlier play.

And unfortunately reviewers influence not only other reviewers but audiences too—both the audience that stays away and the audience that comes. Whiting could only have succeeded as a playwright if an audience had been created for him, as an audience was created for Beckett and for Pinter. If theatre critics had liked Whiting and if the Royal Court had put his plays on, he could possibly have become fashionable. George Devine committed himself in 1951 to the view that *Saint's Day* 'splits wide open the conventional forms of playwriting and allies itself with the other modern arts in a way that no other play has done. It helps the theatre to bridge the gap of time which exists between itself and other forms of artistic expression.' In 1956, when he was made artistic director of the Royal Court, his intention was to put on plays by Whiting there, but in fact he never did.

At this stage, after the failure of *A Penny for a Song, Saint's Day* and *Marching Song,* it wouldn't have been easy to build up an audience for Whiting. But it wouldn't have been impossible and it should have been done. Had he gone on writing in the way that he started, he could have become a great playwright. But for six years he stopped writing for the theatre and when he started again with *The Devils* it was in a totally different vein. Quite apart from being an adaptation, *The Devils* is written like a screenplay.

What happened in the six years? *The Gates of Summer* was finished in 1954, just before *Marching Song* was put on. Thanks to his agent he'd started to earn some money by writing for the cinema as early as 1952 and between 1954 and 1960 he wrote ten complete screenplays. In August 1956 *The Gates of Summer* started its chaotic tour, which folded in Leeds in October. In November he started to write notes for a novel called *Noman.* In 1957 Peter Hall commissioned him to write a curtain-raiser for the translation he'd done of Anouilh's *Le Voyageur sans Bagages.* He wrote *No Why* but Peter Hall said it would empty the theatre and instead Whiting did a translation of Anouilh's *Madame de* . . . In 1958 he wrote the first half of the play *Noman,* abandoned it, wrote the first half of another play and abandoned that too, writing nothing else for the theatre till Peter Hall commissioned *The Devils.* Then in September 1961 he started trying to rewrite *Noman* as *The Nomads.* He made four abortive attempts. The last is dated January 1963 and in June he died of cancer.

Strictly speaking, this isn't a collection of Whiting's plays but of Whiting's scripts. A play is only a play when it's in performance and a script is only a score for a sequence of theatrical effects, some of which are made through the words. There are three ways of reading a script:

(1) you can be remembering a performance you've seen;

(2) you can be imagining a performance; or

(3) you can just read the words.

In practice you can't do any one of these things. You're always doing at least two at the same time, if not all three.

These plays of Whiting's belong to the future but they also belong specifically to the time when they were written and staged. This is why I have prefaced each play with a few notes on its stage history so far. I hope these notes will soon be out of date.

BIOGRAPHICAL OUTLINE

1917   born in Salisbury on 15 November, the son of an army captain.

1918   his father was discharged from the army because of an injury to his lung. He moved, with the family, to Northampton, where he started a legal practice.

1930   John was sent to school at Taunton.

1934–6   at R.A.D.A.

1936–7   a series of acting jobs including repertory at Aberystwyth and small parts for Robert Atkins at Regent's Park Open Air Theatre.

1937   repertory at Bideford, where Jackie Mawson was a member of the company.

1939   joined the anti-aircraft section of the Royal Artillery.

1940   got his second stripe just before he married Jackie.

1942   commissioned.

1944   discharged because of sinus trouble.

1944–6   repertory in Peterborough for three months, followed by a season at Harrogate.

       wrote the unpublished novel *Not a Foot of Land.*

1946   his father died five months after Jonathan, the first of his four children, was born.

       played in Sean O'Casey's *Oak Leaves and Lavender* at the Lyric, Hammersmith.

       wrote a one-act comedy *No More a-Roving* and started writing stories and plays for radio, including a play called *Paul Southman.*

1947–51   repertory in York and Scarborough.

1947   wrote the radio play *Eye Witness* and started on *Saint's Day.*

1948–9   wrote *Conditions of Agreement.*

1949   two of his stories, *Stairway* and *Valediction,* were broadcast. the play *Eye Witness* was broadcast on 18 February and the play *The Stairway* on 30 December.

       finished *Saint's Day* and started *A Penny for a Song,* which he finished before the end of the year.

1951   *A Penny for a Song* at the Haymarket.
        he joined the Gielgud company at the Phoenix to play a
        Gaoler in *The Winter's Tale*.
        Saint's Day won the Festival of Britain play competition at
        the Arts Theatre and he started work on *Marching Song*.

1952   finished it and through his agent (A. D. Peters) got work
        writing for films.
        played a Sexton in the Gielgud *Much Ado about Nothing* at
        the Phoenix and played the Abbot of Westminster in
        Gielgud's production of *Richard II* with Paul Scofield. It
        opened on 24 December at the Lyric, Hammersmith.

1953   started writing *The Gates of Summer*.

1954   finished the first draft just before *Marching Song* was put on.

1957   wrote the one-act play *No Why*.

1960   Peter Hall commissioned *The Devils*.

1961   it opened in February at the Aldwych and went into the
        repertoire.
        in June he started reviewing plays for *The London Magazine*.

1962   cancer was diagnosed in the winter and he was treated as an
        out-patient at the hospital.

1963   he went into hospital a week before he died on 16 June.

CONDITIONS OF AGREEMENT

INTRODUCTORY NOTE

THIS WAS written in 1948–9 while he was also working on *Saint's Day*. *Conditions of Agreement* wasn't performed until October 1965 when Christopher Denys directed it for the Bristol Old Vic at their Little Theatre with Eithne Dunne (Emily), Terence Hardiman (Peter Bembo), Frank Middlemass (A.G.), David Burke (Nicholas) and Jane Lapotaire (Patience).

Irving Wardle wrote in *The Times*:

John Whiting gets frequent acknowledgment as a progenitor of the new British drama but if any play of his pre-figures the comedy of menace it is this unknown early piece. . . . The affinity with Pinter is particularly close.

PERSONS

EMILY DOON

PETER BEMBO

A. G.

NICHOLAS DOON

PATIENCE DOON

The scene is laid in the living-room of Emily Doon's house, in the present.

ACT ONE

Time is the present.

The scene is the large living-room on the ground floor of Mrs Doon's house in a small town near Oxford.

The house was built in 1740. The room is of great beauty. Details of decoration are a massive fireplace with plasterwork overmantle and an exceptional rococo doorcase for the only door into the room. The wooden panelling of the walls is painted white. Four windows are set to look over the street: the room, although on the ground floor, is set above the street. The furniture is of a period: there is a piano. Set beside the fireplace is an oil-painting of a woman.

It is the afternoon of a Thursday in September. The sun is shining strongly through the drawn curtains.

EMILY DOON *is asleep in a chair, her feet resting on a low stool. A thin woollen shawl covers her. As she sleeps, her mouth slightly open, there is only the faintest whisper of a snore from her. A small, cheap alarm clock stands on the arm of her chair. On a low table before her a tray of tea is set with a silver kettle over an unlit spirit-lamp.*

EMILY *is fifty-eight years of age. Beneath her shawl covering she is gaily dressed.*

The alarm clock rings, waking EMILY. *She starts up: 'What!' she cries and then, realizing her position and that no one has spoken, taps herself reprovingly on the forehead. She switches off the alarm of the clock. Rising, she takes up the shawl, folds it and places it beneath the cushion of the chair. She stands before the tea-table taking a rapid inventory of the contents: she is satisfied. She goes to the mantelpiece, looks at herself again and grimaces. She then replaces both spectacles and mirror on the mantelpiece.* EMILY *goes to the window and, slightly drawing back the curtain, looks into the street. She is blowing her nose when she sees someone known passing in the street. She hurriedly steps back and regards this person furtively until they are out of sight. She pulls back the curtains and then comes down to her former chair and takes up the alarm clock: this she puts to her ear as she carries it to, and places it away in, the desk. From the desk she takes a*

5

powder-box and powders her face, running her fingers over her lips. After putting the powder back in the desk she goes to the table and takes up the tea-pot and the kettle. She goes out of the room. The telephone rings immediately. EMILY *returns to the room and carries the kettle and tea-pot to their places before answering the telephone.*

EMILY: Hullo—yes, this is Emily. That's A. G., isn't it? You might have known it would be me. You know there's no one else in the house. What? I don't know anything about that. You'd better ask Nicholas—he made it. Yes, I expect him this afternoon. Well, I suppose so. It's usual to bring one's wife back from the honeymoon, isn't it? Look, A. G. It seems absurd for you to ring me up as much as you do when you live next door. Five times in the last two days. I mean, if I go to the window now I can see you talking on the phone. Why don't you call and talk to me? Yes, I know that, but—What's that? Coming to my door now? On the steps? Is it anyone you know? What's he look like? Yes, I am expecting someone. (*The front door bell rings.*) He's just rung the bell. I must go and answer it. Yes, well, come and see Nicholas about that, A. G. Any time. I must go now. (*The door bell rings again.*) Yes. Yes. Goodbye.

    She puts down the receiver and goes quickly out of the room, leaving the door open. There is a pause. PETER BEMBO *enters. He slowly crosses the room. A moment later* EMILY *returns, coming into the room and shutting the door behind her.*

PETER (*he turns, smiling, to face her*): How are you, Emily?

EMILY: I'm well, thank you, Peter.

PETER: You expected me this afternoon, didn't you?

EMILY: Yes. That is, I didn't know it would be you. I knew someone was coming but I didn't know who.

PETER: You got my letter.

EMILY: Yes. This morning. But you know I always found your signature completely illegible and you can't expect me to remember your handwriting after twenty-three years.

PETER: I'm sorry. I wrote the letter in a train—perhaps it was worse than usual. It is my precaution always to type the envelopes.

EMILY: Surely there's no point in that as when the letter arrives it can't be read. Sit down. (PETER *sits.*) We'll have some tea. (*She puts her hands to her eyes.*) I'm so sorry but I've been asleep and I'm not really awake. Yet I am awake, aren't I, Peter?

PETER: Oh, yes. Twenty-three years since we've seen each other but in this moment we are both here, both awake and I'd like some tea very much indeed. (*He takes up a small hand-bell from the tray and rings it.*)

EMILY: I'm alone here. I must go myself. (*She takes up the tea-pot and kettle. She indicates the spirit lamp.*) That thing never works. (*She goes out of the room.* PETER *rises to look at the portrait of the woman. He reverses the picture to examine the frame. An opened letter is on the mantelpiece. He picks this up, peeping into the envelope. He takes two snapshots from the envelope, and looks at them. He does all this unhurriedly, with no secrecy and it is only by coincidence he has returned the photographs and letter to the mantelpiece when* EMILY *re-enters.*)

EMILY: I found your letter in the kitchen. (*She unfolds it.* PETER *returns to his chair.*)

PETER: Should I pour this out?

EMILY: No. Leave it for a moment. I've only just made it. Now! How anyone could be expected to read that signature as Peter Bembo is beyond me. It looks like a prescription for something.

PETER: If it's so very peculiar I should have thought you'd have remembered it—or remembered me—

EMILY: In the three years I knew you your signature changed about fifteen times.

PETER: Unintentionally. Probably my signature lacked uniformity because my life lacked stability.

EMILY: You must have been the despair of your bank.

PETER: I didn't have a bank.

EMILY: Have you one now?

PETER: No.

EMILY: Anything in the old sock or under the mattress?

PETER: If that is a joke I don't understand it.

EMILY: Have you any money?

PETER: No. (EMILY *rises and goes to the window. She stands looking down into the street. There is a pause.*) Can I have some tea now?

EMILY: Of course. I'm sorry. (*She returns slowly to the tea-table.*) What has happened to your eye? (*She refers to the black patch worn by Peter over his left eye.*)

PETER: It's a permanent loss. From about ten years ago.

EMILY: How? (*She is pouring the tea.*)

PETER: A long and, I think, very funny story—

EMILY: Bembo would have sawn off his legs to make the children laugh so it is only right he should think losing an eye very funny. You're still the clown.

PETER: One cannot follow the profession of circus clown and for forty years rely on physical deformity and grotesque mischance for success without retaining some—

EMILY: There's been no mention of you for years. In the Press.

PETER: I am old: done with. (*Pause.*) Still laughable, perhaps. Yes?

EMILY (*she smiles*): Yes. When did you retire?

PETER: About fifteen years ago.

EMILY: And what have you been doing since?

PETER: Nothing. I've been living in Armenia.

EMILY (*she looks at the envelope of Peter's letter*): I hadn't noticed this. It's not addressed to Emily Doon but to Emily Heitland.

PETER: What?

EMILY: My name is Doon now.

PETER: Oh, yes. Lambert mentioned your marriage—

EMILY: Lambert? Good gracious!

PETER: Yes. I went to see him to get your address.

EMILY: I haven't seen him since I—Of course, he was our only mutual acquaintance. What's he doing now?

PETER: He's editing a hairdresser's trade journal.

EMILY: Poor Lambert! Probably still combining the brain and manners of a sparrow with an abundance of misdirected energy. I remember my mother telling me one day, 'If you're lucky you'll marry a man like Mr Lambert.' That's what she said. Lambert was nineteen at the time. Worthy! Oh, dear me, worthy! (*She pauses.*) I married John.

PETER: John, was it?

EMILY: John Doon. He was a soldier.

PETER: You—

EMILY: He was killed. He was a hero.

PETER: What?

EMILY (*loudly*): He was a hero. (*She takes up Peter's letter again.*) This letter of yours came and I thought at first it was a bill or circular. I nearly didn't read it immediately. No one except tradesmen address their letters to me on a typewriter.

PETER: Don't you look at bills?

EMILY: Of course I do. And I pay them.

PETER: He left you money?

EMILY: Don't be a fool, Peter. What soldier has ever died and left any money?

PETER: Soldiers and circus clowns, eh? The understanding of their affinity might be difficult by any but their widows.

EMILY: Listen. Is there anything in this to indicate who you might be? (*She reads.*) 'Dear Emmy—'

PETER: That should have been a clue. Does anyone else call you Emmy?

EMILY: Sometimes my son.

PETER: Ah! You have a son?

EMILY: Yes. Nicholas.

PETER: The dark boy with the girl in the photographs? (*He indicates the mantelpiece.*)

EMILY: What? Oh, yes. Yes, that's his wife. They're on their honeymoon. They come back today. (*She pauses.*) When did—?

PETER: I had a look at them when you were out of the room. (*He points to the portrait.*) Who's that?

EMILY: Me.

PETER: I'm so sorry. I—(*breaks off*) Nicholas is a good-looking boy.

EMILY: I suppose you must say that. Yes, he's—I don't like him very much. (*She reads.*) 'Something hotel. Something Street, London. (*She makes a resigned gesture.*) Dear Emmy—I am in London after—'

PETER: Yes. I remember exactly what I said. More important, I remember exactly what you said the last time we met. You said, 'Goodbye, you damned old clown.' Those were your last words to me before I went to—Where on earth was I going that time?

EMILY: You were fooling about to the last moment.

PETER: Never thought I'd see you again. I have not come back to disturb you but I can tell you your first words to me. 'Please stand up.'

EMILY (*she begins to laugh*): At the Charity Dance for Crippled Children. 'Mr Peter Bembo, the famous clown,' the Lady Mayoress said, introducing us.

PETER: 'This is Miss Emily Heitland, one of our committee,' she said.

EMILY: And you said, 'How d'you do,' and stood on your head. Your trousers slipped down to your knees and showed your yellow socks. I stood before you, your face at my feet, with my hand stretched out like a fool. All around us the children laughed and clattered their little wooden legs.

PETER: Such antics were expected of me.

EMILY: Yes, I remember. (*She pauses.*) Dear Bembo. I was a little afraid of you and I couldn't understand then why the children were not afraid.

PETER: The children were never afraid.

EMILY: I only realized that from performances. There was your trick of leading a child from the audience whilst the band—what was that tune?

PETER: 'The Hill where Melchen Lives.' A child's song—forgotten now.

EMILY: You led the child out to hold your paper hoop. Never once in all the times I saw you do that was the child afraid.

PETER: Never once at any time was the child afraid. There was never a tear shed, except of laughter, at my performances.

EMILY: You're boasting.

PETER: God knows, Emmy, I have little enough to boast of now. Leave me that.

EMILY: I meant it most gently. (*She looks towards the window.*)

PETER: You are expecting someone. Who is it?

EMILY: Nicholas and Patience.

PETER: No one else? (EMILY *does not answer.*) Someone else is expected here. (*He rises, speaking.*) So, quickly! My intention was to talk about the present, not the past. And so, Emmy, my love—
    There are three short, nervous rings at the door-bell. Simultaneously with the first ring of the door-bell the telephone begins to ring.

EMILY: Nonsense, Peter! (*She points to the portrait.*) You had forgotten me.

PETER: No! (*There is a pause.*) Which shall I— (EMILY *goes quickly from the room.* PETER *answers the telephone.*) Hullo. Yes, this is Mrs Doon's house. No. No, I am not A. G. My name is Bembo. Would you like to—Who is that? Nicholas? Oh, yes; your mother will only be a moment—I say she'll be back in a moment. What? Very well. I'll tell her. (EMILY *and* A. G. *enter.*) Here she is. Will you speak to her? Oh. Oh, very well. A quarter of an hour. Yes. Yes, I'll tell her. Goodbye. (PETER *puts down the receiver and turns to Emily. He is startled to see A. G. standing beside Emily who he thought to be alone.*) I—Your son, Emily—Nicholas. He'll be here in a quarter of an hour. I asked him if he would speak to you but he said, no.

EMILY: Thank you, Peter. This is A. G. Our neighbour. He lives on that side—No! on that side. A. G., this is Peter Bembo, a very old friend of mine.

A. G.: How do you do.

PETER: How do you do.

They shake hands.

A. G. (*there is a pause*): Emily, I really came to return this. (*He is carrying a strange piece of machinery.*) It doesn't work.

EMILY: So you said on the phone. Did you try it clamped to the edge of a table?

A. G.: Yes. I followed the instructions you wrote out for me most carefully but I can't get it to work at all.

EMILY: The electric current is the same in both our houses, isn't it?

A. G.: I think so. I don't really know.

EMILY: It worked all right in this house. We'll ask Nicholas when he comes in. Have you had tea?

A. G.: Yes, thank you.

EMILY: Well, sit down. You're not in any hurry, are you?

A. G.: No. (*He sits, holding the machinery on his knees.*)

EMILY: More tea, Peter?

PETER: No, thank you. (*He turns away to the window.*)

A. G. (*after a pause*): It's a special reading lamp Nicholas has invented for me.

PETER (*suddenly realizing he is being spoken to and not having heard*): What's that?

A. G. (*louder*): It's a special reading lamp Nicholas has invented for me. My eyes are not at all good now and I am engaged on work needing much reading and writing.

PETER: I see.

A. G.: Yes, I am writing my memoirs and I had hoped this lamp would help me when I work at nights but I can't get it to light. I clamped it firmly to the edge of the table and followed the instructions. (*He takes a slip of paper from his pocket.*) These are the instructions Emily wrote out for me. One: clamp to edge of table by means of screws. Two: connect—

EMILY: You still have your hat on, A. G. Take it off.

He does so, placing it on the lamp on his knees.

A. G.: I did all this and yet it wouldn't work.

EMILY: We'll ask Nicholas when he comes in.

A. G.: I'll leave the instructions too. Nicholas may find them wrong.

EMILY: He dictated them to me. I wrote exactly what he said.

A. G.: I'll leave them, though. (*He puts the lamp, his hat and the instructions on the floor beside his chair.*) Mrs Barton tried it but it didn't work.

EMILY: How is Mrs Barton?

A. G.: She's very well, thank you. She had a cold but she's better now.

EMILY: I haven't seen her for some time. (*To* PETER.) Mrs Barton looks after A. G. She's quite an oddity. How many children has she now, A. G.?

A. G.: Nine. Do you know, I have to give each of them a birthday and a Christmas present. Eighteen presents a year and each one different. I am just beginning to note down ideas for Christmas presents now, three months before: but I've got two birthdays before Christmas. It makes it almost a life work. (*He begins to feel for his notebook but* EMILY *interrupts him.*)

EMILY: Is the husband out of prison yet?

A. G.: Barton? Oh, yes. He does odd jobs for me.

EMILY: Are you sure you won't have some tea?

A. G.: Quite sure, thank you. (*Speaking very much louder than he had intended to Peter.*) Who are you? What are you doing here?

PETER: I beg your pardon.

EMILY: A. G.! You mustn't shout at Peter like that.

A. G.: I'm so sorry. I thought Mr Bembo was deaf.

    PETER *and* EMILY *look at each other.*

PETER: What gave you that idea?

A. G.: I don't really know. You gave the impression when I first spoke to you that you didn't hear me.

PETER: You spoke very quietly.

A. G.: Yes, I suppose so. I'm sorry. Tell me, are you—? But it was years ago. There was a circus clown, Bembo. He was called, 'Bembo, The Clown'—almost as if to—well, to imply there was no other clown in the world. I saw him once as 'Bembo, El Bufoncillo'. That's Spanish. Many years ago now. Must be dead now.

PETER: I am 'Bembo, The Clown'.

A. G.: Are you? Not dead, then?

PETER: Not yet, no.

A. G.: But you haven't performed—

PETER: For fifteen, sixteen years. No, I am, as they say, retired.

A. G.: It is most startling. (*To* EMILY.) My wife, you know— (*To* PETER.) She died many years ago before I came to live here. She—

EMILY: Of course! But not at one of his— (*As she indicates* PETER *she is interrupted by* A. G.)

A. G.: She died, sir, at the circus during one of your performances. *There is a pause.*

PETER: What did you say?

A. G.: She died, sir—

PETER: A death! It was never mentioned to me.

A. G.: Please! You mustn't distress yourself.

PETER: Distress myself! But this is most important. 'Never a tear except of laughter.' (*To* EMILY.) You remember I said that was the only remaining boast I could make.

EMILY: Ask him.

PETER: I will. Now, sir. I want you to tell me when and where this death of your wife occurred. The remembering of such things may make you unhappy but it is important to me. I am a stranger to you and I realize such things are difficult to retell to a stranger. But if I can impress upon you the importance of this knowledge to me I am sure—

A. G.: Certainly I will tell you.

EMILY *suddenly laughs aloud.*

PETER: Thank you.

A. G.: Twenty years ago. I was forty. I had been married three years.

PETER *is listening intently.*

EMILY *lights a cigarette. As she is doing so* A. G. *stops speaking until the cigarette is lit.* PETER *regards her during the interruption with a sudden hostile irritation.*

Helen—the name has never become strange to me— (*He stops.*)

PETER: Go on.

A. G.: Helen was ten years younger than me. We had wished during the three years of our marriage for children. In that third year Helen underwent an examination which proved that she was unable to bear children.

PETER: I can dispense, sir, with these more personal details. I only wish to know—

A. G.: The knowledge of this distressed her considerably.

PETER: But of course. I understand. It is natural in a woman—

A. G.: This distress, probably not apparent to a casual observer at the time, manifested itself in a highly nervous state. So much so that I determined to take her for a holiday in an attempt to divert her brooding. I was also determined to prove to her that she and I, alone, were self-sufficient and could live full and definite lives although childless. We travelled to Spain. For the first few weeks it appeared that my resolves generally were to be realized. She was almost happy. My mind was at rest as to my business in England— my brother was left in charge—and I was able to attend to her and give her my interest and understanding. After the third week we went to Burgos. When we entered the city by car we saw the advertisements for the circus. 'Bembo, El Bufoncillo' greeted us. There was one show to be given in the evening of the following day.

PETER (*with almost a shout*): Yes! I remember! Yes!

A. G.: She had a strange liking for the circus—

PETER: Ha!

A. G.: —and an almost childlike understanding of the clown's antics which have always remained completely incomprehensible to me. We spent that night at an hotel and I remember that, although we were both tired after the journey, I made love to her. The last thing she said to me before falling asleep was, 'Will you take me to the circus tomorrow?'

There is a long pause until A. G. *continues.*

The following evening we went to the circus. You say you remember, Mr Bembo. Perhaps you remember the stands around the open-air ring you used that day.

PETER: The local authorities would not—

A. G.: There was a fault in the erection of those stands. It went unnoticed. Helen and I were forced by being late to sit far from the ring and high in the back row of the stand. Thirty feet up—would you say thirty feet, Mr Bembo?

PETER: Don't be absurd! You can hardly expect me to remember. (*He speaks to* EMILY *in defiance.*) This is only a most trivial incident to me.

A. G.: I should say quite as high as that. We sat and watched the beginning of the performances. Mr Bembo, the stands were most ill-constructed for Helen's feet as she sat were clear of the planking —a fact which touched me considerably at the time. Admittedly, she was a small woman but you must confess, Mr Bembo, it is not comfortable to sit without your feet firmly planted. (*He pauses.*) You, sir, had begun your antics. You had crawled beneath the horse, examined its mouth and had been snapped at, examined its feet and had been stamped upon. You had mounted and fallen;

remounted with aid and again fallen. The child had come forward from the audience to hold that great paper hoop before you. The horse had charged forward, halted, and you had sailed from his back, through the air, through the hoop and had landed in the sand. There was such laughter at that! It was then, during the laughter, that Helen turned to me and complained of sickness. She said she could not hear the laughter she recognized in the faces around us. Immediately I took her hand to lead her away but the passage on the high stand was narrow and she was forced to loose my hand and go before me, alone. Then she fell. From the narrow passage-way above the seats she fell outward. The shoe on her right foot caught in a brace of the stand structure and she hung, head downward, above the drop of—oh, I should say quite thirty feet. I went towards her: I was mortally afraid of the height. Looking down I could not see her face as her skirts had fallen about her head. I could make no attempt to raise her. I was not a strong man: I have grown stronger since then to meet a similar eventuality which may never arise. I could make no attempt to hold her to her position for the terror of the notion that she might drag me down. She made no sound. I appealed for help to some men and women sitting below us: they were half-turned to watch our antics but had made no movement towards us. My Spanish was poor—I can now speak it well—but there must have been some implication of my terrible position in my face and manner. The response of these men and women—I can never be quite sure of this—but I believe their response to my call was laughter: the sound was laughter and the grimaces seemed to be caused by mirth. It was not until some years after that I came to the charitable conclusion that their not coming to my aid—indeed, sir, they turned back to watch you at your antics—was because they could see me gesticulating but could not see Helen hanging by her heels. Then the strap of Helen's shoe— an old shoe, worn for comfort—broke and she fell. They tell me she was killed instantly—her hat was driven into her head. When I climbed down to her she lay terribly disordered in the sand. The soldiers picked her up—

PETER: Did you cry?

A. G.: —and arranged her. I could not—

PETER: Did you cry? There at the circus—did you cry?

A. G. *does not answer.* PETER *speaks with great urgency.*

Tell me, did you cry?

A. G.: You must remember my position.

PETER: It is a well-known fact, is it not, that shock caused by an incident such as you have just told us does not occasion precipitate tears? Was this so in your case? Did the emotional impact causing tears or grief strike you immediately or—Do you understand me? Did you stay and weep or wait until you had left the crowd?

A. G.: Yes.

PETER: Well, which?

A. G.: I wept bitterly on being told she was dead. I was told by an official of the circus. Perhaps you remember him? A garish uniform with buttons of—

PETER *is obviously not listening.*

A. G. *makes an appeal to his understanding.*

You must remember. It was the death of my wife. She was beloved of me.

PETER: I quite understand.

PETER *moves to the window. There is a pause.* A. G. *picks up his hat and looks at* EMILY. *She is staring at her hands stretched on her lap.* A. G. *puts down his hat again on the reading lamp.*

(*To* EMILY.) A car has just driven up.

A. G. *rises.*

A. G.: I must be going, Emily.

EMILY: What? Oh, very well, A. G. Goodbye.

A. G.: Goodbye. (*They shake hands.*) Goodbye, Mr Bembo.

PETER *murmurs an inaudible goodbye.* A. G. *goes to the door. As he reaches it the door is opened and* NICHOLAS *stands there.*

NICHOLAS: Hullo, A. G. Going?

A. G.: Yes, I—

NICHOLAS: Back in a minute. Patience has gone to her room. (*He goes.* A. G. *hesitates a moment.*)

A. G.: I shall not wait. No. (*He goes, unanswered.* EMILY *looks up at Peter and smiles.*)

EMILY: Peter.

PETER: Yes?

EMILY: Turn round.

He turns from the window.

You must not allow it to affect you so deeply.

PETER: Emily. Emily, it was always understood that any incident among the audience of my performance should be reported to me. If they kept this from me what other things may have happened without my knowledge? Always I was told, 'Success! Success and nothing but laughter!' You remember, Emmy, my only boast.

EMILY: Don't worry, Peter. You can still vaunt the greatest talent.

PETER: Can I? The mechanics, Emmy. If I were to jump from that chair now I'd probably break both my legs. I'm an old man now. I pity myself. Who is he?

EMILY: A. G.?

PETER: Yes.

EMILY: A neighbour.

PETER: What is he?

EMILY: A retired grocer.

PETER: He's a friend of yours?

EMILY: I suppose so. Nicholas—

PETER: I presume that was Nicholas who came in just now?

EMILY: Yes. Nicholas says A. G. calls so often and stays so long because he's in love with me. It may be true. Nicholas plays jokes on him—he won't leave A. G. and me alone together. One night A. G. made no attempt to go until two-thirty and then it was Nicholas who showed him to the door. But again Nicholas has been away for ten days and I've been alone in the house but A. G. hasn't called here. He waited until you arrived. He saw you come in from his window.

PETER: All this about his wife—

EMILY: Pay no attention to that. He loves telling the story. He must have told me twenty times—without the references to you, of course.

PETER: Is it true?

EMILY: I should think so. The details never vary. He showed me some photographs of her once. She looked a dowdy little thing. I believe she served behind the counter in his shop or something. Did he tell me that or did I imagine it from looking at her? I don't know.

PETER: Have you known him long?

EMILY: About three years now. He introduced himself to me one morning. It was not until some time afterwards I knew that that in itself was an extraordinary thing. I really know very little about him.

    NICHOLAS' *voice is heard off, calling.*

NICHOLAS (*off*): I can manage. I'm very good on these stairs.

PETER: Emily, may I stay here for a while?

EMILY: Why, yes, I suppose so. Yes, of course.

PETER: If you, with your ever passionate demand for motives—

EMILY: No, no!

PETER: —want my reasons they are these: (*He is hesitant, unsure.*) I have travelled a long way—I am tired—it is natural at my age— I have no money but I expect a small sum to be made available to me in a matter of a week or so—there is you and—I want to interest myself in others—perhaps your son—I want—

EMILY: Have you been very lonely?

PETER: Not so much lonely as alone. I am not, by nature, taciturn. My work as a clown demanded that I should amuse by my very silence. And recently, in my retirement, there have been incidents too horrible to—

> NICHOLAS *and* PATIENCE *enter.* NICHOLAS *is a giant of a man who walks with the aid of a heavy stick. He limps badly.* PATIENCE, *his wife, aged seventeen, is attempting to support him when they enter the room. When they are within the room he, without speaking, pulls himself from her.*

PATIENCE: I was only trying to help, dear.

NICHOLAS: Hullo, Mother. (*He makes no movement towards her.*)

EMILY: Hullo, Nicholas.

NICHOLAS: Have you any cigarettes? We ran out on the journey and haven't yet had time to get any.

> *As* EMILY *indicates the cigarettes on the tea-tray* NICHOLAS *becomes aware of* PETER BEMBO *standing by the window. For a moment the two men stare at each other.*
> Emily.

EMILY: My son, Nicholas. Mr Peter Bembo. And—

NICHOLAS (*pointing at her with his stick*): My wife, Patience. How do you do.

> PATIENCE *and* PETER *greet each other.* NICHOLAS *turns to the tray, takes and lights a cigarette.*

EMILY (*to* PATIENCE): Come and sit down.

> PATIENCE *and* NICHOLAS *sit.*

NICHOLAS: Whose cup of tea is this?

PETER: I think it must be mine.

NICHOLAS (*he holds the cup out*): Here you are.

EMILY: It must be quite cold by now.

PETER: Yes, it is.

NICHOLAS: Patience will go and make some more—and we shall need another cup.

EMILY: I'll—

NICHOLAS: Patience will go. Run along.

PETER: I'll go and get it. (*He picks up the tea-pot.*)

NICHOLAS: Oh, all right.

EMILY: The kitchen is— (*but* PETER *has gone.*) Did you have a nice time?

   There is a pause.

PATIENCE: Very nice, thank you.   (*They speak together.*)

NICHOLAS: Who is he?

EMILY: Good. What did you say, Nicholas?

NICHOLAS: Who is he?

EMILY: Who?

NICHOLAS: Mr Rainbow.

EMILY: Bembo: Peter Bembo.

NICHOLAS: Well, Bembo then. Who is he? He's gone out to give you an opportunity to say something about him.

EMILY: He's a very old friend of mine. I knew him many years ago— before you were born.

NICHOLAS: Another one, eh?

EMILY: Don't be silly, Nicholas. (*To* PATIENCE.) Did you like Bath? You hadn't been there before, had you?

NICHOLAS: You will find, Patience, that we are often attended by elderly gentlemen with a kind of fading love-light in their eyes.

EMILY: Shut up!

NICHOLAS: They will be introduced and explained to you by Mother as, 'A very rare old friend of mine. I knew him many years ago— before you were born.' That formula introduces each one. There was Harry or Henry or whatever his name was—ten years ago when I was a child—Harry died but he didn't leave us any of his money. Then there was Andrew—one of the hearty kind—he used to frighten me—he died but he didn't leave us any money: it wasn't until after he was dead that we found he hadn't any money to leave, was it, Emmy? There were others in varying stages of wealth and penury. All acquaintances of my mother until she met my father and became respectable. I must say she still appears to possess great charm. There's A. G. next door who in the last three years has become passionately attached to her. Poor old A. G. He thinks Mother is 'such a lady'. He told me so.

EMILY: Have you taken the car back to A. G.?

NICHOLAS: Mother has given up saying to me, as she used to say to me when I was a child, 'Be nice to So-and-so. Behave yourself in front of him and show him what a sweet, clever little boy you are.' Implying that So-and-so had money and that we were very poor and that if by some artifice I could touch a streak of sentimentality in So-and-so by my charming antics So-and-so might be very kind and give me fifty pounds down and remember me in his will when he died.

EMILY (*to* PATIENCE): Are you hungry?

NICHOLAS: I used to sing for them, the Harrys and the Andrews. A little song called, 'The Hill where Melchen lives'. Emily used to accompany me on the piano while I piped away in a whining falsetto and Harry or Andrew used to sit in a state of profound embarrassment. I tell you now, Emmy, that singing—I used to round it off with a little dance, remember?—it was a mistake.

EMILY: I realize that now. You've always been very nice as long as you kept your mouth shut.

NICHOLAS (*laughs*): Good for you. Cheer up, Emmy. I forgive you everything.

PATIENCE: Can I have a piece of cake?

EMILY: Do, my dear. (*She passes the cake.*)

PATIENCE: I'm really very hungry.

NICHOLAS: What are we going to do with Bembo?

EMILY: What do you mean? What are we going to do with him.

NICHOLAS: I mean is he staying at an hotel in the town or what?

EMILY: He's staying here. (*She suddenly laughs quietly.*)

NICHOLAS: What are you laughing at?

EMILY: I think you two should get on well together.

NICHOLAS: Do you mean Patience and I should get on?

EMILY: No, no! You and Bembo.

NICHOLAS: What on earth makes you say that?

He is staring at EMILY *when* PETER *comes in with the tea-pot which he puts on the table.* EMILY *begins to pour out the tea for* PATIENCE *and* NICHOLAS.

Thank you, sir.

EMILY: Will you have some tea now, Peter?

PETER: No, I think not, thank you. (*To* PATIENCE.) I hear you two have just got married.

PATIENCE: Yes.

PETER: My congratulations to you both.

PATIENCE: Thank you.

NICHOLAS: Have you come far today, sir?

PETER: From London.

NICHOLAS: By road?

PETER: No, train. I arrived this afternoon.

EMILY: I'll go up and get your room ready in a minute, Peter.

PETER (*after a pause*): Thank you. Thank you, Emily.

The realization that this is a definite invitation to stay at the Doon's house has a perceptible physical effect on PETER. *He leans back in his chair and rests his head, his arms stretched and relaxed before him.*

It is very pleasant to be—

The telephone rings. NICHOLAS *answers it.*

NICHOLAS: Hullo. Yes, Nicholas here. Hullo, A. G. You've left what? The reading lamp? Oh, yes. Why didn't you wait?

As he is speaking he holds out his burnt-through cigarette. PATIENCE *rises and takes an ash-tray to him.* EMILY *is speaking to* PETER.

Well, come round some time. You're what? Going to bed? Oh, I'm very sorry. What's the trouble? I see. Is Mrs Whatshername there—Mrs Barton? Would you like one of us to come round? No. Very well. Goodbye. (*He puts down the receiver.*) A. G. is not feeling well so he's going off to bed.

EMILY: I'm sorry to hear that.

NICHOLAS: Have you upset him?

EMILY: I don't think so. I'll go up and get your room ready, Peter.

PETER: Thank you.

EMILY: Will you come and help me, Pat?

NICHOLAS: Who are you speaking to?

EMILY: Your wife.

NICHOLAS: Pat! Pat! This damned use of diminutives making nonsense of names. Her name is Patience and she will be called so.

PETER: You are inconsistent. (*He speaks quietly.*) I believe you sometimes call your mother Emmy.

NICHOLAS *does not reply.*

EMILY: Will you come and help me make the bed, Patience?

PATIENCE: Of course, Mrs Doon.

EMILY *and* PATIENCE *go out.*

NICHOLAS: Has Mother been talking to you about me?

PETER: No.

NICHOLAS: She does to most people—at length.

PETER: Does she?

NICHOLAS *waits for* PETER *to continue.*

Why? Are you an interesting person?

NICHOLAS: She doesn't like me, you know.

PETER: She mentioned that she didn't.

NICHOLAS: Did she? You must be a very 'old friend' to be told that. With most people she has a fine attitude of affection for me. Did she say anything else about me?

PETER: No.

NICHOLAS: She said something rather odd to me.

PETER: What?

NICHOLAS: She said she thought you and I would get on well together.

PETER: Really?

NICHOLAS: Yes.

PETER: I wonder why she should think that?

NICHOLAS (*after a pause*): Should we try and find out? You're staying here for a while, aren't you?

PETER: You're thinking that—Yes, your mother has been kind enough—

NICHOLAS: You invited yourself.

PETER *takes out a cigarette case.*

PETER: Yes.

They both take and light cigarettes.

NICHOLAS: Why?

PETER: Have you your mother's passion for reasons?

NICHOLAS: I like behaviour that is understandable.

PETER: And mine is not?

NICHOLAS: Frankly, no.

PETER: I shall not explain. I can see no foundation for your mother's assumption that we should have anything in common. Indeed, I am beginning to find your attitude detestable.

NICHOLAS: What are your interests?

PETER: Very few. Eating and sleeping.

NICHOLAS: At least your digestion has survived. How old are you?

PETER: Sixty-eight.

NICHOLAS: I'm twenty-two. Do you drink?

PETER: Not excessively.

NICHOLAS: What is your job?

PETER: I've retired.

NICHOLAS: What was your job?

PETER: I was a clown.

NICHOLAS: A what?

PETER: A clown in a circus. 'Bembo, The Clown'. Have you never heard of me?

NICHOLAS: No.

PETER: Has your mother never spoken of me?

NICHOLAS: Never. (*He pauses.*) There's nothing there. I have never been to a circus in my life and if I had I'm sure I'd have disliked it intensely—especially the clowns.

PETER (*he leans forward*): And what are your interests?

NICHOLAS: Well, I—You must realize that at my age they are constantly changing.

PETER: Do you work at anything?

NICHOLAS: No. I am slightly incapacitated. (*He hits the lower part of his right leg with his stick.*) It is artificial below the knee.

PETER: Not a very great incapacity.

NICHOLAS: No, but it is an excuse. I see your eye—

PETER: Yes. An accident some years ago. (*He smiles: pointing to Nicholas' leg.*) How did it happen?

NICHOLAS (*he smiles*): They all think I lost it in a war.

    PETER *laughs.* NICHOLAS *laughs.*

But it must be something more than that. The loss of an eye and the loss of a leg are not enough foundation for an understanding between us.

PETER: I think you place too much importance on it.

NICHOLAS: Not at all. Emily has an acute mind. She is not given to making loose remarks. Have you a lot of money?

PETER: I have none at all.

NICHOLAS: Then why? Why? Why? (*He moves away from Peter.*)

PETER: I don't think we want to prolong this any longer. I shall go up to my room.

NICHOLAS: Wait a minute! (*He stops.*)

PETER: Well?

NICHOLAS: What did you and Emily talk about?

PETER: When?

NICHOLAS: When you were along together. You must have arrived before A. G.

PETER: Mostly about ourselves.

NICHOLAS: And the past. It's always in the past, isn't it, with you people?

PETER: Why not? It is a healthy memory.

NICHOLAS: Nonsense!

PETER: Really! I cannot see what—

NICHOLAS: The past for me as you old people consider it is corrupt but terrifyingly productive of one thing. That one thing is hope. Hope that some incident of the past will produce us some money for the present. Hope that some acquaintance of the past will offer me some sedentary job in the future. For years now Emily and I have lived together in this house supported by her pension and the small sums I have managed to earn by the very odd jobs I have done. I have been brought up to believe that the past is our god and that that god will provide. But my faith is failing. None of the supposed benefactors have come forward with money or jobs or even common acts of kindness. And it was on these people my childhood trust and affection were squandered. (*He pauses.*) In affection I have recently made a gesture to the present by my marriage. Do you know what my wife, Patience, is? She was brought up in an institution because she was born a bastard: she was completely friendless. I met her at a local dance hall where she was working as a cashier. We were married and she has nothing to remember before the day she met me. This makes her an ideal companion for Emily, whom I love. But you! You people of the past sometimes come this way: all you wish to do is to talk of the past. You revify Emily's memory and her faith in the better dead and forgotten. And that is a most criminal thing to do! (*He turns sharply away from* PETER *and in doing so his leg buckles and he falls to the floor.* PETER *makes no movement to assist him. After a slight cry of pain* NICHOLAS *looks up at* PETER.) Will you help me? I am unable—

PETER *moves to help him.*

Very kind of you—now I can manage—sometimes happens this—distressing—I can manage now. (*He is on his feet.*) Thank you. May I sit down for a minute? (*He sits.* PETER *picks up the cigarette* NICHOLAS *has dropped in his fall and puts it in an ash-tray.*) Well, Mr Bembo, I hope you enjoy your stay with us. As you have undoubtedly noticed I shall do my best to make it entertaining for you. Emily was quite wrong. If you and I talk we shall only do so at cross purposes. But A. G. will suit you. You must meet A. G. He has a fund of anecdote both comic—

PETER: I have already met him.

NICHOLAS: Of course, he was here when—

PETER: I hate him.

NICHOLAS (*after a pause*): Poor little man. Why? (*pause*) What did you say?

PETER: I hate him.

NICHOLAS: I'm so sorry. I thought you said you hit him.

PETER: I very nearly did.

NICHOLAS *is about to speak.*

I shall give you only one reason. To tell you it is based (*he covers his face with his hand*) in some half-forgotten professional pride that he has destroyed. Unforgivable clumsiness.

NICHOLAS: In return for this confidence I shall give you my definite reason for hatred of A. G. I hate him because in his ignorance he cannot see our want. He avails himself of our company because he is a lonely man: we prove ourselves friends by giving him an audience for the continually reiterated story of the death of his wife: we allow him the impression that he is associated with gentle-folk—

PETER *laughs.*

an intentional irony, Mr Bembo—we give A. G. all this and in return get nothing. He continually tells us he is fond of us but his stupidity does not allow him to see how he can practically express that affection—by hard cash. Even for a wedding present—an excellent opportunity for him—he gave Patience the most God-awful sort of water-jug. We cannot parade our poverty before him in any more obvious way than we do at present. He is aware of my dislike but again his stupidity is such that he cannot understand the cause. Undoubtedly, if ever the light did dawn on him he would present us, quite happily, with a cheque for several hundred pounds. But, Mr Bembo, the apparent lack of pride allowing me to tell you this is counterbalanced by a fierce and active pride preventing me from telling, in plain terms, a retired grocer the direction in which his duty lies.

PETER *stands shaking his head.*

Well?

PETER: A more prolix and fantastic reason than mine. You realize, I hope, that neither of these are sane causes. For hating a man, I mean.

NICHOLAS: I realize nothing of the kind.

PETER: Good.

NICHOLAS: My hatred is the only active thing within me. (*In sudden despair.*) I must attempt a future as well as a present.

A pause.

PETER: Can I help you?

NICHOLAS (*in complete acceptance*): Shall we begin our acquaintance from here? How do you do, Mr Bembo.

PATIENCE *enters.*

PATIENCE: Mr Bembo, sir. Mrs Doon says will you go up now and she will show you your room.

PETER: Thank you. My luggage is at the station. How can I—?

NICHOLAS: I'll go and fetch it for you before I return the car to A. G.

PETER: Thank you.

NICHOLAS: Is there much?

PETER: Three suitcases.

NICHOLAS, *who has his back to* PETER, *smiles.* PETER *gives* NICHOLAS *the cloakroom tickets.*

NICHOLAS: All right.

PETER *goes out.* PATIENCE *moves to the window and looks into the street.*

PATIENCE: When are you going to fetch the luggage and take the car back?

NICHOLAS: In a few minutes. (*He takes a small notebook from his pocket and begins to write.*)

PATIENCE: Can I come with you?

NICHOLAS: Of course.

PETER *can be heard calling 'Emily! Emily!'*

PATIENCE: It was nice of the gentleman next door to lend us his car for the honeymoon.

NICHOLAS *continues to write.*

NICHOLAS: Patience.

PATIENCE: Yes?

NICHOLAS: Come here.

PATIENCE *comes down from the window and stands directly before* NICHOLAS *who continues to write. He speaks with great gentleness.*

Try not to behave as if you were a servant. You are a married woman now and this is your home. The people who happen to stay here are as much your guests as they are Emily's. There is no need to call them 'sir'—and when you come into a room come right in, don't stand just inside the door. (*He puts the notebook back in his jacket pocket and looks up at her.*) Why don't you talk more?

PATIENCE: I don't seem to have anything to say to people like that. Mr Bembo, I mean.

NICHOLAS: You talk nineteen to the dozen to me when we're alone. What is it about other people?

PATIENCE: I don't know.

NICHOLAS: When we were having tea, for instance. Hadn't you anything definite to say then except whatever it was you said— about the cake? What were you thinking?

PATIENCE: Oh, I don't know. Why Mr Bembo wears that black patch over his eye. Whether I should call your mother Mrs Doon or Mother or what. Whether I couldn't have some more sugar in my tea—I like a lot of sugar in my tea. (*She takes hold of the walking-stick and pulls* NICHOLAS *from the chair.*) And I was thinking about you.

NICHOLAS: What about me?

PATIENCE: Nothing.

NICHOLAS: Why didn't you say any of these things?

PATIENCE: You were talking too much.

NICHOLAS (*laughs*): Yes! Yes, I do, you know. (*He goes to the desk and taking out a small knife begins to sharpen the pencil with which he has been writing.* PATIENCE *goes to him and receives the parings in her cupped hands.*)

PATIENCE: Who is Mr Bembo?

NICHOLAS: A friend of Emily's, a friend of yours and a friend of mine.

PATIENCE: He's old, isn't he?

NICHOLAS: Nearly seventy.

PATIENCE: I say! As old as that!

NICHOLAS (*he mimics her*): I say! Yes! Over two and a half times older than you.

PATIENCE: I say! That's some age, my man, some age!

NICHOLAS: How right you are.

They laugh. NICHOLAS *replaces the pencil in his pocket and the knife in the desk.* PATIENCE *carries the wood parings and throws them into the fireplace.*

PATIENCE: Does he make you want to laugh?

NICHOLAS: Who? Bembo?

PATIENCE: Yes.

NICHOLAS: Not particularly.

PATIENCE: He does me.

NICHOLAS: You should have told him.

PATIENCE: That I wanted to laugh at him? No!

NICHOLAS: He likes being laughed at.

PATIENCE: Even when he's being serious?

NICHOLAS: At all times.

PATIENCE: Nicholas! Nobody likes being laughed at.

NICHOLAS: Shall I tell you a secret? About Emily and Peter?

PATIENCE: Yes, please.

NICHOLAS: Come here.

She moves to him and he whispers to her.

PATIENCE (*she screams with laughter*): But they're old!

NICHOLAS: They weren't always old. Ssh! Don't make such a row.

PATIENCE *is on sure, known ground with this mention of the physical. She moves to* NICHOLAS *and puts her hands into his jacket pockets, pressing her body to him, sure of her behaviour.*

PATIENCE: But, there, you see, Nicholas, I can never imagine old, cold bodies doing what we've done, can you? It's like a true story I once read of two people in love, loving. It wasn't until the end of the book I found out they were both dead and that made it horrible.

NICHOLAS: 'Peace, good reader, do not weep;
        Peace, the lovers are asleep.
        They, sweet turtles, folded lie
        In the last knot that love can tie.'

PATIENCE: What's that?

NICHOLAS: It was written by a bloke who lived round here. Don't worry. He's dead, too.

PATIENCE *has pulled the notebook from Nicholas' pocket. She holds it in her hand. The conversation between the living of the dead is beyond her limited understanding. She takes her only refuge.*

PATIENCE: Kiss me.

NICHOLAS (*he kisses her*): Oh, my own lass. God save us both.

PATIENCE: God save us indeed.

They embrace. She speaks to him, returning his gentleness.

There is no cause to be afraid of the night. Why are you shy with me? You must have no shame with me. Together, we must be gay and impudent—and it must be you who comes to me to demand and be bold. I want that.

She steps back from him. He stands motionless, leaning forward on his stick. Suddenly he looks up at her.

I had to say that.

NICHOLAS: I'm all right, really, you know.

PATIENCE: Of course you are. Come along.

NICHOLAS: Are you going to put on a coat?

PATIENCE: No. (*She holds up the notebook.*) What were you writing in this?

NICHOLAS: How much I've spent today. Patience.

PATIENCE: Yes?

NICHOLAS: Pay attention.

She is reading the notebook.

PATIENCE: I'm listening.

NICHOLAS: You remember I explained to you the other morning about your behaviour now we're married with regards to money and things like that?

PATIENCE: Yes.

NICHOLAS: We must be careful.

PATIENCE: I don't spend much.

NICHOLAS: No, I don't mean that at all. You remember what I said —you mustn't let anyone know we're poor.

PATIENCE: Are we? Mrs Doon gave me ten pounds for the honeymoon. I've never had so much money.

NICHOLAS: Yes, I know, but— (*He stops, realizing the impossibility of an explanation.*)

PATIENCE: What are you trying to tell me? I'm listening.

NICHOLAS: It doesn't matter. Don't use that dreadful perfume you have on, there's a good girl.

PATIENCE: It's 'Sweet Jasmine'.

NICHOLAS: I don't care what it is.

PATIENCE: It was a present from the girls at the hall. I've got ever such a lot left. Seems a pity to waste it.

NICHOLAS: I'll buy you some more.

PATIENCE: Will you? I'll put it down in your book. 'La-di-da perfume for Patience—twenty pounds.'

NICHOLAS: Behave yourself.

PETER *comes in.*

I'm just going to fetch your luggage.

The telephone rings.

PETER: Thank you. Shall I—? (*He goes to the telephone.*) Hullo—oh, hullo, A. G. (PETER *has an easy familiarity.*) How are you feeling? Good. You haven't gone to bed yet? This is Peter Bembo.

 EMILY *enters.*

EMILY: How long will you be, Nicholas?

NICHOLAS: Not long.

PETER (*at phone*): He can bring it round. (*To* NICHOLAS.) You can take the reading lamp round to A. G., can't you? He wants you to try it there.

NICHOLAS: Certainly, certainly. (*He picks up the lamp from the floor.*)

PETER: He'll bring it round now.   } *Spoken together.*
NICHOLAS: Can we have a fire, Emily?

EMILY: I'll light one.

 PATIENCE *has been staring at* PETER. *She suddenly bursts into laughter.*

PETER: You must take care of yourself, you know, A. G. (*To* PATIENCE.) What are you laughing at?

PATIENCE: You.

 PETER *makes a clown's grimace at her which increases her laughter.* NICHOLAS *and* EMILY *also laugh.* PETER *increases his facial antics also elaborating strange, stilted gestures. He pulls a false nose from his pocket and puts it on. He continues to speak on the telephone to* A. G. NICHOLAS *and* PATIENCE *begin to move to the door.*

PETER: What's that you say? What's that? No. No, we're all laughing here, A. G. So hurry up, get better and come round: come round.

CURTAIN

ACT TWO

The same, three days later: that is, the Sunday. The time is ten-thirty in the morning.
The sun is shining into the room with an unnatural brightness. Church bells are ringing.
A. G. is sitting alone in the room. He is wearing an overcoat and holds a hat and stick. Beside him, on the arm of the chair, is a large, ivory-bound prayer-book.
After a moment A. G. turns his head to stare at the portrait of Emily. As he stares at the picture his lips begin to move but the words are inaudible. He rises to move towards the picture and in doing so knocks the prayer-book to the floor. He picks up the book and putting it beneath his arm moves to stand before the portrait. He stretches out his hand and touches the face of the picture. In sudden, unreasoning panic he turns to the door.

A. G. (*his voice thin with fear*): Emily! Emily! (*He remains staring at the door.*) (*In a whisper.*) Emily!
    There is a sudden strident burst of laughter from beyond the door. A. G. moves slowly towards the door: he opens it. Standing in the hall-way with their backs to the room are PETER BEMBO *and* NICHOLAS DOON. *They are talking together. When the door is fully open they turn to face into the room but they do not enter.*
NICHOLAS: Good morning, A. G.
A. G.: Good morning, Nicholas. Good morning, Mr Bembo.
PETER: Good morning.
    There is a pause whilst the two men silently regard A. G.
NICHOLAS: Are you better?
A. G.: Oh, yes.
NICHOLAS: You were never really very ill, were you?
A. G.: You mean—When?

31

NICHOLAS: On Thursday. When you rang up to say you were going to bed and rang again asking me to come round and then wouldn't see me when I arrived.

A. G.: Why do you say that?

PETER: You were afraid.

A. G. (*pauses*): Do you know if Emily is ready? We haven't much time.

NICHOLAS: Why were you afraid, A. G.? Why have you stayed away?

A. G.: You should grow up, Nicholas. That's what you should do—grow up.

PETER: That's not applicable to me. What should I do?

A. G.: You, Mr Bembo, should practise tolerance and—

PETER: Yes?

A. G.: —and respect.

PETER: Tolerance and respect.

A. G.: Yes.

PETER (*to* NICHOLAS): And you must grow up.

NICHOLAS: Yes.

> PETER *and* NICHOLAS *move away.* A. G. *returns to his chair.*

A. G.: If all trumpeters blew such cracked tunes— (*He takes up the prayer-book and begins to read.* EMILY *and* PATIENCE *can be heard calling to each other.* A. G. *listens intently. After a moment* PATIENCE *enters to stand in the open doorway.*)

PATIENCE: Please, will you—

A. G.: What? Oh, hullo, my dear.

PATIENCE: Hullo. Mrs Doon says to tell you she'll be down in a moment, and—

A. G.: Thank you.

PATIENCE: And if you would like some sherry please to help yourself.

A. G.: Right-o.

PATIENCE: It's in there.

A. G.: Won't you stay and talk to me until Emily comes down.

PATIENCE: I'm sorry. I'm very busy. (*She makes no attempt to move.*)

A. G.: I see. Well, in that case, I mustn't keep you here.

> PATIENCE *remains motionless.*

You may go. I shall be all right. Quite all right.

> PATIENCE *goes, leaving the door open.*

PATIENCE (*off*): He's in there.

EMILY (*off*): Thank you. Run and get my gloves from my room. (EMILY *comes in, closing the door behind her*.) Goodness, A. G. You look very handsome this morning.

A. G.: Do I?

EMILY: Did you have some sherry?

A. G.: No.

EMILY: Well, I'd like some—wouldn't you?

A. G.: If you're having some.

EMILY: It's in there.

> A. G. *takes the sherry and pours out two glasses.*

Do you know, it's about six years since I went to church.

A. G.: Is it?

EMILY: Yes. Which one are we going to this morning?

A. G.: St John's.

EMILY (*she takes the sherry*): Thank you. That's the one—

A. G.: On the corner—

EMILY: I know. Opposite Woolworths.

A. G.: That's right.

EMILY: We've got time for this, haven't we? (*She holds up her glass.*)

A. G.: Oh, yes. It's just six minutes' walk.

EMILY: How do you know?

A. G.: I— (*He shrugs his shoulders.*)

EMILY: What a precise person you are.

> *There is a pause.*

I can't remember any prayers, I'm afraid, except—'From Ghoulies and Ghosties and Long-Leggedy Beasties and things that go Bump in the night, Good Lord deliver us'. Will that do?

A. G.: I should think it will be very suitable.

> PATIENCE *enters with Emily's gloves.*

EMILY: Thank you, darling.

> PATIENCE *goes out.*

What do you mean by 'suitable'? (*Before he can reply.*) I shall want a prayer-book, shan't I? Now where—?

A. G.: I'd like you to have this one. (*He holds out the ivory-bound prayer-book.*)

EMILY: But that's yours.

A. G.: I have another. (*He takes a small leather-bound book from his pocket and holds out the other to* EMILY, *who takes it.*)

EMILY: What a beautiful book. (*She opens it at the fly-leaf and reads.*) 'To Helen, on her birthday, from Mummy. September—'

A. G.: Today is her birthday.

EMILY *stares at him for a moment and then snaps the book shut.*

EMILY: Dear God! Do you want me to cry? Is that what you want?

A. G.: No!

EMILY: Is all this premeditated?

A. G.: No!

EMILY: Why do you work on my feelings with your dead wife?

A. G.: Please—

EMILY: What is your object, A. G.? You ask me to go to church with you on her birthday. Very well. I'll go to church with you and I'll pray for the peace of her soul. I'll speak of her to you. You may remember her with me. You may tell me again and again of her dreadful death but—to give me, a stranger, this most intimate possession—

A. G.: Stranger?

EMILY: —and expect me to remain unmoved—no, A. G. No!

A. G.: Emily!

EMILY: What is your purpose?

A. G.: It was not to distress you.

EMILY (*holding out the prayer-book*): Why? Why this one?

A. G.: It was my intention that you should keep it. It is a present to you. (*He pauses.*) Apart from its associations you said yourself it is a beautiful book.

EMILY: Do you wish to part with it?

A. G.: To you, yes.

EMILY: Why to me?

He does not answer.

Why to me?

He is silent.

Answer me. Why do you give this to me?

A. G.: As to your suggestion that I'd purposely give you cause for tears—

EMILY: A. G.!

A. G.: —and I am shocked by your lack of understanding.

EMILY: Why do you give this to me? (*She pauses.*) Do you love me?

A. G.: No.

EMILY: Well, that's a plain answer to a—

A. G.: Twenty years is not a long time.

EMILY: Meaning—?

A. G.: Meaning that love for me—

EMILY: Yes?

A. G.: Love for me is—

    EMILY *waits for him to continue.*

Meaning that love for me is contained within one night.

    EMILY *holds out the prayer-book to him.*

Keep it. At least for this morning.

    EMILY *retains the book and as* A. G. *continues to speak she opens it and turns the leaves.*

The bed, very large, with coarse linen sheets—comfortable though —we had travelled a long way that day, you remember—we washed in the water from the jug—heavy, stone-cold jug—No one had come near us since we entered the room— (*He speaks quietly.*)

EMILY: I can't hear what you're saying.

A. G.: Helen and I were afraid. We laughed but we were afraid. That's why we made love.

EMILY: I don't want to hear about it.

A. G.: But you understand me?

EMILY: Yes.

A. G.: Do you?

EMILY: Yes.

A. G.: Then will you answer me this? Although I love no one must I live without friends? You can't answer that?

EMILY: You're a nice person, A. G., but—

    A. G., *looking at the clock, interrupts.*

A. G.: We haven't drunk the sherry.

EMILY: Leave it.

A. G.: You're ready?

EMILY: Yes.

A. G.: Come along then.

    They move towards the door. A. G. *takes the large prayer-book.*

I'll carry that for you. I thought you would like to walk.

EMILY: Yes, I do.

    A. G. *stops.*

A. G.: When was that painted? That picture of you.

EMILY: Just before Nicholas was born.

A. G.: I see. I can get the car now if you would prefer.

EMILY: No, I'd like to walk.

    They go out. There is a pause. The front door shuts. After a moment NICHOLAS *and* PETER *enter. They go quickly to the window and look into the street.*

NICHOLAS: There they go. That strut of A. G.'s is more comic seen from the rear. I want you to observe the angle of his hat—jaunty, I believe, is the term. Notice the swing of the cane—Yes, look! A full circle. Ah! He tips his hat to an acquaintance. (*Mimics.*) 'How d'you do. How d'you do.' (*He pauses.*) And note, please, Peter, Emmy's grace.

The church bells cease to be replaced by a single bell.

A little quicker. They mustn't be late. It is obviously some kind of occasion. Did you notice the ostentation of the prayer-book? Ivory-bound. I doubt if it contains his single, reiterated prayer— 'Thy kingdom come, Thy will be done on Earth as it is in Helen'.

PETER *moves from the window.*

They are crossing the road. Mind the horse dung, A. G. He has offered Emily his arm so neatly crooked at the elbow. (*He laughs.*) She has refused.

PETER *has taken up the two glasses of wine left by* EMILY *and* A. G. *He takes one to* NICHOLAS.

They are about to turn the corner. (NICHOLAS *takes the wine.*) Thank you. They are gone. (NICHOLAS *stands staring through the window.*) (*Quietly.*) That child will be run over. (*He bangs the window with the handle of his stick and shouts.*) Look out, little boy! (*Pause.*) All right. He has fallen. Well, at least he can cry. (*He turns from the window.*) There is a certain pathos in the actions of a person unaware he is observed. Presumably the child in the adult—the child playing a silent, lonely and mysterious game. From what I could see of A. G. whilst he was alone in this room—that key-hole is badly placed; too high—I gathered he spoke a little to himself. He was clumsy, knocking something—I couldn't see what—to the floor. He moved towards that wall and put his hand in a strange gesture towards—would it be that picture of Emily?—and then came the cry of her name. I couldn't be sure what would follow and so I gave the signal to reveal ourselves by laughing.

PETER: And what better way to reveal ourselves?

NICHOLAS: No. No, the fear in A. G. was there at that moment. It was not caused by our laughter. It was there in the call of Emily's name. What was the cause?

PETER: Perhaps he knew he was being watched.

NICHOLAS: I doubt it. Was it the portrait? His outstretched hand on the varnish—cold to the touch—

PETER (*laughs*): No!

NICHOLAS: It doesn't really matter, does it? I mean, the fear is there. The origin doesn't concern us.

PETER: I'm not sure the fellow is frightened. He showed some spirit when he found us listening at the door—I am presuming he knew we were listening. I must practise tolerance and—and, what was it?—humility?

NICHOLAS: No. Respect. And I must grow up.

PETER: How right he is.

NICHOLAS: How right.

They laugh.

But the spirit of attack in him at that moment was because of his fear. An animal—

PETER: At bay? Oh, no! I can't have that. No. He's just a dear little lonely old man.

NICHOLAS: The greatest of all his fears is that someone will disclose the fact that he is afraid.

PETER: Absurd!

NICHOLAS: Why have you begun to ridicule me? You said yesterday that—What's the matter?

PETER: Nothing.

NICHOLAS: Oh, come on. Now, come on. There's something wrong this morning. Since Thursday, when you came here, you have been angry and defiant—only too willing to discuss the A. G. affair with me. It's true we made no definite plans but you were loud in your support of anything I might do—anything. You remember you definitely offered me your co-operation. Until last night you were malicious and violent towards A. G. It was only last night you said of A. G., 'It is his innocence we must destroy,' and, you said, 'That cannot be achieved by intimidation,' and then you yawned and went to bed saying we'd discuss it further this morning. Here is this morning and you are taking my conjectures, my attempts at a solution to our problem, my tentative, inexperienced, efforts to put A. G. in his rightful place and you are laughing at them—and, I suppose, at me. I am not a pathetic character. Don't think that. I am strong and I can do without your support.

PETER: I am sure of it. I'll tell you the truth. I had a bad dream last night.

NICHOLAS: Well?

PETER: You must have experienced the dream that comes so near nature that the first waking hours must be spent in disentangling reality from the fantasy.

NICHOLAS: Was the dream about us—this place?

PETER: No.

NICHOLAS: Did you scream in the night? I heard someone. It might have been Emily.

PETER: Possibly it was me.

NICHOLAS: Will you recover?

PETER: Yes.

NICHOLAS: You will recover your feelings towards A. G.?

PETER: There is a change.

NICHOLAS: I know! Why? Because of me?

PETER: Now, listen, Nicholas.

NICHOLAS: Why? Because I have—

PETER: Listen to me. I've explained to you the immediate impact on me of the story of the death of this man's wife. You know the tears he shed in that place at that time attacked my greatest conceit. You know that and you understand.

NICHOLAS: Yes, I understand and sympathize. I'm no artist but I understand.

PETER: But consider: the woman's death was so fantastically comic in its elements. You admit? To hang by the heels, skirts about her head, distraught lover fluttering around in an agony of indecision and dismay while a clown in a circus ring below flew through a hoop and the immense audience howled with laughter. The woman fell, was killed. (*He laughs.*) No, Nicholas, it's too much. I can't take it seriously. Perhaps, after all, A. G.'s tears were tears of laughter.

NICHOLAS: Then you can no longer—? Do you find it cold in here?

PETER: Not really, no.

NICHOLAS: The sun should warm the room but— (*He moves to the door.*) We must talk about this, Peter. (*He calls.*) Patience!

PETER: I'm quite willing, Nicholas. I want to help you.

NICHOLAS: Patience!

PATIENCE (*off*): Coming! Coming!

NICHOLAS (*mimics viciously*): Coming! Coming!

    PETER *looks up in surprise.*

PETER: What's that?

NICHOLAS (*he moves back into the room*): I want you to listen to me. Patience has—I have been gentle and considerate but her violence to me—No. This is what I wish to say. When you offered me your help you remember I said the only active thing within me was my hatred of A. G.

PETER: I'm trying to understand you, believe me. You say, your wife—

NICHOLAS: No. My—my love for Patience is passive. It is she who takes any initiative in such matters. I don't wish to speak of that.

PETER: Why not?

NICHOLAS: Yet I can speak of it to you.

PETER: Certainly.

NICHOLAS: It is relevant.

PETER: Then tell me, child.

NICHOLAS: The girl has degraded me beyond expectation. (*He turns away from* PETER.) I was prepared as a necessity of marriage to give myself to a degree but she has made me debase myself until—I—don't—sucking at—in the violence of—look at her hands, you look—Before, I'd only limited knowledge—walking home through the park at night I had seen the couples linked on benches, lying among bushes, plucking at each other's clothing in an aimless passion like dying people. Even the sight of this attacked my—my—yes, innocence. Yes! my innocence. Now this girl, my wife, has made me—My bedroom which we share has been my refuge for many years. The shelves still hold my childhood books, the cupboard beside the bed still contains my toys. The decorations and furnishing have remained unchanged within my memory.

PATIENCE *enters. She stands in the doorway.*

And it is in that room this girl has made me do such things—

PETER: Here's Patience.

NICHOLAS (*to her*): What are you doing now?

PATIENCE: I've just finished making the beds and clearing up.

NICHOLAS: Will you light a fire in here, please.

PATIENCE *goes out. There is a pause.*

PETER: What do you want to do, Saint Nicholas?

NICHOLAS: I don't know, Peter, I don't know. (*He is terribly distressed.*) I want some kind of revenge.

PETER: Now we're getting down to elementals. Revenge for what?

NICHOLAS: For my weakness.

PETER: Good. And on whom?

NICHOLAS: A. G.

PETER: I see. But why A. G.?

NICHOLAS: Because he is weaker than I am.

PETER: Should I kill him?

NICHOLAS *does not answer.*

Should we dress up as ghosts? He—

NICHOLAS: You have no need to dress up.

PETER: He has a belief in the supernatural.

NICHOLAS: No.

PETER: Pity we're not clever enough to swindle him out of all his money.

NICHOLAS: Yes.

PETER: Let's burn down his house.

NICHOLAS: Too close. Damn it! It's next door. (*He begins to smile.*)

PETER: Let us invent some facts, evidence that his wife was an immoral woman before her marriage.

NICHOLAS *looks up.*

I was joking.

NICHOLAS: Were you?

PETER: Yes.

NICHOLAS: Were you?

PATIENCE *enters with a bucket of coal and firewood. She proceeds to lay and light the fire.*

PETER: Some kind of practical joke. What do you say to that?

NICHOLAS: Yes. Yes, but no dressing up as ghosts, no physical violence. Something about his wife—?

PETER: Be careful, Nicholas.

NICHOLAS: Of course. Something about Helen. Of course. (*His excitement grows.*) But there must be some preliminary. His attention must be directed to an unknown that threatens him. Now! What do we know? What do we know of him to his discredit?

PETER: Nothing.

NICHOLAS: Nothing.

PETER: But do we need to know anything?

NICHOLAS: What do you mean?

PETER: There is the old trick.

NICHOLAS: What old trick?

PETER: An anonymous letter.

NICHOLAS: Yes, I see. Explain what *you* mean by it.

PETER: There is a formula. 'All is discovered—' or 'All is lost. Flee for your life. A Well-wisher.' Simple. We know nothing. If there is something that letter will explode A. G.'s ingenuousness. If there is nothing—if nothing happens we can—we can send him some poisoned chocolates.

NICHOLAS: We—

PETER: But I forgot. You don't want him dead, do you?

NICHOLAS: This is urgent.

PETER: Perhaps just enough to give him tummy-ache. No?

NICHOLAS: No. Be serious. This letter. We can do it at once. We can deliver it to A. G.'s house now whilst he is at church. He is invited to tea and will probably stay for the rest of the evening— he always does. The rest can come then.

PETER: What is the rest?

NICHOLAS: I know. Really, I know what to do. You. Why shouldn't I profit by the presence of a famous clown?

PETER: By all means do so.

NICHOLAS: Thank you.

PETER: But tell me what you propose to do.

NICHOLAS: Later. Let's get this letter done. (*He moves to the desk, speaking. He continues to speak as he writes.*) Tell me, Peter, were you really amused by A. G.'s defiance at the door just now?

PETER: Not amused. Touched.

NICHOLAS: Do you mean emotionally moved?

PETER: Yes. Children—

NICHOLAS: I know nothing about children.

PETER: No. Well, children have the same quality of defiance. I remember once—

NICHOLAS: Are you defending A. G.?

PETER: No. I remember I—

NICHOLAS: The defiance of children, I should imagine, is always in defence of their integrity.

PETER: It is with child or man. A long time ago now but I remember quite—

NICHOLAS: Some other time, Peter, some other time. There. (*He holds up the letter.* PATIENCE *goes out.*)

PETER: What have you written?

NICHOLAS (*reads*): 'You are discovered, therefore you are lost. She died in vain. Actum est.'

PETER (*smiles*): Oh, what villains we are.

NICHOLAS (*with mock ceremony*): Mr Bembo. Do you sanction this note being sent to A. G.?

PETER: I do. What is more I will carry it myself.

NICHOLAS: Thank you, sir. I will seal it. (*He turns to the desk, puts the letter into an envelope and begins to seal with wax.*) Why did you insist I leave Emily and A. G. alone together this morning? I've never done so before.

PETER: Emily asked me to arrange it.

NICHOLAS: What?

PETER: Emily asked me to arrange it.

NICHOLAS: I see. Now why?

PETER: What are you talking about?

NICHOLAS: Why should Emily want to be left alone with A. G.?

PETER: You think she should have asked you?

NICHOLAS: No, no! She doesn't trust me. She'd never ask me. (*He holds up the sealed letter.*) This must go at once. Peter, I trust you.

PETER: You may do so.

NICHOLAS: I have to go to London tomorrow to have a fitting for a new leg. I shall take Patience with me. I shall go by an early-morning train and I shall be back by night. It is an appointment that is difficult—impossible to break.

PETER: Yes.

NICHOLAS: I shall be back as soon as—

PETER: You needn't hurry.

NICHOLAS: Of course I must hurry back. (*He indicates the letter.*) Is this the way, I wonder? Whether or not it is a beginning. We must have faith in it.

PETER: I have faith. (*He moves to* NICHOLAS *and nudges him.*) Hey! (*He puts up the index finger and thumb of one hand and makes of them a small 'O'.*) Look through there.

    NICHOLAS *peeps through.*

That's me. I have faith.

NICHOLAS: I understood you to say your faith had evaporated with your bad dreams.

PETER: You have misunderstood me again.

NICHOLAS: Have I? I am not always bright.

PETER: The dreams destroyed any remaining faith I possessed in my powers to hold affection for—that is, I suppose, at my age, to love—any person. And for that matter to hate any person with an active, destructive abhorrence. All that is finished: done with. But you are young and very brave. Carry on! I will give you all I can even if it is nothing more than my applause. I can give you that. See! (*He begins to clap his hands.*) Bravo! Bravo!

NICHOLAS: Promise me this. Promise me you have considered us. All of us. Myself, my wife, my mother, yourself and A. G.

PETER: All of us. In every way. I have observed A. G. in my mind. I have reconstructed a satisfactory past—one to include the story of his wife—and a suitable present life for him. I have arrogated myself to imagine his weaker moments and debased myself to observe—as at the door—his stronger moments. I have included you in your misery, Emily in her kindness, Patience in her ignorance and myself in my boredom and my conclusion is this: I will entirely endorse any action of yours because you are young and very brave.

NICHOLAS: You can think all this and retain your reason?

PETER: Yes.

NICHOLAS: Good. (He smiles.)

PETER: My sanity is secure but I confess to a slight tension of my scalp and neck muscles—excitement, do you think?

NICHOLAS: I should think so. You are an excellent friend. Forgive my doubts.

PETER: I forgive them.

NICHOLAS: But remember, there must be no violence towards A. G.

PETER: Don't be silly! He is younger than I am and he could probably beat me blindfold. Anyway, my last sight of him in his happiness with Emmy moved me so much that I couldn't now harm a hair of his head.

NICHOLAS: There is this to deliver. What's the time?

PETER: About eleven.

NICHOLAS: His house will be empty. I know his habits. Mrs Barton, his woman-help, arrives today at eleven-thirty.

PETER: I'll go with it. (He takes the letter.)

NICHOLAS: One more thing.

PETER: Yes?

    NICHOLAS does not speak.
Yes?

NICHOLAS: What do you hope to gain from this?

PETER: Another ten years of life. Come along, you moody fellow, the scheme is under way with this letter. What more do you want?

NICHOLAS: The ending.

PETER: Already?

NICHOLAS: I have been completely honest with you, Peter.

PETER: And do you doubt my honesty?

NICHOLAS: No.

PETER: You do. You think I am unreliable. You think I should do something more than applaud.

NICHOLAS: I do not.

PETER: You lie. But it is understandable, this—defiance. Not only your leg lets you down, eh? By the way, have you forgotten what you told me about your wife?

NICHOLAS: No.

PETER: You have. What has she made you do?

NICHOLAS: Peter, in God's name—!

PETER: Was it done in God's name? (*He winks.*) Why, most certainly. You are married. What did you tell me about your wife? Must I tell you?—Must I?

NICHOLAS: Yes, please.

PETER: How she was brought here as a bride, loved but friendless. Left to her own devices, treated as a servant. Given by necessity a share of your bed in the room containing your toys and fairy-tale books—articles which could only intimidate and terrify her by reason of your unknown past. You condemn her actions directed against the weakness of your body. You are a fool. She is a child and every invitation which you are too weak to resist arises from her love for you. Realize the delicacy of her spirit and imagine the repugnance she forces herself to overcome on seeing you, nightly, minus a leg. A deformed creature. You imply she's not human. Take away that contraption (*he points to Nicholas' leg*) and what becomes of you?

   There is silence.

Now let's hear no more of honesty and trust.

NICHOLAS: What can I do to please you?

PETER: Accept with gratitude all qualities of kisses and demonstrations of love no matter from whom they may come. Be grateful for memory: it is the booby prize for those who have failed or are ruined. (*He holds up the letter.*) Do I drop this through the letter-box?

NICHOLAS: I should think so.

PETER: Yes. The delivery in the normal way of a normal letter. I shall walk on through the town for a while. Is there anything of interest to see?

NICHOLAS: Nothing except a brass band playing in the public gardens.

PETER: How do I get there?

NICHOLAS: Go down past Elliots, the builders, over the way.

PETER: Will you come with me?

NICHOLAS: No.

PETER goes out. He returns after a moment carrying his hat and coat.

PETER: Shall I send your wife to you?

NICHOLAS (*after a pause he laughs*): How very sweet and gentle of you, Peter. But you're wrong. There's been no 'lover's tiff'—there is nothing to 'make up'. We haven't quarrelled. Goodbye.

PETER goes out. NICHOLAS sits before the fire. He takes out his notebook and pencil. PATIENCE opens the door.

PATIENCE: Can I come in?

NICHOLAS: Of course.

She enters carrying a child's teddy-bear which she places on the piano out of Nicholas' sight.

PATIENCE: Has everyone else gone out?

NICHOLAS: Yes.

PATIENCE stands looking out of the window.

PATIENCE: Why is Peter going to A. G.'s house?

NICHOLAS: He's taking a letter from me to A. G.

PATIENCE: You've never written a letter to me.

NICHOLAS: Haven't I? But we've always been together.

PATIENCE: Are you cross with me?

NICHOLAS does not reply.

You haven't spent any money today.

NICHOLAS: No.

PATIENCE: Your book—

NICHOLAS: I do my week's accounts on Sunday mornings. And then on Mondays I pay my bills and collect any debts.

PATIENCE: I see.

NICHOLAS: We shall be starting early in the morning.

PATIENCE: All right. (*She sits on the arm of Nicholas' chair.*)

NICHOLAS: Pull your skirt down. And if you want to sit down sit properly in a chair. Don't lounge about on the arms.

PATIENCE goes to a chair and sits.

Now about tomorrow. As I said we shall be starting early and we'd better arrange—You've finished your work, haven't you?

PATIENCE: Yes. Emily gave me some dresses this morning. I've been putting them away.

NICHOLAS: Are they nice?

PATIENCE: They're old-fashioned. I think, perhaps, if I alter them a bit—

NICHOLAS: You're not to alter them.

PATIENCE: I shall look very funny if I don't.

NICHOLAS: It was very kind of Emily to give them to you, wasn't it?

PATIENCE: Yes.

NICHOLAS: I hope you thanked her for them.

PATIENCE: Yes, I did.

NICHOLAS: And I hope you've put them carefully away.

PATIENCE: Yes, I have. That's what I've been doing. I'd just finished when you asked me to light the fire in here. (*She holds out her hands. The palms are black with coal-dust.*)

NICHOLAS: Haven't you washed your hands?

PATIENCE: Not yet. I cleared out that big cupboard beside our bed for the dresses. It was full of your old toys. I discovered him. (*She points to the toy on the piano.*) He's funny, isn't he?

  NICHOLAS *turns and sees the toy-bear.*

PATIENCE: The rest of the toys and the books I packed carefully away in my trunk. I think we might send them all to the orphanage, don't you? The kids would dearly love them even though they are a bit out of date. (*As she speaks* NICHOLAS *goes quickly from the room.* PATIENCE *sits motionless until he returns from the bedroom. He comes back into the room. The girl watches him.*) What did you want to arrange about tomorrow?

NICHOLAS: You didn't know, of course.

PATIENCE: What didn't I know?

NICHOLAS: I can't scold you because you cannot be expected to realize what a wrong thing you have done.

PATIENCE: I've done nothing wrong. Really, Nicholas. I've done nothing.

NICHOLAS: It would have been useless to have attempted an earlier explanation to you.

PATIENCE: An explanation of what?

NICHOLAS: You slut. You'll go upstairs to my room and unpack those toys and books and put them back exactly as you found them.

PATIENCE: I can't remember how they were. What did you call me?

NICHOLAS: You can't remember how they were?

PATIENCE: No, not exactly. I'll put them back if you want me to do that. I didn't know—

NICHOLAS: You can't remember how they were.

PATIENCE: I've told you, no. They were in such a muddle.

NICHOLAS: You have destroyed them.

PATIENCE: Of course I haven't. I told you. I've put them carefully away in my trunk.

NICHOLAS: You have destroyed them. Just as if you had burned them.

PATIENCE: I think you're making an awful fuss.

NICHOLAS: Am I?

PATIENCE: I think so.

NICHOLAS: Have you no regard for other people's property?

PATIENCE: But you are my husband—

NICHOLAS: Yes.

PATIENCE: —and they are your baby toys. But you're not a child now, Nicholas.

NICHOLAS: And my only excuse for you is that you are a child.

PATIENCE: Well, come to that, you're only about five years older than me—

NICHOLAS: Shut up!

PATIENCE: I'll go and put them away, the toys, as nearly as I can remember, in their old places.

NICHOLAS: No, it's finished: done with. Even you with your limited understanding must realize that. It's done with. They can never be put back.

There is a pause.

PATIENCE: Will you explain to me what I've done wrong? (*She pauses.*) I don't understand. (*She pauses.*) I was very careful with them. Don't you know how delighted I am by the seeing and the touching of the toys that belonged—still belong—to you? Do you think I could destroy them? I suggested they should go to the kids at the orphanage to pass on, continue, the happiness, that was all. I shouldn't send him (*she indicates the toy bear*) because I think he's funny. I brought him down to ask you if I might keep him for myself. I'll love him as much as you've loved him. When I was taking the toys from the cupboard and the books from the shelves I thought of you as a boy. (*She laughs.*) Come, Nicholas! Tell me what you were like. Were you handsome or ugly? Naughty or good? Noisy or quiet? (*She goes to embrace him.*) Were you ever in love with any little girls then? Who were your friends? What did you think about at nights, alone, in that room before—?

NICHOLAS *turns and strikes her across the face. After a pause*
PATIENCE *bursts into howls of pain.*

You've hurt me!

NICHOLAS *stands watching her as she cries.*

Why did you hit me? You've hurt me very much. Why did you
hurt me? Have I deserved it? You have never been angry with me
before. Never once. What did I say? 'Who were your friends?
Were you ever in love? Noisy or naughty or—' Did I give offence?

NICHOLAS *goes to her and puts his arms about her. As the girl's sob-
bing dies a brass band can be heard playing in the distance.*

God! How you frightened me.

NICHOLAS *leads her to the door.*

You want me to go? I will. I'll go and put back the toys and the
books in their places. At once. I'll go now. Don't worry. They
shall all be put back as they were before. I can remember. (*She goes
out.* NICHOLAS *returns to the room. He sits. After a moment he rises
and moves towards the door.*)

NICHOLAS (*he shouts*): Patience! Patience!

There is a pause.

Patience!

PATIENCE (*off*): What is it?

NICHOLAS *returns from the door. He stands by the toy bear. Suddenly,
dropping his stick, he snatches up the toy and holds it to him in an embrace.
He is whispering endearments to the toy as* PATIENCE *calls again.*

Yes? I'm listening. What is it?

CURTAIN

SCENE 2

The same: late afternoon of the same day.
Present are EMILY, PETER, A. G. *and* PATIENCE.
PATIENCE *is wearing one of the dresses given to her by* EMILY. *It is of grey
silk and is generally too large for the girl.*
They are finishing tea. PATIENCE *is crossing the room with two cups to
place them on the small table before Emily.*

PETER: Come now. Be cheerful.

A. G.: Be quiet.

PETER: But why? We have cause to be cheerful.

A. G.: Cause?

PETER: Yes.

A. G.: But nothing has happened.

PETER: And isn't that cause enough for us to be happy?

A. G.: Three times in the last half-hour you have said to us, 'Be cheerful'. No one has answered you.

PETER: I didn't expect an answer.

A. G.: Now you tell us we should be happy because nothing of importance has occurred. Did you expect something frightful to happen?

PETER: Oh, yes.

A. G.: What?

EMILY: What, Peter?

PETER: Don't be angry.

A. G.: Take your hand away from your face—let me see you.

PETER *removes his hand; his expression is innocent enquiry.*

PETER: Well?

A. G.: What do you mean?—Well.

PETER: I thought you wished to ask me something.

A. G.: Ask you—?

PETER: Yes. I thought you wanted to ask my advice.

A. G.: This is absurd!

PETER: Not at all.

A. G.: But it is! The conversation is absurd—without reason! (A. G. *moves across the room to return his tea-cup to* EMILY. *He passes before* PETER *who, sitting, puts out a leg and trips* A. G. *who falls to the floor, the tea-cup flying from his hand.*

PETER: My dear fellow! I'm so sorry! Are you hurt? (*He assists* A. G. *to his feet.* PATIENCE *picks up the broken cup.*)

EMILY: Come along, A. G. Sit down. (*She leads* A. G. *to a chair.*)

PETER: Yes. Come along.

EMILY: What a nasty fall.

PETER: Yes. I can't forgive myself. I must watch what I'm doing. Don't look so reproachful, old man. It wasn't intentional. If you were a child I should be inclined to say, 'Temper! Temper! That's where temper lands you.' (*He laughs.*)

EMILY: Are you all right now, A. G.?

A. G.: Yes.

EMILY: Would you like some water?

A. G.: No.

EMILY: Patience, go and get some water.

A. G.: No! (*He shouts.*) I don't want any water.

EMILY: Very well.

     A. G. *rises from the chair and moves across the room staring at* PETER. *The others watch him.*

A. G.: I struck my head.

PETER: Then come and sit down—rest.

A. G.: Yes, rest. Rest and be cheerful.

PETER (*smiles*): Now look. Come and sit down. It wasn't as bad a fall as all that, was it?

A. G.: Bad enough.

EMILY: Would you like to go home, A. G.?

A. G.: No. (*He turns to* PATIENCE.) Why should Mr Bembo wish me to fall?

PATIENCE: I don't know.

PETER: It was an accident.

PATIENCE: It was an accident.

A. G. (*to* PATIENCE): Do you know—you live in this house—do you know of any reason why Mr Bembo should wish to hurt me?

PATIENCE: I don't.

A. G.: He must have a reason, mustn't he?

    The girl does not answer.

Mustn't he?

    PATIENCE *moves to the door.*

Don't go! Please don't go!

    PATIENCE *goes out.* A. G. *turns to face* PETER.

She is afraid of you? Or of me?

PETER: She is afraid of neither of us. She is embarrassed, that's all.

A. G.: Embarrassed! Dear God!

PETER: I tell you it was an accident. The girl realizes that. I'm sorry. It merely happened that when you were passing me I stretched out my leg: you tripped and fell. I can assure you I have nothing against you personally—and if I had anything against you I'd not play schoolboy tricks on you. I am not in any way a malicious person. You remember me? I am an old clown. Reverse the positions. Suppose you had accidentally tripped me and it was I who had sprawled on the floor. What would have happened? Everyone in the room, you with them, would have laughed and shouted, 'Bembo! You old fool!' and then laughed again.

A. G.: And you would have stood up in pain and bowed and fixed a smile on your face.

PETER: You understand me?

A. G.: I understand you deliberately tried to harm me.

PETER: I'm sorry you should think that. I can say no more.

A. G.: And if you would do that how else might you threaten me?

PETER (*in sudden anger*): I've never threatened anyone in my life. (*To* EMILY.) May I put the lights on?

EMILY: Of course.

PETER *does so and then crosses to draw the curtains.*

Come and sit down, A. G.

A. G.: Thank you, my dear.

EMILY *takes the tea-tray from the room.*

PETER (*at the window*): I wonder when they light the coloured lamps in the public gardens. Those hanging from the trees. (*He pauses.*) I say, I wonder when they—

A. G.: Yes. I heard what you said. On Wednesday.

PETER: What happens on Wednesday?

A. G.: A fête. A children's sports meeting and, at night, dancing in the gardens.

PETER: It would be a brave soul who danced in those gardens from what I saw of them this morning. And all this in aid of—?

A. G.: The local British Legion.

PETER: Have you ever fought in your life?

A. G. *does not reply.*

Tell me. In the gardens there is an engraved stone—

A. G.: With my name—yes.

PETER: You—

A. G.: I presented the building where the public can buy tea and refreshments.

PETER: Ah! Refreshments. Do they?

A. G.: What?

PETER: Buy either?

A. G.: No.

PETER: I'm not surprised. Who would imagine they could be refreshed by that dismal hut?

A. G.: I was not responsible for the design.

PETER: You presented it to the town. Now what did you hope to gain by doing that?

A. G.: What do you mean?

PETER: What did you hope to get out of it?

A. G.: Nothing. It was the gesture of a newcomer to the town. It was given in memory of my wife who played in those gardens as a child. You would have known that if you had troubled to read the words on the stone.

PETER: Have you seen it recently?

A. G.: I—

PETER: The stone is defaced. Your name remains but otherwise new hands, new lovers have been at work. No mention of Helen but there is 'Syd loves Lil' and 'Lil loves Syd' cut deep.

A. G.: They can be prosecuted for that.

PETER: Do you do many—many 'good works'?

A. G.: When I—

PETER: Then let me impress upon you the urgent need to aid the charity for Crippled Children.

A. G.: We have no such local charity.

PETER: Then start one.

A. G.: Why do you smile?

PETER: It is of great importance. Emily will help you. I will help you.

    EMILY *has entered the room.*

EMILY: What will I help?

PETER: A. G. to start a charity fund for crippled children. I'll start it here. (*He takes a coin from his pocket.*)

A. G.: A halfpenny?

PETER: Don't sneer at it. Four hundred halfpennies may well buy one little wooden leg. Collect, A. G., collect!

EMILY: Yes, I'll help.

    NICHOLAS *and* PATIENCE *enter.* NICHOLAS *carries the reading lamp.*

NICHOLAS: I shall never invent another damned thing for you, A. G. This lamp has caused endless trouble.

A. G.: I'm sorry, Nicholas.

NICHOLAS: What do you do with it when you get it home?

A. G.: Nothing.

NICHOLAS: Well, if it doesn't work now I give it up. Here you are. (*He hands the lamp to* A. G.)

A. G.: Thank you. (*He holds out his hand to* PETER.)

PETER: What is it?

A. G.: Your halfpenny.

PETER: You refuse to do as I ask. I'm sorry—not for my sake but for the children, A. G., the children.

A. G.: Fool!

NICHOLAS: Are you two playing some kind of game?

A. G.: Shove ha'penny.

PETER: Did you make a joke, A. G.?

A. G.: Yes. Do you mind?

PETER: Not a bit. I'm delighted.

A. G. speaks to EMILY. PETER *watches* NICHOLAS *and* PATIENCE.

PATIENCE: Are you all right, Nicholas?

NICHOLAS: Of course I'm all right.

PATIENCE: Why didn't you come down to tea?

NICHOLAS: I've been in my room mending A. G.'s lamp.

PATIENCE: I haven't seen any of you all the afternoon.

NICHOLAS: No.

PATIENCE: I was afraid to come and look for you.

NICHOLAS: Were you now?

PETER: You mustn't be afraid of us.

PATIENCE: Mind your own business.

PETER: I'm sorry.

A. G. (*to* EMILY): You don't think he'll mind?

EMILY: Of course not.

NICHOLAS: What won't I mind?

A. G.: What?

NICHOLAS: I presumed you were speaking of me.

A. G.: Yes.

NICHOLAS: Well, then. What won't I mind?

A. G.: I should like— (*He stops.*)

EMILY: A. G. would like—

NICHOLAS: Let me hear him. Let him tell me himself. Yes?

A. G.: I'd like to speak to you.

NICHOLAS: Certainly.

A. G.: Alone.

NICHOLAS: Oh. (*He looks about the room.*) Well, we'd better go outside.

NICHOLAS and A. G. *go out.*

EMILY: Did you see much of the town during your walk this morning, Peter?

PETER: What? Oh, yes. The gardens and the town hall and the—the 'Crown', is it?

EMILY: Opposite the town hall?

PETER: Yes.

EMILY: That's right. 'The Crown'. It's the first time you've been out since you've been here, isn't it?

PETER: Yes. (*To* PATIENCE.) Do you like living here? In this town, I mean.

PATIENCE: I've never known another.

PETER: You must show me the sights some time.

EMILY: She can take you to the Farthingale Hill.

PETER: We might go out to tea.

PATIENCE: I'd like to.

NICHOLAS *enters. He smiles at* PETER.

EMILY: And what was so secret?

NICHOLAS: Didn't he tell you just now?

EMILY: No. He merely asked if I thought you would mind if he spoke to you alone.

NICHOLAS (*laughs*): And you expect me to tell you?

EMILY: Of course.

NICHOLAS: A. G. wants our help—our advice.

EMILY: What about?

NICHOLAS (*to* EMILY): What's the matter?

EMILY: Nothing.

NICHOLAS: Oh, yes, there is. What is it?

EMILY: A. G.—

NICSOLAS: Yes?

EMILY: His behaviour in church this morning was inexcusable.

NICHOLAS: What did he do?

EMILY *does not answer.*

Spit on the cross?

Pause.

He has received an anonymous and, he says, threatening letter.

EMILY: From whom?

NICHOLAS: Don't be silly.

EMILY: You know. You know who sent it.

NICHOLAS: He wants our advice and our—our guesses as to who it is from and why it was sent. I said we would be more than pleased to help him clear up the mystery.

PETER: Of course. We can't have our little friend threatened by outsiders, by strangers. Of course we must help him.

NICHOLAS: He came to me alone. But I think I convinced him of your sincerity and desire to aid. He seemed suspicious of you. He even hinted that you might have written the letter yourself.

PETER: What did you say to that?

NICHOLAS: I said I didn't think you could write.

EMILY: Where is he?

NICHOLAS: He's gone to fetch the letter. He'd left it at his house.

PETER: He wants our advice?

NICHOLAS: Yes.

PETER: And our pity? That's what he's working for, isn't it?

EMILY: Why should he be pitied?

PETER: A frightened man with no understanding of the threats against him—he feels he requires pity.

EMILY: What are the threats against him?

PETER: We shall know.

EMILY: You already—

NICHOLAS: I cannot pity him. I've never pitied anyone in all my life.

PETER: Yourself?

NICHOLAS: No!

PETER: You have never—?

NICHOLAS: I've sometimes used the word. I am forced to use the common jargon to make myself understood. My meaning has more often been—

The front door is closed. There is a pause. A. G. *comes into the room. He is carrying the letter. He stands before the others for a moment and then speaks to* NICHOLAS.

A. G.: You've told them?

NICHOLAS: Yes.

PETER: We are very distressed. No man likes to be threatened. It is most disturbing. You can be sure of our support and, if necessary, our action against this scoundrel. You have come to us. That is good. It is always to friends you must go in the case of fear.

There is a pause. A. G. *speaks to* NICHOLAS *and* EMILY.

A. G.: The circumstances are these. When we returned from church this morning—(*He pauses and then speaks to* PETER.) I am not afraid.

PETER: Liar!

A. G.: What?

PETER: Any man must be afraid when threatened. Listen to me! We can only give you our advice and help in this matter providing you are honest and give us your faith.

A. G. (*to* NICHOLAS *and* EMILY): When we had returned from church this morning and you had left me I went to my house. This letter must have been delivered by hand in my absence. It lay just within the door and on entering I trod on it—you can see the mark of my sole— (*He holds up the letter.* PETER *shouts with laughter.* NICHOLAS *goes to take the letter but* A. G. *refuses him, withdrawing to a corner of the room.*) The paper and envelope are blue and of a good quality.

PETER (*taking a sheet of the identical paper from the desk*): Something like this?

A. G.: Very like that. It's sealed with red wax. (*Pause.*)

EMILY: And what does it say?

A. G. (*taking out the letter and reading*): 'You are discovered, therefore you are lost. She died in vain—' and then something I can't read.

NICHOLAS: 'Actum est.'

    There is a pause.

A. G.: I must go home. (A. G. *hesitates before running to the door.* NICHOLAS *has meanwhile moved to stand before the door which he shuts.*)

PETER (*speaking immediately*): But where is the threat in that? I don't understand you. No, I don't understand this at all. You have been misleading us. You gave us to believe you were in some kind of danger.

    Speaking through these lines of Peter's, NICHOLAS *has taken* A. G.'s *arm, saying,* 'Come and sit down. Dear oh, dear oh, dear!' *and leading him to a chair.*

You must explain more to us.

NICHOLAS: This has given you a very nasty shake-up I can see.

PETER: Yes. You must rest and recover your senses.

NICHOLAS: You're not well enough to run about like that.

PETER: I take it the reference in the letter is to your wife.

NICHOLAS: Give him time to recover. He has had a bad shock—delayed, you know. Is there anything I can get you, A. G.? A glass of water?

    A. G. *does not answer.* NICHOLAS *takes the letter from him.*

Now what can we make out from this?

PETER: May I see?

NICHOLAS: Certainly.

    They stand together examining the letter.

A good-quality paper—yes.

PETER: A man—

NICHOLAS: Or woman—

PETER: —of taste.

NICHOLAS: From the handwriting?

PETER: From the paper.

NICHOLAS: The wax—is that a thumbprint?

PETER: Perhaps.

NICHOLAS: A clue.

PETER: The handwriting—

NICHOLAS: A trace of affectation.

PETER: Indeed, yes.

NICHOLAS: More than a trace.

PETER: There is arrogance.

NICHOLAS: Yes.

PETER: That initial Y.

NICHOLAS: A flourish.

PETER: Dear me, yes.

NICHOLAS: It is obvious we—

PETER: Yes?

NICHOLAS: We have to deal with a dangerous fellow.

PETER: I'm afraid so.

NICHOLAS: But perhaps a trifle careless.

PETER: Why do you say that?

NICHOLAS: The paper was folded—

PETER: —before the ink was dry.

NICHOLAS: Careless.

PETER: Yes.

NICHOLAS: We may catch him in that.

PETER: We may.

NICHOLAS: His meaning. He writes—

PETER: 'You are discovered—'

NICHOLAS: Meaning A. G. is discovered.

PETER: Obviously.

NICHOLAS: '—therefore you are lost.'

PETER: Meaning A. G. is lost.

NICHOLAS: Quite.

PETER: So far, so good. 'She—'

NICHOLAS: A. G.'s wife.

PETER: Well—

NICHOLAS: You seem doubtful.

PETER: I suppose it must be.

NICHOLAS: Who else?

PETER: We'll take it as being his wife.

NICHOLAS: 'She died in vain.'

PETER: The cause was not enough.

NICHOLAS: No.

PETER: Pity.

NICHOLAS: Unfulfilled.

PETER: 'Actum est.'

NICHOLAS: 'Actum est.'

    There is a pause.

PETER (*to* A. G.): Better? (*To* NICHOLAS.) He is badly shaken by this. (*Shouting.*) The blackguard! How dare he intimidate helpless men! How dare he play upon the emotion and sensitivity of a man like this! (*He indicates himself.*)

NICHOLAS: Peter! This situation—

PETER (*to* A. G.): You are in great danger.

NICHOLAS: Yes.

PETER: You must behave naturally, however.

NICHOLAS: We—

PETER: Casually.

NICHOLAS: The situation calls—

PETER: You must not—*must not* betray the slightest anxiety or fear.

NICHOLAS: I agree.

PETER: You must laugh. Be—be—

NICHOLAS: Devil-may-care.

PETER: But I do not.

    PETER *and* NICHOLAS *laugh.*

Yes. That is how you must behave.

NICHOLAS: Better?

PETER: Feel better, A. G.?

NICHOLAS: Well enough to discuss our plans? For we have plans to help you. Haven't we, Peter?

PETER: We have.

NICHOLAS: Yes, you look better. Listen to me. Can you hear me? (*To* PETER.) Do you think he can hear me?

PETER (*shouting at* A. G.): Can you hear us?

    A. G. *gives no indication.*

Yes, he can hear us.

NICHOLAS: Right.

PETER: It is obvious from this letter that you are threatened. Oh, yes.

I understand the threat. Foolish of me not to realize it from the first instance. Now! Have you any idea who wrote this letter?

NICHOLAS: He can't hear us.

PETER (*kneeling by* A. G.'s *side*): Yes, he can. Do you know who wrote this letter?

In the silence A. G. *raises his arm and points at* PETER. PETER, *purposely misunderstanding, moves to leave* A. G.'s *finger pointing at* EMILY. Emily? Absurd! You didn't send this letter, did you, Emmy?

EMILY *goes quickly from the room.* A. G.'s *finger remains pointing until* PETER *slaps down his hand.* Don't point. It's rude.

NICHOLAS: No matter who sent it you can rely on our help.

PETER: You shouldn't have accused Emily like that. Even in fun. I expect you've upset her.

NICHOLAS: We'll help you. You've come to us as your friends and we shan't disgrace you. I promise you dear, dear A. G., we shan't fail you.

PETER: We are extraordinarily capable—hardly used, of course, but capable of dealing with things like this.

NICHOLAS: Our plans are these. Shall I tell him or will you?

PETER: Carry on.

NICHOLAS: We're going to protect you.

PETER: We'll stay with you.

NICHOLAS: So don't worry.

PETER: If you are afraid to be alone—

NICHOLAS: Yes, alone in your house—

PETER: You can come and stay here. Can't he?

NICHOLAS: Of course he can.

PETER: You can move in and close up your own house.

NICHOLAS: And live with us until it is all over.

PETER: We won't desert you.

There is a pause.

NICHOLAS: This has upset you, of course.

PETER: It would have upset me. But we must be cheerful.

NIHOLAS: You need taking out of yourself for a while. Doesn't he?

PETER: Yes.

NICHOLAS: Have you any suggestions?

PETER (*pauses*): Let's all go and have a drink.

NICHOLAS: Fine. There you are, A. G. What about that, eh? We'll all go and have a drink.

PETER: Then come back here with us and we'll amuse you. Keep your mind occupied until bed-time.

NICHOLAS: Yes. Let's do that, shall we, A. G.?

PETER: Just a moment. Let him recover himself. Give him a few minutes.

NICHOLAS: Yes. Take your time, A. G. We're in no hurry.

> NICHOLAS *and* PETER *move apart from* A. G. *and speak quietly together*.

What a damned thing to do. Attack him through the memory of his wife. We all know how fond he was of her.

PETER: We do. No one who has heard the story of her death could fail to be moved by the gracious memories he has of her last hours.

NICHOLAS: The cruelty of 'She died in vain'.

PETER: Ah, yes.

NICHOLAS: When by her very death she made A. G. what he is now.

PETER: Don't speak of it. (*He fingers beneath his eyeshade.*) Are we ready?

NICHOLAS: Give him a moment longer.

> *They stand in respectful silence.*

PETER: He is moving.

NICHOLAS: Yes. I think he's all right now.

> PETER *moves to* A. G. *and, taking his hands, raises him from the chair.*

PETER: Ups-a-daisy. Has he a hat and coat?

> NICHOLAS *indicates the hallway.*

Come along then.

> *The three men go out—*A. G. *between* NICHOLAS *and* PETER. PATIENCE *remains still until the front door is heard to close when she moves to the window. She draws back the curtain and stands staring into the street.* EMILY *comes into the room.*

PATIENCE: Are they going to murder him?

EMILY: No, of course not.

PATIENCE: Why did they send that letter?

> EMILY *has seated herself at the piano. Looking at* PATIENCE *she strikes a chord and then speaks.*

EMILY: What a pretty child you are.

PATIENCE (*very pleased*): Am I?

EMILY: Yes, very pretty.

PATIENCE: Thank you. (*She bobs a little mock curtsey.*)

CURTAIN

ACT THREE

The same: 9.30 the same evening.

EMILY *is sitting in an armchair; she is holding a book.* PATIENCE *is seated on a low stool set at Emily's feet.* EMILY *puts down the book, leaving it open. She then puts an arm about* PATIENCE'S *shoulders in a gentle, affectionate gesture.*

EMILY: How charming we must look to anyone who could see us.

PATIENCE: Do you ever think of how you look to other people?

EMILY: Don't you?

PATIENCE: No. I've never really bothered. Nick—Nicholas says—

EMILY: Yes?

PATIENCE: He says I've no pride.

EMILY: Have you?

PATIENCE: No, I don't think so.

EMILY: You are not so aware of yourself as he would like, is that it?

PATIENCE (*not understanding*): I suppose so.

EMILY: When did he say that?

PATIENCE: I don't really—What?

EMILY: When did he say you had no pride?

PATIENCE: Oh, I don't know.

EMILY: Well, how did it come up?

PATIENCE: When I asked him if he'd like to come and watch me have my bath.

There is a pause. EMILY *then speaks with tenderness.*

EMILY: Poor Nicholas.

PATIENCE: Will you read some more to me?

EMILY: No more this evening. The men will be back soon.

EMILY *is tidying* PATIENCE'S *hair.*

PATIENCE: You have a lovely voice.

EMILY: Thank you.

PATIENCE: You have a lovely face. How old are you?

EMILY: Fifty-eight.

PATIENCE: That's not old, is it?

EMILY: To you, at seventeen, it must be.

PATIENCE: Does anyone flatter you?

EMILY (*calling out*): Who's there?

PATIENCE: What is it?

EMILY: Didn't you hear the door?

PATIENCE: No.

 They sit listening. There is silence.

 What's the matter?

EMILY: Nothing. I'm expecting the men, that's all.

PATIENCE: They'll be home soon, won't they?

 Again they listen.

EMILY: One of us must go. (*She goes out of the room. After a moment she returns.*) Nothing. I shall leave the lights on. For their return. (*She closes the door.*)

PATIENCE (*picking up the book*): Who wrote that last thing? You mustn't be afraid.

EMILY: No. John Donne.

 PATIENCE *laughs.*

PATIENCE: I'm sorry.

EMILY: I don't mind.

PATIENCE: Funny name. Is he dead?

EMILY: Oh, yes.

PATIENCE: All the poets seem to be dead.

EMILY: What did you say?

PATIENCE: I said, all the poets seem to be dead.

EMILY: Nicholas put it another way.

PATIENCE: What?

EMILY: Many years ago, when Nicholas was small—about ten or eleven—I was reading to him. At the end, on his way to bed, he turned at the door (*she indicates the door*)—it was this room—and asked me if the poet was dead. Yes, I said. Of course, he said, only dead men could write like that.

PATIENCE: That's the only story you've ever told me about Nicholas. He remembers some of the things you read to him.

EMILY: Does he? He never speaks of them to me.

PATIENCE: Did you read these poems to him?

EMILY: I can't remember. Probably.

 There is a pause as PATIENCE *refers to the book.*

PATIENCE: I didn't know such things were written.

EMILY: What? Things like—?

PATIENCE: Such as the poems you read to me. About love.

EMILY: What poetry have you known?

PATIENCE: 'Marmion'.

EMILY (*smiles*): What?

PATIENCE: 'Marmion'. I remember that. A long poetry story in a red cover.

EMILY: School? (PATIENCE *nods*.) Did you like it?

PATIENCE: No. But this— (*She indicates the poem*) —such things as this are thought by men about women but surely most secretly.

EMILY: That poem was probably written most secretly.

PATIENCE: But it is here, in print, for anyone to read. How is that?

EMILY: The man was a poet.

PATIENCE: Teachers! You won't find me being guided by old, dead men.

EMILY: I didn't mean that.

PATIENCE: This girl he writes about—she's dead?

EMILY: Yes. She's dead.

PATIENCE: And all the men whose poems are in this book—they're all dead?

EMILY: All dead.

PATIENCE: 'O my America! my new-found-land.'

EMILY: Don't break the book like that!

PATIENCE: Well, I'm alive. Very much so. Say it again.

EMILY: What?

PATIENCE: That I'm pretty.

EMILY: You're pretty.

PATIENCE: I'm prettiest when—Nobody flatters me, either. Let's talk about such things.

    EMILY *moves away.*

Nicholas said you'd probably try to educate me. He warned me about it. (*She pauses to study Emily's reaction to this.*) Did you hear what I said?

EMILY: Yes, I heard you. Should we both have a drink? They must be back soon. (EMILY *moves to pour out the wine.*)

PATIENCE: Nicholas made me drunk on our honeymoon.

EMILY: Did he?

PATIENCE: On whiskey. I could hardly stand.

EMILY: Couldn't you?

PATIENCE: The hotel porter had to carry me to the bedroom.

EMILY: Oh?

PATIENCE: I was sick. I was sick all over the bedroom floor.

EMILY: Poor Patience!

PATIENCE: Have you ever been drunk?

EMILY: Yes.

PATIENCE: Really drunk?

EMILY: Here you are. (*She holds out the glass of wine to* PATIENCE.)

PATIENCE: What's the time?

EMILY: Just after twenty to ten.

PATIENCE: Oh.

    Pause.

EMILY: Where did they say they were going?

PATIENCE: They just said to have a drink. No special place.

EMILY: They can't be far away.

PATIENCE: Why not?

EMILY: Nicholas' leg.

PATIENCE: Of course.

EMILY: He can't—

PATIENCE: No, of course not. He won't—A. G. has the car though and—Ought I to get some food ready for them?

EMILY: There's some cold meat and salad.

PATIENCE: Very well. (*She goes to the door and then turns to* EMILY.) Aren't you coming?

    EMILY *shakes her head. After a moment of indecision, then fear,* PATIENCE *returns quickly into the room.*

What? What?

    EMILY *is silent.*

Well, we can get it when they come in. It won't take long. Meat and salad. (*She takes up her glass of wine.*)

    Looking at EMILY, PATIENCE *sees that in her abstraction her glass is tilted and the liquid spilling.*

Hey! You're spilling your drink. (*She takes out her handkerchief and wipes the wine from Emily's dress.*) Clumsy. You mustn't be clumsy. You are always so delicate. (*She laughs and kisses* EMILY.) Mustn't be clumsy.

    EMILY *suddenly takes* PATIENCE *in a close embrace.*

What is it? Dear Emily.

    PATIENCE *returns the embrace.*

Don't look so amazed. (*She laughs again.*) No harm done. I only kissed you. Look at me. I've enjoyed this evening very much.

Thank you for it. Did you mean to please me? Because you have. So you see—no harm done. (*She disengages herself from the embrace and puts down the two glasses.*) So. Here, I say! Why do you look at me like that? (*She laughs.*) Have I said something foolish?

EMILY *shakes her head.*

What's the matter? You do look unforgiving.

EMILY: Come and sit down again.

PATIENCE: I don't want to sit down.

EMILY: I have something to tell you.

PATIENCE: What?

EMILY: Something I've been asked to tell you.

PATIENCE: By Nicholas?

EMILY: Yes.

PATIENCE: I guessed that. Clever, eh? I seem to have annoyed him. He won't speak to me.

EMILY: I'm sorry.

PATIENCE: Well, come on. What is it?

EMILY: Nicholas—

PATIENCE: Yes?

EMILY: He has suffered great disappointment.

PATIENCE: Yes?

EMILY: It is only human.

PATIENCE: You mustn't talk to me like that. Human. Men and women do this and that. I am myself and I behave as Patience Loratt—Patience Doon. He is Nicholas Doon and as Nicholas Doon he must be expected to behave. I don't need excuses for him.

(*She pauses.*) Go on. (*She pauses.*) Go on!

EMILY: He is going to kill himself. (*She goes quickly on.*) Himself. Nicholas. Himself. He says he intends to kill himself. It is part of a plan that I don't understand: to kill himself. Do you believe me? Do you, child?

PATIENCE: Child! I am a child and you make fun of my innocence.

EMILY: No!

PATIENCE: I meant—

EMILY: I'll forget that you're a child. I'll ignore your innocence.

PATIENCE: I meant to say ignorance. I am not innocent. I am foul.

(*She wanders to the door and goes out of the room.* EMILY, *following, stands in the open doorway, calling after her.*)

EMILY: He has had great provocation.

PATIENCE (*off*): What?

EMILY: Don't go. I've more to tell you. It is a defensive act. Don't you understand, the secrecy and the joking are directed against himself. The plot is against himself.

   PATIENCE *returns to the room.* EMILY *stands aside to allow her to enter.*

EMILY: For any of us to take, at any time, an instrument of suicide is easy. (*She is silent.* PATIENCE *has moved into the room. She picks up her glass of wine and puts it down again, untouched. She moves about the room.* EMILY *watches her.*)

PATIENCE: Now, look. You say he's told you this?

EMILY: Yes. It's true. Do you believe it?

PATIENCE: Do you?

EMILY: There's nothing to be done.

PATIENCE: Do you believe it?

EMILY: I don't know.

PATIENCE: It's a joke, isn't it?

EMILY: I don't know.

PATIENCE: Did it seem as if he was joking?

EMILY: Peter laughed.

PATIENCE: And Nicolas?

EMILY: He wasn't laughing. It's something to do with A. G.

PATIENCE: But he's a joke. I mean, they laugh at him. When did they tell you this?

EMILY: This afternoon. They—

PATIENCE: Sit down.

   EMILY *sits.*

EMILY: Nicholas asked me, just before he went out this evening with Peter and A. G., to tell you. He wanted you to know.

PATIENCE: Forget my innocence! (*She laughs. The two women stare at each other in silence. Into the silence the telephone rings.* EMILY *remains unmoving and it is* PATIENCE *who answers it.*) Yes. Yes; Patience. Very well. (*She puts down the receiver.*) Peter. Phoning from a close-by box. They'll be home in a minute, he said.

EMILY: Nicholas—

PATIENCE: They're all together, he said. Did Nicholas say anything about me?

EMILY: Then he's not in the house. (*She moves quickly to the door.*)

PATIENCE: Did he? Did he talk about me? Tell me. It's important.

   EMILY *returns to* PATIENCE.

EMILY: Give me your hands. (*She takes Patience's hands.*) No, he didn't talk about you. Just asked me to tell you. (*She raises and kisses Patience's hands, laughing.*) Funny! Now I see the mortality in everything. I've not thought of it before. My husband died away from me—miles away. But now I see it as you appear to see it. You talk about your innocence—your ignorance. I am as ignorant of this experience as you. But now, Nicholas—You are young and strong and if it is his intention to—You say it. Go on. You say it.

PATIENCE: Nicholas is going to kill himself.

EMILY: If that is his intention you must exercise your strength and surrender yourself to the lack of comprehension that is the blessing of your youth. By attempting to understand you may, by chance, succeed and that will destroy you.

PATIENCE: What do you mean? You talk like a book.

EMILY: I mean soon Nicholas will kill himself. We must not obstruct his designs or we shall distort the pattern of our lives. You must attempt, therefore, not to understand but to accept.

PATIENCE: But it wouldn't be friendly not to try to save him. Besides, it's against the law.

EMILY: You must know—Rather. How can you tell who are friends and who enemies? That is the basis of Nicholas' suspicion.

PATIENCE: When I married him—

EMILY: Very well, then. Don't believe it. It's not true. It is a joke. But remember, some people see quite clearly—

PATIENCE: They are here.

EMILY: —that a man has no other—

The front door is heard to open and the sound of the men's voices is also heard for a moment: the door is heard to close. There is silence. The two women stare at the closed door of the room.

PATIENCE: I was lying about my being drunk. I made it up to frighten you.

Pause.

EMILY: Why don't they come in?

After EMILY *has spoken there is another pause: the door then opens and* PETER, A. G. *and* NICHOLAS *enter.* A. G. *is in the centre, his arms linked with those of the other two men. All three are in a state of great exultation but, although they have been drinking, they are not drunk. They come fully into the room.*

A. G.: I have two friends!

NICHOLAS: Hullo, Mother.

A. G.: Emily!
EMILY: Hullo, Nicholas. } *Spoken together.*

A. G.: Did you hear me, Emily? I have two friends! } *Spoken*
PETER: Only just in time. I think it's going to rain. } *together.*

EMILY: Yes, I hear you, A. G. Have you walked far?

NICHOLAS: We've been to the 'Crown'.
A. G.: The three of us have been talking together. } *Spoken together.*

PETER: What's the time?

EMILY: You're not tired, Nicholas?

NICHOLAS: No. (*To* PETER.) Getting on for ten.

A. G. *is touching* EMILY'S *arm and speaking her name quietly in an attempt to gain her attention.*

PETER: We should have been home earlier but when we came out of the 'Crown' there was an accident and we couldn't drag A. G. away from the spectacle.

A. G. (*laughing*): I say!

EMILY: What happened?

NICHOLAS: A car ran into a horse drawing a cart.

PETER: We saw it happen and A. G. insisted on staying until they put the beast away.

A. G.: Really, I was— (*Laughs.*)

PETER: And so we stood there—just watching the dying animal.

NICHOLAS (*pointing to* A. G.): Is that blood on your shoes?

A. G. (*laughing*): No, no! Of course not. (*He bends down to wipe his shoes.*)

PETER: So that's— (*he smacks* A. G.'s *behind*) —why we're late.

A. G.: It was Nicholas who said, 'We may as well wait until the end.' I was quite willing to come away. (*He laughs.*) Good gracious me! You speak as if it were some kind of entertainment.

PETER: Your face was, as they say, 'a study'.

A. G. (*to* EMILY): Peter sat by the animal's head and talked to it. Most extraordinary.

EMILY: Are you hungry? I mean, do you want supper now?

NICHOLAS: No, later. You'll stay, won't you, A. G.?

A. G.: I'd like to, Nicholas, I'd like to.

NICHOLAS: Good. Let me take your hat and coat. (*He takes* A. G.'s *hat from his head and assists him with his coat.* NICHOLAS *and* PETER *then go out to remove their own coats.*)

A. G.: Emily, I have something to tell you.

EMILY: What?

A. G.: It's secret.

EMILY: What's that?

A. G.: Not really, I suppose. They've told me. You know it was Nicholas and Peter who sent that letter to me. (*He laughs.*) The rascals!

EMILY: Why?

A. G.: Eh?

EMILY: Why did they send it?

A. G.: Because of Helen. We had a talk about it. They say I am always going on about her and that I bore people—people like you—with my stories of her. I must admit I didn't realize it but now they have mentioned it—been completely honest about it—I believe it must be true. Nicholas says I'm to ask your forgiveness. Will you forgive me, Emily?

EMILY: Of course.

A. G.: I'll take back the prayer-book from you.

EMILY: I hadn't accepted it.

A. G.: No, but—well, I'll take it back. I suppose the memory of her has obsessed me. But there was no one else. You do understand that, don't you? No one. But now—Nicholas. He says he will find me interests to occupy my mind.

EMILY: Good.

A. G.: I have spoken to you about my child.

EMILY: What?

A. G.: The unborn.

EMILY: Oh, yes.

A. G.: May I—? (*He stops.*)

EMILY: You may do anything you wish so long as you don't make a fuss about it.

A. G.: Nicholas says I can see more of him and he wants me to drive him out in my car. (*To* PATIENCE.) You too, of course, my dear.

EMILY: That's good.

A. G.: Yes, I think it will be good for both of us. You see, Emily, Nicholas' assurance of friendship gives me a future. It is good, isn't it? Forgive me, Emily.

EMILY: Yes, I'm sure it will be very good for you.

A. G.: So, you see, that letter and all the fuss was a joke. (*He pauses.*) A cruel joke. (*He laughs.*) Of course, I had a pretty good idea who sent it. I mean the paper was—

PATIENCE: You have never told me about your wife.

A. G. (*unsurely*): Haven't I?

PATIENCE: Will you?

A. G.: Perhaps: some time. Nicholas says the memory is unhealthy. He says I should not speak or write of her. She's dead, he says; there must be no more about her. Even the memoirs I am writing —Nicholas says I must put, 'At this time I was married'—'In this month my wife died'. That is all.

  NICHOLAS *and* PETER *have entered, unseen by* A. G.

It won't be easy. I had already written much about her—a pity I have to destroy it. Her name was Helen. (*He moves to* PATIENCE, *speaking to her.*) She was about your height—her hair was fair though—she had a scar on her arm, just there— (*he touches* PATIENCE'S *left arm*) —an accident when she was a child playing in the gardens. (*He pauses.*) That dress you are wearing—is it fancy dress?

PATIENCE: It's one of Emily's old frocks. A present from her to me.

A. G.: That explains it. (*He touches the dress.*) Grey silk. That would have been a fine dress to Helen. She loved—She died, you know. She was killed at a circus by falling from—

  PETER *has moved to* A. G. *and now puts an arm around* A. G.'s *shoulders.* A. G. *turns to see the two men.*

Hullo, Nicholas. You were wrong. Here's someone (*he laughs and indicates* PATIENCE)—who has never heard my stories about Helen.

NICHOLAS: Now, I've warned you. If you keep on about it I've warned you what will happen.

PETER: One of these days, now our curse is upon you, you'll open your mouth, say, 'Helen', and—Puff!—you'll disappear.

A. G. (*laughing immoderately*): Yes, Peter.

NICHOLAS: What have we got for supper?

EMILY: There's some cold meat and salad.

NICHOLAS: Will that suit you, A. G.?

A. G.: Anything will do. I'm not very hungry.

  PETER *still has his arm around* A. G.'s *shoulders and he is whispering:*
A. G. *giggles.*

NICHOLAS: I met Gerald Hussey in the town.

EMILY: Oh?

NICHOLAS: He was with some girl. He's just got back from India.

EMILY: It must be years since you saw him.

NICHOLAS: Yes. When we were at school.

There is renewed giggling from A. G. NICHOLAS *laughs.*

Shut up, you two! Ah! I feel pleasantly tired. I haven't walked so far for a long time. (*He yawns.*) Delightfully tired—and no pains.

PETER: Does your leg ever hurt you?

NICHOLAS: The actual leg, no—

PETER: I—

NICHOLAS: —but I am easily tired. Where is my darling wife? (*He speaks without irony.*)

EMILY: Patience!

NICHOLAS: Come here.

PATIENCE *moves to him.*

And what have you been doing since I've been away? (*To* EMILY.) Has she behaved herself?

EMILY: Oh, yes.

NICHOLAS: Have you been talking about me? Has Emily been telling you what a beautiful baby I was—with two fat legs? Did she say I was noisy or quiet? Naughty or good? Did she tell you I was in love with Caddy Jellyby? Well, I wasn't. Nor was the diary I kept—

A. G.: Would you like a game of cards? We could play bridge.

NICHOLAS: Me?

A. G.: Yes.

NICHOLAS: I don't want to play. Emily?

EMILY: No.

NICHOLAS: Peter?

PETER: No.

NICHOLAS: No, A. G. We don't want to play bridge.

A. G.: I don't mind.

NICHOLAS (*to* PATIENCE): Those were the things you wanted to know, weren't they?

A. G.: I only thought it would be something to pass the time.

NICHOLAS: Don't mutter, A. G. (*To* PATIENCE.) Caddy Jellyby was—

A. G.: But, of course, we can talk about anything now, can't we? (*He laughs.*) Except one subject.

NICHOLAS: That's right.

PETER *is turning out the contents of his pockets on to the desk.*

A. G.: I've told Emily.

NICHOLAS: What? (*To* PETER.) Looking for something?

PETER: Yes. An address.

A. G. (*laughs*): Going to write another letter, Peter?

PETER: That's right.

A. G. (*to* NICHOLAS): I told Emily about—the things you said—about my wife— (*He stops.*)

NICHOLAS: And—?

A. G.: She understands and she has forgiven me.

NICHOLAS: Emily?

A. G.: Yes. You remember you told me to ask her forgiveness?

NICHOLAS: Did I?

A. G.: Yes. Don't you remember?

NICHOLAS: I expect I did. (*He yawns again.*)

A. G.: But surely! You made a great point—

NICHOLAS: Yes, yes, A. G.; that's all right. We'll go out together. You can take me out in your car.

A. G.: I will, yes.

NICHOLAS: There are many places I should like to see again that—I can't walk to them now but you will take me in your car. To the places I want to see again. Farthingale Hill—

A. G.: Yes, Nicholas, we arranged all that.

NICHOLAS: Did we?

A. G. (*in sudden fear*): You haven't had too much to drink, have you?

NICHOLAS: No.

A. G.: We arranged all those things. Don't you remember?

NICHOLAS *nods.*

I said—You remember I said I admired you?

PETER: Yes. We remember everything you said.

NICHOLAS (*he is sitting, his eyes closed*): I'd like my supper.

EMILY: I'll get it.

NICHOLAS: No. Later.

EMILY: Very well.

NICHOLAS: Later. You're staying, A. G.?

A. G.: Well, yes. You asked me to and I said yes.

NICHOLAS: Of course.

There is silence. PETER *is sitting at the desk writing a note. Suddenly* A. G. *begins to chatter.*

A. G.: Farthingale Hill. I haven't been there myself for some time. A famous local beauty spot, Peter. Perhaps you've heard of it? When the rhododendrons that cover the south side are in bloom it's a picture. I didn't see them this summer. As I say I haven't been there for—oh, I don't know—it must be eighteen months. One doesn't, you know.

NICHOLAS: Well, you shall go there again with me.

A. G.: Thank you, Nicholas.

NICHOLAS: Not at all. Thank you, A. G.

A. G.: You can have the car—

NICHOLAS: What?

A. G.: You can have the car without me if you like. I mean, I won't come unless you want me.

NICHOLAS: No, you must come and drive. That's part of the agreement.

A. G.: Say you want me to come with you.

NICHOLAS: I do want you to come with me.

A. G.: I've never understood why you've not borrowed my car before. I've offered it several times. It was Emily who accepted it for your honeymoon. I thought you'd like it then because—well, it's better than going by train, eh?

NICHOLAS: Much better. It was very kind and generous of you to think of it, A. G. You're a very kind person and your generosity is alarming—as alarming as your exaggerated pathos. But I forgive you: Emily forgives you: we all forgive you. Don't worry. We are going to find common interests and exploit them. You know, I've found you suddenly, much as I found Peter here. We're going to be friends, A. G., friends! Think of that!

A. G.: What is it?

NICHOLAS: What?

PETER (to NICHOLAS): You can't hope to— } *Spoken together.*

PATIENCE (to A. G.): Don't!

A. G.: Just a moment, my dear. (To NICHOLAS.) What is it?

NICHOLAS: What is what?

PATIENCE: Look here!

A. G.: Ssh!

PETER: What's the matter, A. G.?

There is a pause.

A. G.: There's nothing the matter with me.

PETER: Well, why did you suddenly shout out like that?

A. G.: I'm sorry. I thought you were making a fool of me again. You're not, are you?

PETER: No.

A. G.: I'm speaking to Nicholas. I don't mean the remarks about my kindness and exaggerated pathos—that's a joke, isn't it? I mean, I see that but—you're not making a fool of me again?

PATIENCE (*to* A. G.): Listen to me!

NICHOLAS: I have a proposal to make.

PATIENCE: Don't listen to him. Go home now. Go home.

NICHOLAS: Peter. (*He turns to* PETER *who is still seated at the desk.*)

PETER: Yes?

PATIENCE (*to* A. G.): I'll walk home with you. Come along.

A. G.: I don't want to go home.

NICHOLAS: No, of course he doesn't want to go home.

A. G.: Really I don't, Nicholas. I don't.

NICHOLAS: Of course not. (*To* PATIENCE.) Leave him alone, you silly girl. (*To* EMILY.) Send her to bed.

PATIENCE: No.

EMILY *moves towards her.*

No!

EMILY *stops: there is silence.*

PATIENCE *and* A. G. *are standing together staring at* NICHOLAS.

NICHOLAS *taps twice on the floor with his stick and then extends the handle towards* A. G. *who takes it. By this means* NICHOLAS *guides* A. G. *to a chair where* A. G. *sits.*

NICHOLAS: Don't get excited. Nothing to get excited about.

PETER *comes from the desk carrying the note he has written sealed in an envelope.*

PETER: You said you had a proposal to make.

NICHOLAS: Yes.

PETER: I can only make a suggestion.

NICHOLAS: Well?

PETER: 'That passion may not harm us, let us act as if we had only eight hours to live.'

NICHOLAS: And how do you do to you. (*He laughs.*) You're old, you know, really quite old.

PETER: Ah! You've mistaken the meaning. (*To* PATIENCE.) Hasn't he?

NICHOLAS: I've told you I'm not very bright at times.

PETER: I shan't tell you the qualification of the suggestion. I'm afraid it would be useless.

NICHOLAS (*mocking his solemnity*): Ah, yes, indeed. Now let me see. See if I can guess. Something about a long life.

PETER: A hundred years, if I remember rightly.

NICHOLAS: Oh, a very long life.

A. G. (*to* PATIENCE): What are they talking about? (*To* EMILY.) Emily!

PATIENCE: They're talking about the day Nicholas will die.

A. G.: What a thing to talk about.

NICHOLAS: Yes. And this was going to be a quiet evening with your friends, wasn't it, A. G.?

A. G.: Yes.

NICHOLAS: Well, then, what else can we talk about?

PETER: I must go and post this.

NICHOLAS: The post will have gone.

PETER: Never mind. The box is outside the house, isn't it? I noticed—

NICHOLAS: That's right.

PATIENCE: I'll take it for you.

PETER: No, it's all right.

NICHOLAS: Well, now. What shall we talk about?

PATIENCE (*to* A. G.): Tell me about your wife.

NICHOLAS: Shall we talk about Emily and Peter many years ago? You don't know about that, A. G. (*He pauses.*) No? What about Patience and myself in the present? (*He pauses.*) No? Come on, what shall we talk about? Sit down, Peter.

PETER: I'm going out.

NICHOLAS: Let Emily read some poetry to us. (*He picks up the book of verse and snaps it shut.*) Not that? (*He pauses.*) Well, come along. Let's have some other suggestions. Peter?

    PETER *shakes his head.*

Let's talk about the things A. G. and myself are going to do together.

A. G.: Yes.

PATIENCE: Tell me about your wife.

    There is a pause.

NICHOLAS: Very well. Go on. Tell her. You may as well.

    A. G. *is silent.*

Well? (*He suddenly appears furiously angry.*) Well? How do you begin? Don't sit there like a mute. She is waiting to hear your story. That's what you want to talk about, isn't it? Very well, then, let's have it. How will you begin it? 'Once upon a time— Once upon a time—'. Say it! 'Once upon a time—.'

PETER: 'Once upon a time—'

A. G.: 'Once upon a time—'

NICHOLAS: '—twenty years ago—'

A. G.: '—twenty years ago—'

NICHOLAS: '—when I was young and handsome. When I was—'

A. G.: '—when I was young and handsome.'

NICHOLAS: '—I was married to a girl named Helen.'
Come along, old man. Her name was Helen. Remember?

A. G.: '—I was married to a girl named Helen.' (*He speaks to* PATIENCE.) Helen Dyson before I married her. Helen—

NICHOLAS: Yes?

A. G.: Helen was ten years younger than me. At the time of which I speak I was forty and we had been married for three years. I had known her for eight years before our marriage. She worked as a cashier in one of our shops. When she came to work for us my father was still alive—we were grocers, you know—and my brother and myself held only minor positions. But in the year my father died—

NICHOLAS *turns to* PETER *who is still holding the letter.* NICHOLAS *takes the letter and says, 'I'll take that.'* PETER *says, 'Very well.' They smile at each other.* NICHOLAS *goes out.* A. G. *continues uninterrupted.*
—I took sole charge of the shops and Helen and I were married. She left the shop then, of course. (*He pauses.*) She was a pretty girl but shy, very shy. (*He smiles.*) Are you shy? We were married for three years. We were happy—lived very quietly—not in this town where she was born but near Bristol—my shops were round there. Very happily, very quietly we lived and we wanted children. Do you want children? Yes, we'd have liked a baby very much but it was then we found we couldn't have one. After being married three years Helen was examined and that's what they told us. No children. You understand how disappointed we were? Helen was very distressed and insisted that she had failed me. That was not so, of course, but she said to me many times, 'I have failed you.' (*He pauses.*) She died, you know. She died at a circus performance in Spain. A circus with Mr Bembo here as a star performer. Yes, she died. It was very tragic. I'll tell you about it. (*He edges forward on his chair.*) We had travelled to Spain, you see, on a holiday. After the third week of the holiday we came to a town one night and we saw the advertisements for the circus. Mr Bembo's name was in large letters—he was famous then. Helen was very fond of the

circus. Are you?

PATIENCE: I've never been to one.

A. G.: Haven't you? Anyway, Helen was very fond of them and that night before going to sleep she said to me, 'Will you take me to the circus tomorrow?' Of course, I did, and the following evening we went to the performance. Now I want you to understand this quite clearly. The stands—set around the ring, you know—those stands had a fault in their construction. I have spoken to Mr Bembo about this. Helen and I were forced—we were late—to sit high in the back row of the stand. We were, I think, quite thirty feet from the ground. I've spoken to Mr Bembo about this also but he says he can't remember. But I should say we were quite thirty feet up from the ground. We had taken our places and Mr Bembo had begun his turn. You must get him to tell you about it some time. I suppose it was very funny. There was a child who came from the audience—to hold a paper hoop—Mr Bembo jumped through the hoop and then there was the laughter: and then Helen turned to me and complained of illness.

At this point PETER *begins to speak with* A. G. *He speaks to* PATIENCE.

Her face was puckered and I thought she was going to cry. I took her hand to lead her away from the place but we could only go singly on the narrow platform. That is why I say to you the stands were badly constructed. You see, she let go my hand and went on before me, alone. Then she fell.

PETER'S *voice accompanying this last passage has become louder.* A. G. *stops speaking.*

PETER: He turned to her and, indeed, she seemed ill. He was alarmed. Taking her hand he attempted to lead her away but the way of exit was narrow and it was only possible to go singly. He insists the stands were faulty but I can assure you it was the normal method of construction. She went on alone and then fell. She fell outwards away from A. G. and the other spectators.

When A. G. *stops speaking* PETER *pauses and then continues to speak to* PATIENCE *saying:*

As A. G. has told you it was very tragic—she was spared nothing for her fall was not direct. No, for the strap of her shoe caught, by some chance, in the structure and she hung, head downwards, her skirts about her head, while A. G. here stood in understandable indecision. You mustn't laugh! You mustn't!

PATIENCE *shakes her head. She is not laughing.*

No! (*To* A. G.) She is young. She doesn't understand. (*To* PATIENCE.) The shoe-strap broke and she fell to the ground. She was dead when the soldiers—it was soldiers?—

A. G.: Yes.

PETER: —when the soldiers picked her up and A. G. had climbed down to reach her. (*He pauses.*) I was present at that time but I was in ignorance. I was not told of the incident until I met A. G. Now I know. Now all of us here know. I believe today is her birthday?

A. G.: Yes.

PETER: Many happy returns of the day.

EMILY: Where's Nicholas?

PETER: He went out to post a letter for me. (*He again speaks to* PATIENCE.) Which of the many reasons that A. G. has given us made her do such a dreadful thing—that I don't know.

A. G.: Do what?

PETER: Her reasons for—

A. G.: Do what?

PETER: Why, kill herself.

A. G.: It was an accident.

PETER: What's that you say?

A. G.: I say it was an accident.

PETER: Your wife's death?

A. G.: Yes.

PETER: Then you have misled us.

A. G.: No!

PETER: You have always led us to believe your wife was a suicide.

A. G.: Never!

PETER: Oh, yes.

A. G.: No!

PETER: Oh, yes.

A. G.: No!

PETER: But you have implied, if not stated, so many reasons.

A. G.: Not one!

PETER: One: that she was to remain childless. Two: that she regarded herself as a failure in marriage. Three: that she couldn't live with your kindly reproach. Four: that she was afraid to return to England and a life of boredom with you among the sugar and spices. Five: that she was unbearably moved by the sight of the child coming bravely to me from the audience. Six: that my performance that day was so bad that the poor lady went straight off and did away with herself. Which of these reasons was the actual cause I say I don't know. But you've not only given us reasons—there are the various incidents. Her shoe catching and her hanging head downwards: to give her time for the full realization of the act, do you think? The business of love-making on the preceding night: what other motive had you in telling us that, eh? And other things—many other things. For instance—

A. G.: But I didn't mean that.

PETER: Whether you meant it or not—

A. G.: How could you believe such a thing?

PETER (*he follows* NICHOLAS *in an appearance of great anger*): Because we thought it was what you intended us to believe. Our sympathies have been for you because we believed that. Do you mean to say that you didn't know she killed herself? (*He pauses.*) Answer me. Do you really think it was an accident? If so why have you done this to us? We've done you no harm. But you have infected us.

A. G.: But it's not true! What you say is not true!

PETER: We believed you. All of us. (*He appeals to* EMILY *and* PATIENCE.) Didn't we? We believed him. Do you want further proof? From the person who believed in you most fully? (*He goes to the door and, opening it, calls.*) Nicholas! Nicholas! (*He turns back to* A. G.) Would you like to go and try to find him? No, you wouldn't, would you? Now you're afraid, aren't you? Now you're afraid.

A. G.: Yes!

PETER: Nicholas! Nicholas! (*He goes out of the room and can be heard calling Nicholas' name through the house. Then there is silence.*)

EMILY: I don't want to hear again about your wife. Never.

PATIENCE: What is keeping Nicholas? Emily, come here quickly. *Exit.*

PETER *returns. He stands in the open doorway.*

PETER: He's dead or dying.

PETER, *who is carrying Nicholas' stick, stands staring at* A. G. A. G. *falls forward on to his hands and knees and begins to crawl across the room.* PETER *comes into the room.*

PETER: Vile: treacherous: insensate fellow. Evil: unkind: monstrous toad. (*He pushes* A. G. *with the stick.* A. G. *rolls over. There is a disturbance from the room upstairs: no voices are heard.* PETER *goes out, leaving* A. G. *lying on the floor. After a few moments* A. G. *gets to his feet. For some time he stands apparently trying to rub some stain from the knee of his trousers with his bare hand. Then he goes to the door and switches off the lights. He goes out. In the lit hallway he can be seen putting on his hat and coat. When he is dressed he turns to look up the stairs. He calls. After a pause Nicholas' voice is heard to call distinctly.*)

NICHOLAS: Goodnight, A. G., my dear.

A. G.: Goodnight. (*He leaves the house: the front door is heard to close.* PETER *and* NICHOLAS *enter.* PETER *switches on the lights of the room and together he and* NICHOLAS *go to the window.* NICHOLAS *pulls aside the curtains and looks into the street.*)

NICHOLAS: There he goes. (*He raps loudly on the window with his stick. Then he and* PETER *stand in silence watching* A. G. *returning to his home.* EMILY *and* PATIENCE *come into the room together.* NICHOLAS *releases the curtains and the two men turn back into the room. They suddenly laugh together.*)

PATIENCE: I knew it was a joke. (*She goes to* NICHOLAS. *She is laughing.*) I knew it was a joke. When Emily told me I said it was a joke. I didn't believe a word of it.

NICHOLAS: Clever girl.

PATIENCE (*she goes to* EMILY): How foolish—how foolish of you not to see the joke. When you told me I could have laughed. Really, I could have laughed out loud. What shall we do tomorrow?

NICHOLAS *shakes his head.*

PETER: I really thought that's how you would employ your time.

NICHOLAS: I was listening to you.

PETER: You really must grow up.

They laugh.

I'll go and post it now. It's quite important.

PETER *goes out.*

NICHOLAS (*calls after him*): But I tell you the post's gone.

PATIENCE (*she has been dancing about the room*): Of course I knew it was a joke.

NICHOLAS: I suppose you must have done.

PATIENCE (*she has picked up the toy bear*): May I keep this, now?

NICHOLAS: No, Patience.

PATIENCE: Oh, very well. (*She throws it down.* NICHOLAS *picks it up.*)

NICHOLAS: What about some supper? (*He looks about the room.*) A. G. seems to have gone home.

EMILY *begins to move to the door.*

I'll get it. (*To* PATIENCE.) Come with me.

NICHOLAS *and* PATIENCE *go out.*

EMILY *picks up the reading lamp and puts it away. She then pulls out into the room a small table on which to set the supper tray.* PETER *is coming back into the room.*

CURTAIN

SAINT'S DAY

INTRODUCTORY NOTE

WHITING started working on *Saint's Day* in 1947 and it took him two years. In the interview he gave in November 1960 to the magazine *Encore* (issue dated January–February 1961) he described it as a 'technical exercise'.

> I think everybody writes one play on which he then draws technically for the rest of his life. You have on paper a sort of anthology of what you can do. . . . Knowing the English theatre as I had done for the past ten or twelve years, I thought it was extremely remote that anybody would actually stage the play. But I thought it was very well worth writing, to see what I could do. And I used all sorts of literary devices and tests such as parody and memories.

But when the Arts Theatre announced a play competition for the Festival of Britain, he submitted it. Out of the 997 plays they received, the judges (Alec Clunes, Christopher Fry and Peter Ustinov) picked three plays which were each to be staged at the Arts for three weeks before they made their final decision. The first two plays, by Enid Bagnold and C. E. Webber, were received unenthusiastically. *Saint's Day* was due to open on 29 August but a fire broke out in the theatre and the first night was postponed to 5 September.

Stephen Murray directed with Michael Hordern as Paul, Valerie White as Stella and Robert Urquhart as Charles. Donald Pleasence was Rev. Aldus.

Here are some of the press reactions:

The Times:

> Of a badness that must be called indescribable . . . fantasy plunging portentously into a sea so dark and wide and stormy that the shores of reality are rarely glimpsed.

John Barber in the *Daily Express*:

> I did not understand a word of the plot . . . and finally, I did not understand why the audience—which included Tyrone Guthrie and Christopher Fry—were so patient with it all.

Alan Dent in the *News Chronicle*:

> It is a strange, mad, baffling little play . . . too startling to be tedious, too scatter-brained to be a bore.

A. E. Wilson in the *Star*:

> My sympathies are with the producer, Stephen Murray, who must have had a fearful task trying to infuse some order into this crazy rigmarole.

R.P.M.G. in the *Daily Telegraph*:

> The message seemed to be that we should prepare not to live but to die, or something equally distressing.

Evening Standard:

> His venture into the depths of religious parable has sunk him with only a slight bubble on the surface to mark his attempt.

When the judges announced their decision to award *Saint's Day* the first prize, Arthur Bollenden wrote in the *News Chronicle*:

> I am more than surprised, I'm amazed. . . . No play since the war has been so unanimously damned by next day's dramatic critics. It has excited all of us to nothing but fury and stimulated most of us to the desperate yell of the patient onlooker who can suffer no longer in silence.

And the Sunday critics were no kinder.

Ivor Brown in the *Observer*:

> If the other entrants were no better than this belaurelled curio you can knock me down with a bay-leaf.

Harold Hobson in the *Sunday Times*:

> This is solely a universe of grotesques, and for that reason uninteresting.

In the *New Statesman*, T. C. Worsley wrote:

> The judges of the Arts Theatre play competition were right to award the prize to *Saint's Day*: it is much the worst of the three.

On 12 September a letter appeared in *The Times* above the joint signatures of Tyrone Guthrie and Peter Brook:

> Its passion and its unbroken tension are the products of a new and extraordinary theatrical mind . . . we only want to record our own deep faith in his talent, integrity and promise, and beg everybody truly interested in the theatre to go and see for themselves.

Two weeks later John Gielgud and Peggy Ashcroft wrote to *The Times*:

We found it moving, beautiful and fascinating.

And on 3 October, a letter from George Devine appeared in the *Radio Times,* protesting against the way The Critics had handled it:

To me, it splits wide open the conventional forms of playwriting and allies itself with the other modern arts in a way that no other play has done. It helps the theatre to bridge the gap of time which exists between itself and other forms of artistic expression.

In August 1958 it got a production in Paris at the Théâtre du Vieux Colombier directed by Roger Dornès, but London audiences didn't get another chance to see it till May 1965 when David Jones's production was put on at Stratford East with Michael Hordern again playing Paul, Sheila Allen as Stella, Barry Justice as Charles and James Bree as Aldus. It ran from 10 May till 5 June at Stratford, transferring to the St Martin's Theatre on 21 June, where it closed on 10 July.

In a lecture he gave on John Whiting to the Royal Society of Literature in 1963, Christopher Fry said '*Saint's Day* stands, at the start of his work, as close to a masterpiece as almost any first play has come.'

PERSONS

STELLA HEBERDEN, *Paul's grand-daughter*
CHARLES HEBERDEN, *her husband*
PAUL SOUTHMAN, *an aged poet*
JOHN WINTER, *his manservant*
ROBERT PROCATHREN, *an admirer of Paul*
GILES ALDUS, *a recluse*
CHRISTIAN MELROSE ⎫
WALTER KILLEEN ⎬ *three soldiers*
HENRY CHATER ⎭
HANNAH TREWIN ⎫
MARGARET BANT ⎪
EDITH TINSON ⎪
FLORA BALDON ⎬ *people of the village*
JUDITH WARDEN ⎪
A CHILD ⎪
THOMAS COWPER ⎭

*The play is in three acts, and the scene is laid in a room of
Paul Southman's house in England on the twenty-fifth day
of January.*

ACT I. Morning.
ACT II. Early afternoon.
ACT III. Night.

ACT ONE

The day is the twenty-fifth day of January: it is morning.
The scene is a room in Paul Southman's house CHARLES *and* STELLA
  HEBERDEN *are present, motionless. The woman is standing by one of the
  three large central windows. The source of light behind the drawn curtains
  of the room is an oil-lamp carried by the man.*

STELLA: Listen!
  They stand listening to the chimes of a distant church. The chimes end.
CHARLES: Half-past.
STELLA: Nine?
CHARLES: Must be.
STELLA: Might be eight.
CHARLES: No.
STELLA: Surely not ten.
CHARLES: No, nine. Half-past nine. Is it raining now?
  STELLA *has moved to set the clock.*
STELLA: It might be any time, really. No, it's not raining now.
CHARLES: It was earlier this morning. (*He yawns.*)
STELLA: The key's not on the ledge.
CHARLES: Look behind the clock. There?
STELLA: Yes. There wasn't—
CHARLES: It slips down. Can you get it?
STELLA: Yes. There wasn't any trouble in the night, was there?
CHARLES: No. (STELLA *begins to wind and set the clock.*) How long
  have you been up?
STELLA: Twenty minutes or so.
CHARLES: I didn't hear you.
STELLA: You were asleep. I shan't wind the strike.
CHARLES: No, don't. It's wrong, anyway. (*He calls.*) John Winter!
  John Winter! (*To* STELLA.) Where is he?
STELLA: I don't know. I haven't seen him this morning.
CHARLES: John Winter! (CHARLES, *wearing a woollen dressing-gown*
  89

*over his shirt—he is without trousers—stands on one leg chafing a bare foot
between his hands. He is below a narrow stairway, set within a wall,
leading to an upper floor.*) I'm cold.

STELLA: Go and dress.

CHARLES: John Winter!

STELLA: If he could hear you he would've come by now.

CHARLES: He's up, I suppose.

STELLA: Now, Charles—don't shout again.

CHARLES: What?

STELLA: We don't want Paul to wake early. He's going to have a
tiring day.

CHARLES: He's already awake. I heard him moving. (*He has opened
the only door of the room and calls down the stairs to the kitchen, 'John
Winter!'*) I heard him moving in his room as I came down. (*From
his room above the narrow stairway* PAUL SOUTHMAN *calls, 'John
Winter!'*) There he is.

STELLA: Damn! I wanted him to sleep as late as possible this
morning. Go up and—

CHARLES: Get John Winter to make a fire when he comes in.

STELLA: All right. Go up and try to persuade Paul to go back to bed
for an hour.

CHARLES: He won't.

STELLA: Try to persuade him. I'm worried— (PAUL SOUTHMAN
calls again: 'John Winter!') All right, Grandpa! (*To* CHARLES.) I'm
worried as to whether the journey will tire him. I hope to God
they don't give him anything to drink when he gets there. I'm
sending John Winter with him—don't you think that's a good
idea?

CHARLES: Yes. (*He is at the window drawing aside the curtains.*) It's
going to be a fine day.

STELLA: Go up to him, will you, Charles. I don't want him to shout
again or he'll start coughing.

CHARLES: All right. (*He takes up a man's bicycle which is lying in the
centre of the room and props it against the wall.*) How are you this
morning?

STELLA: All right now.

CHARLES: Sickness gone off?

STELLA: Yes. Yes, it goes when I've had a cup of tea and a biscuit.

CHARLES: Have you made some tea already?

STELLA: Yes.

CHARLES: Where is it?

STELLA: In our room. (CHARLES *goes towards the stairs.*) Didn't you
you see it?

CHARLES: No.

STELLA: Leave the lamp.

CHARLES: Sorry. (*As he goes up the stairs* PAUL SOUTHMAN *calls
again:* '*John Winter!*') I'm coming.

PAUL: I want John Winter, not you. I want dressing.

CHARLES *goes up the stairs.* STELLA *clears some dirty plates and
cups from a central table and puts them on an ornate but filthy tray. She
picks up a bicycle pump from the floor and fixes it into place on the bicycle.
Going to the windows she draws back the curtains. The room is large: the
building of the year 1775. There are three windows opening on to an iron
balcony—entrance to the room can be gained by any of these windows. The
balcony has iron steps leading down to the garden. There are two other
entrances to the room: one, a door opening on to a small landing above
stairs which lead to the kitchens and also to the main door of the house—
two, a narrow stairway leading to the upper floors. This gives the room an
elevation of being above the ground floor and yet below the main first floor.
It stands alone, an architectural freak having no ceiling but a roof directly
above it. There is an empty fireplace. The furnishing of the room is
minimum for habitation: a table, and about it four chairs—two chairs
and a low bench before the fireplace. The furnishings together with the
various utilitarian objects about the room—the silver tray, the cups and
dishes on the table—are of excellent quality but have lost their grace by
neglect and misuse. Several hundred books are piled on the floor in a corner
of the room. From the right window the wall of the room is curved and on
the plaster surface of the wall is an unfinished painting. This painting
represents five human figures and a dog—greater than life-size—grouped
about an, as yet, unspecified sixth person. Executed in oils, it is harsh in
texture, garish in colour. Below the picture stands a small scaffolding with
painter's materials: there is also a ladder. The floor of this part of the
room before the painting is raised six inches by means of a half-circular
rostrum.*

The curtains withdrawn, STELLA *puts out the lamp. It is light and
promises to be a fine clear day.*

*The front door is heard to open and close; footsteps sound on the
uncarpeted stairs from below.* JOHN WINTER *enters.*

STELLA: Good morning, John Winter.

WINTER: Good morning, Miss Stella.

STELLA: You've been out already.

WINTER: Yes.

STELLA: Where?

WINTER: To get stuff for the fire.

STELLA: Surely you keep that in the cellar.

WINTER: You may remember—

STELLA: What? Speak up.

WINTER: I say you may remember I moved it some days ago. I moved it from the cellar to my shed because of the damp—it's mostly wood.

STELLA: I didn't know you'd moved it.

WINTER: Mr Charles will remember. He helped me.

STELLA: Anyway, you've got the stuff for the fire.

WINTER: I've left it at the door. I didn't want to bring it in until the room—

STELLA: Very well.

WINTER: —until the room had been tidied. I've already cleaned the grate.

STELLA: You look frozen.

WINTER: It's very cold out of doors.

STELLA: Well, don't stand there! Grandpa—Mr Southman has been shouting for you. My husband has gone up to him.

WINTER: Should I light the fire first or go up and dress Mr Southman?

STELLA: I don't know. I— (*They stand silent for a moment.*) Oh, go and dress him but try to keep him in his room for a while. I want him to rest this morning. Just a minute! I want to talk to you. This man who is coming to visit us today—

WINTER: Mr Procathren.

STELLA: You know about him?

WINTER: Mr Southman mentioned him to me yesterday.

STELLA: You know today is Mr Southman's birthday?

WINTER: Yes.

STELLA: In fact, you know all about it.

WINTER: That is all I know—that this gentleman is arriving on Mr Southman's birthday. I think I should go up now. (*He looks towards the stairs.*)

STELLA: Wait a minute! You may as well know it all. This Mr Procathren—Robert Procathren—is a famous poet and critic. He is coming here to do honour to my grandfather on his birthday—

honour as a poet. Late this afternoon Mr Procathren, Mr Southman and you will drive to London by car. You will go with them, do you understand? You will go with them to London.

WINTER: Yes.

STELLA: Those are the arrangements.

WINTER: Very well.

STELLA: There is to be a dinner in London tonight—Are you listening to me?

WINTER: Yes.

STELLA: You are not! Please pay attention. There is to be a dinner tonight in London in honour of Mr Southman. It will be attended by very famous men and women. You will go with Mr Southman. You won't go in to the dinner, of course, but wait outside. You will stay the night in London and be driven back tomorrow. Have you any better clothes than those?

WINTER: I have a blue suit.

STELLA: Wear it. One more thing—I shall cook the meal today. What food have we got? (WINTER *is silent*.) Have you any food at all in the house?

WINTER: There's some bacon and vegetables.

STELLA: We shall want some meat and something for—is there any fruit?—is there anything? And coffee—is there any coffee?

WINTER: No.

STELLA: Then you had better go down to the village this morning —early—and get these things. Do you understand?

WINTER: Yes.

STELLA: Go as soon as Mr Southman has finished with you.

WINTER: I shall need money.

STELLA: Here you are. (*She takes a ten-shilling note from her pocket and gives it to* JOHN WINTER.) That's all right, then? (JOHN WINTER *does not reply*.) Don't be so sullen, John Winter! You may be the servant but you know the position as to money as well as I do. We cannot pay those bills in the village at present—but we will in time. Promise them that. You can tell them—promise them— you—because they respect you down in the village—yes, they respect you.

WINTER: They hate me.

STELLA: Nonsense.

WINTER: Truth.

STELLA: Hate you?

WINTER: Of course—why not?—despise me—hate me, they do. I say, why not? A beggar—I have to go to them—a little food—say, a little meat—a little bread—later—a little more bread—a little more meat—Please!

STELLA: John Winter!

WINTER: One day they'll stop—or I'll stop—and then what will happen?

STELLA: Are you threatening me? (*He is silent.*) I say, are you threatening me? (*He shakes his head.*) Come now, you wouldn't like to see Mr Southman or his guest go without food, would you? Would you? No, of course, you wouldn't, because you love him as I love him, and we'll fight for him, won't we? We'll put our pride in our pocket and we'll fight for him. We've got to look after him, you know. There's no one else. Just you and me, that's all. Now, go along. (CHARLES *comes down the stairs: he is dressed and carries a cup of tea.*) John Winter. (STELLA *goes to* JOHN WINTER *and puts her arms about him.*) John Winter, I want you to go with my grandfather today—go with him to London—because I trust you. Remember, he will be among strangers—all his friends have gone—and he may be frightened. And if he is afraid he will appear ridiculous. I want you to see that he is not frightened—that by his age he is great and not ridiculous. That he is Paul Southman.

WINTER: He is a great and famous man.

STELLA: Of course he is. And today we have an opportunity to remind the world of that. Now, go up and get him dressed, but try to keep him in his room.

WINTER: I've put out his best clothes.

STELLA: He's waiting for you.

CHARLES: He's sitting on his bed cleaning a pistol. You'd better be careful, John Winter.

JOHN WINTER *laughs and goes up the stairs.*

STELLA: I told you I'm sending John Winter up to London with Paul, didn't I?

CHARLES: Yes. Are you going to light a fire?

STELLA: Later.

CHARLES: I'm so cold.

STELLA *fetches an oil-stove from a corner of the room. She lights it.*

STELLA: Sit over this.

CHARLES: Look! (*He points to the ornate pediment over the door.*)

STELLA: What?

CHARLES: There's a bird—above the door. It's hiding there—behind the scroll.

STELLA: They fly in sometimes. They don't come to any harm.

CHARLES: What was all that just now?

STELLA: When?

CHARLES: With John Winter.

STELLA: Oh, a minor revolt—over getting food from the village. He says they hate him down there. I suppose it's true. They hate us all. Is that stove alight?

CHARLES: Yes.

STELLA: They hate us because they don't understand our isolation. They don't understand us and so they fear us. They fear us and so they hate us.

CHARLES: But only passively. They—

STELLA: Not at all. Do you know that three years ago—before you came here—there was a plan among the villagers to attack this house. Everything was arranged, but on the decided night they sat drinking to get up their courage and when the time came they were all too drunk to walk the half-mile to the house. So the attack didn't come off that time. It may some day.

CHARLES: What would they do?

STELLA: Paul says they'd kill us.

CHARLES: It must be hard for John Winter. He has to go down among them—we don't.

STELLA: Well, I've given him some money this morning so he'll be all right.

CHARLES: By the way, I've got this. (*He takes some coins from his pocket.*) You'd better have it.

STELLA: Thank you.

CHARLES: Do you think John Winter could do something for me in London?

STELLA: What?

CHARLES: If he has time.

STELLA: Well, what?

CHARLES: I've got a small canvas I think I can sell—might get ten pounds for it—if John Winter could take it round to the dealers for me tomorrow.

STELLA: Charles! Will you? Will you really try to sell it? Ten pounds would help so much.

CHARLES: It's that small oil I did of you three months ago. You
don't want it?

STELLA: If you sell it we shall be able to—

CHARLES: You don't want it?

STELLA: No, I don't want it. We shall be able to—

CHARLES: Very well! (*A pause.*) Then that's settled.

STELLA: Yes. I'll tell John Winter. (STELLA *moves to* CHARLES.)
I'm sorry, Charles, but we must have money.

    CHARLES *moves away from her.*

CHARLES: I know.

STELLA: If only Grandpa would begin to write again. Anything!
I'm sure they'd take it. Take it on his name alone. People haven't
forgotten him.

CHARLES: Of course they have.

STELLA: They haven't! If they've forgotten him why should this
man Procathren be coming down today to take him to London?

CHARLES: The whole thing is probably a stunt. Listen, Stella. Who
is going to be at that dinner tonight? I'll tell you. Fashionable
people. Poets, painters, novelists and critics à la mode. The kind
of people who, twenty-five years ago when Paul wrote his
pamphlet 'The Abolition of Printing', turned against him and
drove him into this exile and silence. Those are the people who
will be receiving him, applauding him tonight. (*There is a pause.*)
I don't think you understand, Stella. We've had all this so often
before. Why can't you leave the old man alone? For him to
attempt to begin again—No, I don't think you could understand.

STELLA: Of course I understand.

CHARLES: Let me put it this way. Go to London today and ask a
hundred people who know of Paul—ask them about him—and
ninety-nine of them will say he died years ago. I tell you even
those who haven't forgotten him think he's dead. His name in a
newspaper tomorrow would cause nothing but surprise. Let the
few eminent people who do remember him enjoy the entertainment tonight. It won't do them or Paul any harm, but don't you
build anything from it—useless and unkind.

STELLA: Charles, this is a chance we've never had before. He'll
be remembered by this dinner. Now is the time for him to
start writing again. We needn't bother about the physical effect
on him—I can do the writing if he'll dictate. Anything! Articles,
satires—any of the things that made him famous—made him

Paul Southman, the pamphleteer and lampoonist, the poet and revolutionary.

CHARLES: He's eighty-three.

STELLA: I know.

CHARLES: All those things—useless—he's an old man—quite out of touch—he has no idea what has happened in the outside world in the last twenty-five years. There have been changes, you know.

STELLA: Then we'll start taking the newspapers again. I'll try to get him out, even if it's only to the village. We'll buy some new books and I'll read to him.

CHARLES: You know he can't concentrate for two minutes either reading or being read to. You know he will never go to the village. You know—you must know he's a very old man and he's finished. Finished! I'm trying to explain in such a way that you can understand. (*Pause.*) It won't work, Stella. (*Pause.*) Let him die in peace. (*Pause.*) Let him alone. (CHARLES *goes to the door.*)

STELLA: Charles, I want to speak to you. Charles! (*He stops at the door.*) I've lied to you.

CHARLES: What?

STELLA: I've lied to you.

CHARLES: What about this time? (*She does not answer.*) Come along, you know you enjoy the confession more than the lie. I suppose you're not going to have a child.

STELLA: No, it's not that. I've lied to you about my age.

CHARLES: Well?

STELLA: I told you I was twenty-eight last birthday. I was really thirty-two.

CHARLES: That makes you twelve years older than me instead of eight. All right.

STELLA: I don't—

CHARLES: Did you think four years would make so much difference?

STELLA: You look so young.

CHARLES: And who is there to see me but you?

STELLA: This morning there will be Robert Procathren. I was going to suggest that we pretend to him that you're my brother—not my husband.

CHARLES: Don't be absurd!

STELLA: Is it absurd? Well, never mind. Go and get yourself some breakfast.

CHARLES: Yes, I will. And Stella—

STELLA: Yes?

CHARLES: Don't try to get the old man back to work.

STELLA: All right. But I think it would be a good thing—not only for us, but for him.

CHARLES (*in sudden anger*): It would not! It would not be a good thing. It would not be a good thing for any of us. What is it you're hankering after? You want something from it. You're planning something, aren't you—aren't you?

STELLA: Don't speak to me like that! (*In silence* STELLA *picks up the tray and goes out of the room and down the stairs to the kitchens below.* CHARLES *shouts after her.*)

CHARLES: It's only that you don't understand. (*He is unanswered. He goes to the stove and warms his hands: he ties his shoe-laces: he goes to the scaffolding set below the mural painting: he examines the painter's materials set on the scaffolding.* STELLA *returns to the room. She begins to wipe the table with a damp cloth.* CHARLES *speaks.*) I've got a pain in my side. (*A pause.*) Had it last night. Worst this morning. (STELLA *does not reply.*) Here. (*He indicates the position of the pain.* STELLA *ignores this and* CHARLES *turns back to the painter's material.*) Do you think John Winter could get me some stuff in London?

STELLA: I should think so.

CHARLES: Now, what do I want? I want some—

STELLA: Write it down.

CHARLES: What time is this fellow arriving?

STELLA: No special time. Just this morning.

CHARLES: Procathren—Procathren.

STELLA: What do you say?

CHARLES: Nothing. Have you got Paul anything for his birthday?

STELLA: Yes. A pair of slippers.

CHARLES: Where are they?

STELLA: In the table drawer. Why?

CHARLES: When are you going to give them to him?

STELLA: When he comes down, I suppose.

CHARLES *has taken a small parcel from the canvas bag hanging on the scaffolding.*

CHARLES: Will you give him this at the same time?

STELLA: Why don't you give it to him yourself?

CHARLES: No, you. Here you are. It's a scarf—woollen scarf. Take it.

STELLA *takes the parcel and puts it in the table drawer.*

STELLA: Where's the pain?

CHARLES: What?

STELLA: The pain you said you had—where is it?

CHARLES: Here.

STELLA *puts her hand to his side.*

STELLA: Bad?

CHARLES: Rather. I may have strained myself. I fell from there—(*He indicates the scaffolding.*)—yesterday. I called out for you as I fell—you didn't hear me. Just a minute. You've got a cobweb in your hair. Stand still (*His hands go to her head.*) No. No, it's your hair. White. Your hair is—

PAUL: They must go. I have decided—(PAUL SOUTHMAN *can be heard speaking to* JOHN WINTER *as they come down the stairs.*)—we could manage it between us—

CHARLES: Your hair is going white.

PAUL: You think I'm too old, but I could give you a hand.

STELLA: Charles!

PAUL: Away with them. That's what I say—careful!—then we shall have a clear view—

STELLA: Charles!

PAUL: —a clear view if anything threatens.

STELLA: I'm ugly to you, aren't I, Charles?

PAUL (*laughing*): What do I mean by that, eh, John Winter?

STELLA: Charles! Speak to me. I'm ugly to you, aren't I?

PAUL: As it threatens at all times we must be prepared. (PAUL SOUTHMAN *and* JOHN WINTER *reach the foot of the stairs.*) Good morning.

STELLA: Good morning, Grandpa.

CHARLES: Good morning, Paul.

PAUL: What's the time?

STELLA: About a quarter to ten.

JOHN WINTER *puts a chair beside the oil-stove.* PAUL *sits.*

PAUL: Thank you. I've just been telling John Winter about an idea of mine. A precaution. I'll tell you later. I'll have some breakfast now, John Winter. (JOHN WINTER *goes out.*) Is there no fire?

STELLA: We'll have one lit in a few minutes.

PAUL: Good. It's very cold. I've been very cold in bed all night. (*He looks up at* STELLA *and* CHARLES, *smiling.*) It is today I have to play the great man, isn't it?

STELLA: Yes.

PAUL: You notice I'm dressed up?

STELLA: You look very nice.

PAUL: You understand I realize the importance of today?

STELLA: I hope you do.

PAUL: Is the weather going to be fine?

STELLA: I think so.

PAUL: The sun shining?

STELLA: I hope so.

PAUL: The flags hung out in London for me?

STELLA (*laughing*): Perhaps.

PAUL (*laughing*): Excellent.

STELLA: Many happy returns of the day, Grandpa. (*She gives him her present.*)

PAUL: God bless my soul!

STELLA: God bless you, indeed—pretending you didn't expect it.

PAUL: How neatly it's parcelled up—with such a tight little knot. What is it, I wonder? I am supposed to be able to open it, am I? I mean, there is something inside.

STELLA: Let me do it.

PAUL: No, no. I've done it now. (*He has undone the parcel and holds up the pair of slippers.*) For my feet?

STELLA: And this is from Charles.

        CHARLES *turns away.*

PAUL: What is it, Charles?

    JOHN WINTER *enters carrying a cup of tea and a plate of rusks.*

CHARLES: A scarf.

STELLA: You mustn't tell him.

CHARLES: Knitted by myself with wool from a pair of my old socks.

PAUL: Excellent! Now I shall be warm at both ends (*He pauses in undoing the parcel.*) I hope it's not green. I don't like green things. *He takes out the scarf: it is green.*)

STELLA: Put it on, Grandpa. You look very handsome. Doesn't he, Charles?

PAUL: Do I?

STELLA: Of course you do, darling.

    JOHN WINTER *takes a box of cigarettes from his pocket. He holds it out to* PAUL.

PAUL: What's this?

WINTER: Birthday present, sir.

PAUL: Thank you, John Winter. I forgot your last birthday, didn't I?

WINTER: Yes, sir.

PAUL: Good of you to remember mine. Cigarettes. Have one?

WINTER: Thank you.

STELLA: Now, Grandpa, you don't want to smoke. Have your breakfast first.

PAUL: Very well. (*He begins to dip the rusks in the tea.*) Stella, John Winter and I have been discussing—Stella!

STELLA: Yes? (*She has been whispering with* CHARLES *who begins to go from the room.*)

PAUL: John Winter and I have been—Where's Charles going?

CHARLES: I'm going to get some breakfast. Can I pinch one of your cigarettes?

After CHARLES *has taken a cigarette* PAUL *puts the box into his pocket.* CHARLES *goes out.*

PAUL: John Winter. John Winter, where are you?

WINTER: Here.

PAUL: I saw the dog from my window just before I came down. He was limping. What's the matter with him? You haven't been beating him again, have you?

WINTER: I never beat him.

PAUL: I've told you before—I won't have that dog beaten. Do you understand?

WINTER: Yes.

PAUL: He may misbehave himself but he's getting old and he doesn't know what he's doing. He's getting old and a little simple. I suppose you'll be beating me soon. Now remember—

STELLA (*to* JOHN WINTER): You'd better get down to the village. I want those things.

PAUL: Is John Winter going out?

STELLA: Yes. He's going down to the village to get some food. We can't give Mr Procathren bacon.

PAUL: Why not?

STELLA: Go along, John Winter. Meat, bread, dried fruit of some kind and coffee.

JOHN WINTER *begins to wheel the bicycle from the room.* PAUL *calls after him.*

PAUL: O, brave John Winter! Going down among the enemy again.

Would you like to take my pistol? Be careful not to break wind in the High Street or they'll be after you. (JOHN WINTER *has left the room*.) One day they will.

STELLA: What?

PAUL: Kill him.

STELLA: No.

PAUL: Why not?

STELLA: Like them, he's a servant; they would never kill one of their own kind. They hate him, perhaps, but—

PAUL: Are you suggesting that John Winter is working with the villagers against us?

STELLA: No, of course not.

PAUL: Such a thing had never occurred to me. Is it likely?

STELLA: No.

PAUL: Is it?

STELLA: No! Don't get such an idea into your head. I didn't mean to suggest it. John Winter is loyal. He loves you dearly.

PAUL: He beats the dog.

STELLA: He denies that.

PAUL: I won't have that dog beaten. I must exert my authority. John Winter is my servant, and he shall obey my orders.

STELLA: Of course. (*A pause*.) What are you thinking?

PAUL: He moves quite freely among the villagers, you know.

STELLA: To spy on them. So that we can be warned of any danger. Now come, Grandpa. Don't be silly. Of course John Winter is loyal to us. Remember the night when they intended to attack the house and John Winter sat with you out there on the balcony waiting for them. He was prepared to fight with you against them —against his own kind. Remember that. (PAUL *is silent*.) What was it you were telling him before you came down?

PAUL: It is absurd of me to doubt him. Absurd! It was cold that night, you know, but he didn't complain. No, he made jokes—very good jokes too—about the villagers. He's brave and he's loyal. It is ridiculous to doubt his honesty.

STELLA: Of course it is ridiculous. What were you telling him as you came down? I'm interested.

PAUL: What? Oh, yes. Yes, Stella. You know the two trees, the elms—that stand in front of the house—?

STELLA: Tweedledum and Tweedledee—yes?

PAUL: What's that?

STELLA: We used to call them that when I was a child—don't you remember? (*She puts her hands in a defensive boxing attitude.*) Their arms outstretched in constant conflict—remember?

PAUL: Yes, of course. They're dead now.

STELLA: Yes, they're dead now.

PAUL: And I'm going to cut them down.

STELLA: Why?

PAUL: Because they are a danger.

STELLA: To whom?

PAUL: To ourselves. I saw them yesterday as they are—blanched by age—withered, contorted and monstrous. They shouldn't stand before the house. They must be brought down.

STELLA: I played in them when I was a child—with Ellen.

PAUL: You agree they should come down?

STELLA: If you think it's necessary.

PAUL: I believe it is necessary. And it must be done quickly.

STELLA: Very well.

PAUL: That way it will give us less pain. I remember them, too. They were in full leaf the summer morning I arrived here twenty-five years ago. On approach they quite obscured the house and when you were before the door they shadowed you. But now they're dead and must be brought down. I can do it with John Winter.

STELLA: You mustn't do it! Not yourself.

PAUL: With John Winter. You don't think I'm strong enough? I'm quite strong enough. It will have to be carefully done for they must fall away from the house. (*He takes the cigarettes from his pocket.*) I think I might have a cigarette now.

STELLA: Yes.

PAUL: Nice of John Winter. Look! He's written on the box. What does it say?

STELLA (*She reads*): 'Many happy returns of the day. Your obedient servant, John Winter.' (*They laugh.*)

PAUL: Absurd of me to suspect him of treachery.

STELLA: Absurd.

PAUL: Have one?

STELLA: Thank you, I will.

PAUL: I suppose John Winter stole them.

STELLA: I suppose so.

PAUL: Sit down.

STELLA: I have a lot to do.

PAUL: For a few minutes. Whilst we smoke our cigarettes. (STELLA *pulls up a stool and sits by him.*) Have you matches?

STELLA: Yes.

PAUL: You remember the trees from your childhood—Tweedledum and Tweedledee?

STELLA: Yes. Is that foolish?

PAUL: I don't think so.

STELLA: Somehow I—Tell me, are they evil now?

PAUL: Not evil—dangerous.

STELLA: They were most benevolent to Ellen and me when we were children. They were almost our only playthings and gave themselves so willingly to masquerading as other places—other worlds.

PAUL: But they're ugly now—ugly and old and dead.

STELLA: Yes.

PAUL: So I shall cut them down.

STELLA: Very well. When did they die?

   CHARLES, *below in the kitchen, shouts:* Get out! Get out!

PAUL: What? What's that? What?

STELLA Charles. (*She goes to the door and calls down the stairs.*) Charles!

CHARLES (*from below*): All right. It's the dog.

STELLA: It's the dog.

PAUL: Well, what's he doing to it?

STELLA: I don't know.

PAUL: Why do you all hate that dog so much?

STELLA: We don't.

PAUL: You never seem to give him a moment's peace.

STELLA: He's so large and he will come into the house—and he's begun to smell terribly.

PAUL: Probably I do. I'm getting old. I suppose I shan't be allowed in the house soon.

STELLA: Don't pity yourself.

PAUL: What did you say?

STELLA: Nothing.

PAUL: Stella! What did you say?

STELLA: Charles is really very good to him.

PAUL: Then why does he shout at him? And look—look! What's he doing here? (*They turn to look at the painting.*) What does it mean?

What are those monstrous figures? And there's the dog—see? At least I suppose it's my dog. I don't understand such things.

STELLA: He'll say very little about it.

PAUL: Has it a title?

STELLA: I don't know.

PAUL: Things should always be titled. Does he tell you nothing?

STELLA: Very little.

PAUL: I don't understand him. I was nearly sixty when I gave up my work and came to live here—and there was a reason. I was victimised—driven here by my enemies. Charles's work as a painter was recognized when he was—how old?

STELLA: Fifteen.

PAUL: And now he's twenty. There was no attack on him, or on his work. He was acclaimed as a prodigy. Yet he came here, met you, married you—strange, you—and now lives with the old fellow— the poor man. Refuses to show his paintings—except that. What is to go there? (*He indicates the unfinished lower part of the mural.*)

STELLA: There? Oh, another figure—a woman. Charles wants me to model for it but I haven't had time as yet.

PAUL: A woman. Then the other figures—those—will be looking down at her, eh?

STELLA: I suppose so.

PAUL: I don't understand it.

STELLA: Don't—

PAUL: I don't understand it at all.

STELLA: Don't let it worry you. Leave him in peace.

PAUL: Charles? I will. But he mustn't harm the dog. Is that clock right?

STELLA: I think so. I put it right by the village.

PAUL: Procathren should—

STELLA: Oh, Grandpa! (*She laughs.*) I've got something to show you. I found it last night. (*She has taken a page of a magazine from the pocket of her dress and unfolded it.*) It's from a magazine called 'The Tatler'—an old copy—some years ago—look—

PAUL: Who is it?

STELLA: Read it.

PAUL (*puts on his spectacles and reads*): 'The Honourable Robert Procathren, distinguished young poet and critic, photographed last week after his marriage to Miss Amanda Mantess, daughter

of Mr and Mrs Sebastian Mantess of—' it's torn away. What a
beautiful young man!

STELLA: Isn't he?

PAUL: Fancy such an elegant and obviously witty person coming
to see us.

STELLA; Why not?

PAUL: But, I mean, look at him. Look at his clothes. His hair is
trimmed and I'm sure, if you could see them, his finger-nails
would be spotless. His linen is as crisp as the paper on which he
has been writing to me. Oh, dear! He's obviously very famous
and very correct. What on earth shall I say to him? Look at those
dainty feet in the pointed shoes. (*He stamps in his great black boots.*)

STELLA: Are you making fun of him?

PAUL: Indeed, no. He frightens me.

STELLA: What do you mean?

PAUL: Come, child, you know what is meant by fear. I'm afraid of
him—

STELLA: Paul!

PAUL: —his whole appearance is alien to me.

STELLA: His appearance. But, my dear, appearance has never
counted with you. Do you mean his clothes? It doesn't matter
what he wears, but what he is as a man.

PAUL: About tonight, Stella—

STELLA: He is your admirer—he is coming here to express that
admiration. And you can meet him—I give you my word—not
as an equal but as his superior. You see—he'll admit that.

PAUL: How you do talk. But, darling, I'm frightened about tonight.

STELLA: You mustn't be.

PAUL: Why don't you try to understand?

STELLA: You mustn't be frightened.

PAUL: I—

STELLA: Look at me. Do you love me?

PAUL: I do.

STELLA: Then if you love me you won't be frightened.

PAUL: So simple? I'm old. Easily frightened.

STELLA: Paul—Paul! (*She grasps his arm.*)

PAUL: You're hurting me.

STELLA: You are greater than any of them. They understand that
by these last twenty-five years of exile and mortification you have
proved the justice and truth of those opinions expressed in your

pamphlets. You have proved your integrity and saintliness and tonight it is that that they will honour. Paul! You're not going before a tribunal.

PAUL: Ha! They will be in judgement on my table manners.

STELLA: It is your poetry they will be remembering.

PAUL: They'll laugh at my fumbling with the knives and forks.

STELLA: They will remember your political writings.

PAUL: A stupid old man! I shan't be able to eat the food they give me. A glass of wine goes to my head and makes me babble like a baby. I shall want to go to the lavatory during their speeches and I shan't be able to go. I shall wet myself again and then you'll be angry with me. O Stella!

There is a pause—then STELLA *speaks with gentleness.*

STELLA: There is nothing to fear. I promise you that. I've never promised you anything that has not been perfectly fulfilled, have I? Have I?

PAUL: No.

STELLA: Then you can trust in this promise. You will not be afraid today. (*She gives him her handkerchief.*) Dry your tears.

PAUL: I feel giddy.

STELLA: It's the cigarette. Do you remember what you said when you came downstairs this morning?

PAUL: Within twelve hours—

STELLA: Do you remember what you said? 'It is today I have to play the great man, isn't it?' That's what you said.

PAUL: I was joking, dear Stella.

STELLA: Joking or not—that is what you must do. Play the great man. Now, at this moment, you may tell me of your fears. At this moment, because we are alone and I love you. But from the time of Procathren's coming here you must act the great man. You must meet this elegant and witty young man with your own elegance and wit. Good gracious me! From what Mamma told me you were a great one for acting in your day. (PAUL *laughs.*) Were you? Then remember that when you meet these people.

PAUL: I wish I had some better clothes.

STELLA: You look very well as you are.

PAUL: Newer clothes.

STELLA: And Grandpa—

PAUL: Yes?

STELLA: Also remember—this is a new beginning for you. For

twenty-five years—since I was a child, we have been waiting for
this moment. Don't fail! Don't fail, now! Go to London today,
meet these people, show them that you are yet alive and active
and then—then begin to write again. Do this and you won't have
to act the great man—you will be the great man.

There is a pause.

PAUL: And what do you hope to get out of all this, Stella?

CHARLES *comes into the room from below.*

STELLA: Nothing—I swear it! Nothing—I believe in you!

PAUL: Take this cigarette from me.

STELLA: Perhaps they have asked you to return because they need
you. Perhaps they are in trouble out there and want your wisdom,
your advice. Have you thought of that?

PAUL: Why should I give them my advice? They are nothing to me.

CHARLES: Bravo!

PAUL: Hullo, Charles.

STELLA: It is your duty, Grandpa.

CHARLES: Nonsense!

STELLA (*She turns to* CHARLES): You, my precious little fellow—
and what do you know about it?—you being a stranger here.
You, with your paintings stored away unshown—probably un-
showable—and your miserable fears of criticism. Well, Paul, does
not need to fear criticism. He can go out from here into the
world—unafraid—disarming criticism and censure by his genius.
Then how dare you, a stranger—

CHARLES (*shouting*): Stella!

There is a pause.

STELLA: Yes, Charles?

CHARLES: I want to speak to you. (*He goes up the stairs.*)

STELLA: Yes, Charles.

She follows him up the stairs. PAUL *left alone, stares at the newspaper
cutting in his hand. From the head of the stairs the voices of* CHARLES *and*
STELLA *rise together.*

CHARLES: —damnable, damnable things!—

STELLA: —unmeant, unmeant—

CHARLES: —cruel wickedness, most cruel!—

STELLA: —not meant. I never mean to—never mean to—

PAUL, *staring at the newspaper cutting, suddenly cries out.*

PAUL: O God! O God!

There is silence—then STELLA *calls.*

STELLA: What is it, Grandpa? (*She comes down the stairs.*) What is it?
    PAUL *holds up the newspaper cutting.*
PAUL: Stella—Stella, look at this man.
    CHARLES *comes down the stairs.*
STELLA: I've seen it, Grandpa. Your nose is running. Wipe it.
CHARLES: Has John Winter gone out?
STELLA: Yes.
CHARLES: I thought he was going to light the fire before he went.
STELLA: It's more important that we should have the food.
CHARLES: I'm so damned cold. Move over, Paul, and let me have
    a bit of the stove.
PAUL: Charles. I say, Charles, look at this. (*He holds out the cutting.*)
CHARLES: Just a minute, Stella—(*She is combing her hair before a
    fragment of glass set on the mantelpiece*)—when will you have time for
    me to start work on that last figure?
STELLA: I don't know.
PAUL: Charles, look!
CHARLES: Just a moment, Paul. Do you think today, Stella?
STELLA: No, not today. I shan't have a minute to sit today.
CHARLES: Why not, when Paul's gone?
STELLA: Well, I'll see, but I don't know.
CHARLES: I've been asking you for the last three weeks.
STELLA: I know.
CHARLES: Now then—what do you want, Paul?
PAUL: Look at this.
    CHARLES *takes the cutting.*
CHARLES: Who is it?
PAUL: Read it.
CHARLES (*He reads*): 'The Honourable Robert Procathren, dis-
    tinguished young—' Oh!
PAUL: Isn't he a grand young fellow?
CHARLES: Indeed, he is. Stella, have you seen this?
STELLA: I gave it to Paul.
CHARLES: Where did you find it?
STELLA: Among some old magazines of yours.
PAUL: Look! Look, Charles, what do they say?
CHARLES: '—distinguished young poet and critic—'
PAUL: '—distinguished young poet and critic—'
CHARLES (*He nudges* PAUL): Paul, my old one—
PAUL (*giggling with anticipation*): Yes? Yes, sonny, yes?

CHARLES: A splendid young man. Isn't he, Stella? Paul—Paul, tell me—

PAUL: Yes, sonny? Yes, what?

CHARLES: Isn't he the kind of young man Stella admires—very much admires? Clean, upright, bold—

PAUL: Yes? Yes?

CHARLES: —full of a passionate desire—for life. Not like us, my ancient—not like you and me—being, as we are, despised by Stella. No, she'd admire him—this Procathren.

STELLA (*She turns and shouts*): I'm not going to quarrel with you!

CHARLES: —admire him very much for what he is and for what he does—the conduct of his life. Yes, Stella would love him—love him dearly—

STELLA: Damn you, Charles! Damn you!

CHARLES: And what is he, Paul, this Procathren?

PAUL: Tell me—tell me!

CHARLES: He is a man. And being a man may we conjecture what he would say to a woman like Stella? I think we may.

PAUL: Yes, I think we may.

CHARLES: He would say that he looks upon life as an adventure, and upon death as an enemy to be fought with desperation. Age as something to be accepted with dignity—women also. A man lacking in pathos but not lacking in attraction. Therefore, a man clean, temperate, respectable, responsible—

STELLA: I shall leave the room!

CHARLES: —restrained, realistic, reasonable—

PAUL: A lovely man!

CHARLES: A fashionable man. His verse turned out as effortlessly as his personal appearance. Smooth thoughts soothing in their catholic simplicity. Love poems—ah, Stella!—a delicious liquidity—casually inspired by the contemplation of his elegant mistress's inner thighs. Not like your—(*He nudges* PAUL *who giggles*)—not like your blasphemous, bawdy, scraggy limericks. Yes, Stella, I once knew these beautiful poets. They smell. They smell very nice, but they smell.

STELLA: You're jealous.

CHARLES: Yes, my love.

STELLA: You! You lack attraction but, my God! you don't lack pathos. As you are now—as you are sitting there now—I could weep for you—

CHARLES: There's someone—

STELLA: Weep for you!

CHARLES: There's someone on the stairs.

    Footsteps can be heard coming up the stairs from below.

STELLA: Listen!

CHARLES: It's probably him. (*To* PAUL.) Here he comes to take you away.

STELLA: Behave yourselves! Are you ready?

CHARLES: Ready. (CHARLES *rises, and, standing behind* PAUL, *whispers.*) Your flies are undone.

    PAUL *looks, finds they are not undone, and laughs.*

STELLA: Be quiet! (*She is about to move to the door when it is opened from the outside and* JOHN WINTER *comes into the room. He is carrying parcels of food.* CHARLES *and* PAUL *shout with laughter.*)

CHARLES: The distinguished critic!

PAUL: Do I bow, or curtsey, or salute, or—(*Laughing, he proceeds to do all these things.*)

STELLA: You make me look a fool, John Winter.

WINTER: I'm sorry.

CHARLES: Blame me, Stella. Blame me.

STELLA: You've got the food. Good. (*She takes the parcels from* JOHN WINTER.) I've told you I'm going to cook today's meal?

WINTER: Yes.

STELLA: I want you to take Mr Southman upstairs to his room now. He is to rest until Mr Procathren arrives.

WINTER: Very well.

STELLA: Do you hear me, Paul?

PAUL: Yes, but I'm all right.

STELLA: Nevertheless, you're going to rest now.

PAUL: See anything of Procathren in the village, John Winter?

WINTER: No, sir. There's been—(*He is interrupted by* STELLA. *The following conversations between* JOHN WINTER–STELLA *and* PAUL–CHARLES *take place simultaneously.*)

S: This is the meat?	C: Probably lost his way.
W: Yes.	P: No. He's clever.
S: What is it?	C: Perhaps he's changed his
W: Beef.	mind.
S: We have vegetables.	P: Why?
W: Yes.	C: Decided not to come and see
S: Will you prepare them?	a dirty old man like you.

W: Yes. That's the dried fruit.

S: Good. Where's the coffee?

W: I couldn't get any. That's what I—

S: Why not? We've none at all.

W: I know that. If you'll allow me—

S: I suppose they wouldn't let you have it.

W: There's been trouble in the village.

S: What?

W: There's been trouble in the village.

S: Paul! Charles! Do you hear that?

P: Charles.

C: Yes?

P: I don't want to go to rest.

C: Tell her.

P: You tell her.

C: It'll do you good.

P: You think I ought to go?

C: Yes, I think so.

P: All right.

C: You needn't sleep. You can read.

P: Will you come and read to me?

C: John Winter will. I've found a copy of Alice among my stuff? I'll give it to you for an extra birthday present.

CHARLES: What?

STELLA: Something's happened in the village.

CHARLES: Well, what?

STELLA: Come along, John Winter, let's have it.

WINTER (*He speaks directly to* PAUL): The reports in the village are confused, sir, but I have been able to gather a little information.

PAUL. Well?

WINTER: Three private soldiers have escaped from a detention camp. They have made their way to the village, and it is believed they slept last night in the village hall. This morning, at an early hour, they broke out of the hall and began marauding and looting the village. Although unarmed they terrorized the villagers. Having obtained food they retired, and are now hiding at some place in the surrounding country.

PAUL: Thank you, John Winter. An excellent and lucid report.

WINTER: Thank you, sir.

STELLA (*to* CHARLES): He'll salute in a moment.

PAUL: Let us appreciate the situation.

STELLA: Surely—

PAUL: Be quiet, Stella. Well, John Winter, have you anything to suggest?

WINTER: I can see no immediate danger to yourself, sir, from the situation at present. By their actions the soldiers have automatically allied themselves to us, although ignorant of our aims and even of our existence. Indeed, by their actions they caused a diversion in the village admirably suited to the day of your visit to London.

PAUL: You think the villagers might have interfered with my going?

WINTER: I had reports to that effect, sir.

PAUL: And you said nothing?

WINTER: I was prepared, sir.

PAUL: The idea of an alliance with these soldiers against the villagers must be considered. Perhaps we could offer this house as—

STELLA: Stop playing at being soldiers yourselves for a minute, and listen to me. You are both going to London today for an express purpose. This is no time to indulge in your fancy for campaigning. (PAUL *and* JOHN WINTER *are silent.*) All right, Captain Winter. Take General Southman to his room.

PAUL: Stella—I

STELLA: Go along, Grandpa. You can hatch your revolutionary schemes as well up there as you can down here.

JOHN WINTER *takes* PAUL'S *arm and they begin to move to the stairs.*

PAUL: Where's that copy of Alice, Charles?

CHARLES: I'll bring it to you.

STELLA: You're not to read. You're to rest.

PAUL: Charles said I could read.

STELLA: No, you're to rest. (PAUL *and* JOHN WINTER *have gone up the stairs.*) Did you hear them? Ridiculous! Two old men with their stupid attempts at military phrases and reports. Did you hear them? 'Situation—immediate danger—diversion—an alliance.'

CHARLES: Yes, I heard them.

STELLA: Absurd!

CHARLES: But I thought—I may have been mistaken—I thought that you appreciated a very real danger from the villagers.

STELLA: I do. It is a very real danger. If the villagers could organize themselves, or could be moved by a moment's rage they would come here and kill us all. At present they suffer from no more than a grievance. And they have cause—they have cause for grievance and for hating us. When Paul came here—when he withdrew himself from the world that attacked him—he chose the village to be his butt. I remember the things he said—(*she has taken two loose cigarettes from the pocket of her dress. She throws one to* CHARLES)— here—catch!—I remember the things he said about the village when I was a child—unforgivable, beastly and unprovoked. Paul was then no longer in a position to attack his equals and so his abuse, the result of hurt pride, was directed against the villagers. It was unprovoked because he had no quarrel with them but for their sanity and security. Soon they felt—under his attack—they felt their security gone and with it their sanity. The satire that had recently shaken the world was directed against them—against a few miserable peasants in a ramshackle hamlet. They reacted in the way of the world, and as Paul would say, 'declared war on us'. That war has continued since my childhood. It has coloured my life—the threat of violence to this tortured family. And so, Charles, I am frightened to hear such nonsense talked by Paul— with encouragement from John Winter—when we need expert and serious conspiracy to save our lives. Reason tells us that we cannot fight the villagers—we cannot do it, and so we must get away—run away if you like. This is what we must do. But how? I can do nothing—you can do nothing—we are useless, helpless and wretched and must appeal to the one man capable of saving us—Procathren. I know! I know he is a poor specimen in your eyes, but we must appeal to him. He may help us. You must admit that we need help, and I have no pride in such matters. I have no pride at all. But try to remember, Charles, that I am a woman— try to be conscious of that at other times than when I am naked. I am a woman and I have a child inside me. Does that explain anything to you? Pregnant women have delusions, they say. Do they? I know nothing about it. Am I deluded, Charles? Am I? I only know that I am possessed by a loneliness hard to bear—a loneliness which I should imagine attends forsaken lovers. (*She stands silent—then:*) Lovers. I am innocent of such things. I have imagined what they do and what they say—these lovers. It seems they find a great delight in music and solicitude, in whispering and smiling, in touching and nakedness, in night. And from these things they make a fabric of memory which will serve them well in their life after death when they will be together but alone. They are wise, for that is the purpose of any memory—of any experience —to give foundation to the state of death. Understand that what- ever we do today in this house—this damned house—will provide

some of the material for our existence in death and you understand my fear. No one who has lived as I have lived could be
happy in death. It is impossible. They speak of us turning in our
graves when a slighting word is spoken of us. No, the words were
spoken during our lifetime, and it is the memory which causes
the unrest. The family—my mother, my father and my sister—out
there in the row of graves—what did they store up, I wonder?
Dadda who fell from grace in the world when Paul fell and spent
the rest of his life living on the charity of the old man—what
does he remember? Mamma—magnificent angry Mamma—is she
happy in the memory of her justice? Ellen, who died at twenty
years, perhaps happy in the memory of my love for her. As for
myself, if I die today, my eternal happiness will depend on the
tiny memory of you, Charles—you, on your first visit to this place
—standing in the doorway—(*She smiles.*)—consciously picaresque
—and handing me the flowers from your hat. I thought then that
we were to be lovers, but from our marriage you gave me no
understanding—no explanation of the mysteries—only a child
conceived in violence. Therefore, I must ask a stranger. I can use
no female tricks on him. I am not a young girl. I am unused to
laughter and my mind is always slow to understand. I can use
neither wit nor beauty. I can only appeal to his charity to take me
away from this place. Perhaps I can go with him as his servant.
(*She pauses.* CHARLES *is turned away from her. As* STELLA *begins to
speak again there is a single note blown on a trumpet: distant and from
the direction of the village.*) Why don't you speak? Now! Why don't
you speak, now? You could have released me—you could have
freed me from this place if only you could have overcome your
fear of the world out there and returned yourself. Even now you
could kill my black, desperate, damnable fear of all time being
empty if you would tell me—show me how to love. I am human
and I am a woman. Tell me. And, O, Charles, Charles, comfort me!

    *He is about to move to her when the trumpet is blown again. It is nearer
and blatant, raucous, defiant.* CHARLES *and* STELLA, *hearing this,
stare at each other.*

CHARLES: What is it?

STELLA: I don't know.

    The trumpet is blown again.

CHARLES: Listen!

    PAUL *calls from his room upstairs.*

PAUL: What's that?
STELLA: I don't know, Grandpa. O God! I don't know.
CHARLES: It was nearer.
STELLA: Yes. Nearer.
PAUL: What is it? What is that noise?
    The trumpet is being blown.

CURTAIN

ACT TWO

The scene is the same.
The time: four hours later—early afternoon. A fire has been lit.
PAUL *and* STELLA *are sitting at the table; they have just finished a meal.*
A place is laid for CHARLES *who is absent from the room.* JOHN
WINTER *is going about clearing away the remains of the meal.*
There is silence until PAUL, *suddenly turning to* STELLA, *asks:*

PAUL: What did you say?

STELLA: Some minutes ago I answered your question and said, 'It
sounded once more in the distance, then stopped.'

PAUL: What was it?

STELLA: I don't know.

PAUL: It was a trumpet, I know that—but what does it mean? Did
you see anything?

STELLA: We didn't look. (*She puts her face in her hands.*)

WINTER: Have you finished with this, sir? (*He indicates* PAUL'S
plate.)

PAUL: What? Yes. Yes, thank you. (JOHN WINTER *removes the
plate.*) Some trick of the villagers, perhaps.

STELLA: They've never dared to come so near to the house before.

PAUL: No. They're getting really mischievous. Did it frighten you?

STELLA: Very much.

PAUL: Mustn't be frightened. (*He stares across the room.*) What's the
time?

STELLA: Five and twenty minutes to two.

PAUL: You know, I can't see very well now. It isn't so long ago
that I could see that clock from here. Five and twenty minutes to
two. (*In silence he takes up a fork and scores deep marks into the table-
cloth.*) He's not coming, is he?

STELLA: Procathren?

PAUL: Yes.

STELLA: Of course he is. Don't do that. He's probably been—

PAUL: He's changed his mind as Charles said he would. Decided not to come and see me.

STELLA: It's early yet.

PAUL: No. He's changed his mind.

STELLA: Grandpa—would you care very much if he didn't come?

PAUL: Well, yes. Yes, I should be disappointed.

STELLA: Wipe your mouth, darling.

He does so. CHARLES *comes running down the stairs into the room. He carries a book which he throws on the table before* PAUL.

PAUL: Hullo Charles! (*He laughs.*)

CHARLES: That's the copy of 'Alice in Wonderland' I promised you.

PAUL: Thank you, Charles. Stella, can I have something to drink?

STELLA: Water?

PAUL: Yes, please.

STELLA: Get some water, John Winter.

JOHN WINTER *goes out to the kitchen with the dishes.* PAUL *sits looking at the book.*

CHARLES: He's not come yet? (*He stands behind* STELLA *with his hands on her shoulders. Her hands go up to his.*)

STELLA: No.

CHARLES: I hope he comes.

STELLA: For my sake?

PAUL: What's that?

CHARLES: Nothing, Paul, nothing.

STELLA: He should have been here by now if they're going to get to London.

CHARLES: Yes. You thought he'd be here for this meal?

STELLA: Yes, I did. I don't know why.

PAUL: Has John Winter brought the water yet?

STELLA: No, not yet. Oh, here it is.

JOHN WINTER *has entered with a jug of water and some glasses.*

PAUL: I'll pour it out. Have you fed the dog, John Winter?

WINTER: Yes, sir. Some time ago.

PAUL: It must be very cold out of doors. If he wants to come in you are to allow it.

WINTER: He seems to want to stay out.

PAUL: Was he frightened by that noise?

WINTER: I don't know, sir.

CHARLES: Have you heard it again?

STELLA: No. John Winter, will you keep a look-out for Mr Procathren. I suggest from upstairs.

PAUL: He's not coming!

STELLA: Run along, John Winter.

JOHN WINTER *goes up the stairs.*

PAUL (*chants*): He's not coming! He's not coming! He's not coming after all, at all.

STELLA: Shut up, Grandpa! And having made so much fuss about the water, why don't you drink it? Charles, I want you to—

PAUL, *having sipped the water, suddenly reads, from the book.*

PAUL: 'Once I was a real Turtle.' (*He pantomimes a great sigh: the book falls to the floor.*) Then the world wasn't big enough for me to live in. Every time I raised my voice I banged my head. What a fine, brave, gay little chap I was—the world had never seen my like, it said. (CHARLES *and* STELLA *are whispering together.*) How I made them laugh—how they loved me. Have you ever heard—felt the roar of applause—like the thunder of blood in your head? But—pity!—

> Little Southman's come a cropper
> Because he wrote an awful whopper
> Telling Kings and Princes too
> Just how much they ought to do.
> Poor old Paul!
> What a fall!
> Whoo-ah!

That's what they sang when 'The Abolition of Printing' had been written and I was on my way here. And it was true. What a fall! Whoo-ah!

STELLA: Say something, Charles, and stop him rambling.

CHARLES: Boo!

PAUL: What's that? You, who wouldn't say Boo to a goose dare to say Boo to a Southman? I, who was once a real Turtle—am I now less than a goose?

STELLA: You're an old goose to talk such nonsense, Paul.

PAUL: Quack-quack!

CHARLES: Whither do you wander?

PAUL: Upstairs and downstairs and in my lady's chamber.

CHARLES: Not any longer, you don't.

PAUL: It's my legs—they've gone weak.

CHARLES: Only your legs?

PAUL: I know what you mean, you dirty boy. Blank cartridge. But you'd have been proud of me once, ducky. I was full of the stuff of life when I wrote the 'Abolition'. Then I went neither upstairs nor downstairs but straight into my Lady Society's chamber and lifted the skirts of the old whore. A rough customer—but she kindly displayed her deformities. Then it was whoops with the what-d'you-call-'em—Hullo, Mr So-and-so!—why, bless me, here's the thingamegig—ssh!—the tiger's gone into the forest—be a man—be a man—deliver the goods. (*He snaps his fingers.* ROBERT PROCATHREN *has come up the stairs and is standing in the doorway of the room. He is unseen by* PAUL, STELLA *and* CHARLES.) And when I had performed the obscene gesture what a rush there was to restore the disarray of the filthy old bag. What a-neighing and a-braying to assure her that nothing had been revealed to her detriment. Andrew Vince pulled up the knickers and John Ussleigh pulled down the skirts and Arthur Howell took me, the raper, into custody. The accusation against Paul Frederick Southman! (*He beats on the arm of his chair.*) 'Paul Frederick Southman: you are charged with the assault of the well-known and much-beloved whore, Society, in that you did, with malice and humour, reveal her for what she is and not for what men wish her to be, thereby destroying the illusion of youth and the wisdom of age. Also that you employed the perversion of using for this purpose your pen instead of the recognized organ.' Witnesses called for the prosecution. Andrew Vince: this witness testified the poor old body to be sadly shaken by her experience and vehemently denied the defence's suggestion that he had rummaged her after finding her crying in an alley. John Ussleigh: this witness, a publisher, stated that he saw the assault but had been under the impression that it was a case of true love. He had known the prisoner for a number of years, etc., etc. An unnamed young man: this witness, called for medical evidence, admitted intercourse with Society on several occasions. When asked by the defence whether he was not repelled by the malformations of Society, he answered, 'I thought all women were like that.' Witnesses called for the defence: none. Sentence: exile. (*He sees* ROBERT PROCATHREN. *The two men stare at each other across the room.* STELLA *turns to recognize* ROBERT *at once.*)

STELLA: Mr Procathren.

ROBERT: That's right.

STELLA: I'm Stella Heberden.

ROBERT: How do you do.

STELLA: How do you do. This is my grandfather, Paul Southman, and my husband, Charles.

ROBERT: How do you do.

STELLA: Won't you come in?

ROBERT: Thank you. I've left my car some distance away. I could find no road to the house.

STELLA: There isn't one.

ROBERT: I suppose the car will be all right.

STELLA: I'm sure it will be.

There is a pause and then ROBERT *moves towards* PAUL, *and, smiling at him, says:*

ROBERT: Well, sir, this is a great occasion for me.

PAUL: How do you do. Stella!

ROBERT: May I say, Many happy returns of the day.

PAUL: Thank you very much.

ROBERT: I feel there is no necessity for—

CHARLES: Have you had lunch, Mr Procathren?

ROBERT: What? Yes. Yes, thank you—I have. Surely Mr Southman, there is no necessity for formality between us on this occasion, but there are a few things I should like to say. Have I your permission?

PAUL *is silent.*

STELLA: Please go on.

ROBERT: Thank you. I'll be brief. (*He speaks to* PAUL.) What am I doing in coming here today—

PAUL: Did John Winter say he'd fed the dog?

STELLA: Yes, Grandpa. (*To* ROBERT.) You must forgive him.

ROBERT: Of course. I appreciate the honour you do me in allowing me to come here, to this house, today—this house which has been closed to the world for so many years. You withdrew yourself from us, and with yourself your advice and guidance, to punish us for our treatment of you and your ideas. At the time of the attacks on you I was nine years of age and therefore rather too young, actively, to participate in your defence. I have had to wait until today, when I hope—in the following few hours to wipe out the memory of the hatred and violence that was inflicted on you twenty-five years ago by your fellow artists. As a young man my own work was deeply influenced by—

PAUL: What does he say?

ROBERT: No more. I shall say no more. There remains only this: as a material token of our appreciation of your nobility of attitude I have been asked to bring you this book. (*He has taken a leather-bound folio from the brief-case he carries. This book he lays on the table before* PAUL *who makes no attempt to open it.*) With it may I wish you the best of health and happiness and, again, many happy returns of the day.

   PAUL *nods his head.*

STELLA: Well, have a look at the book, Grandpa. (PAUL *shakes his head.*) What do you say? Oh, he hasn't got his glasses.

ROBERT: I'm so sorry. I didn't realize that. May I. (*He takes back the book and opens it.*) In this book you will find some sixty-odd appreciations both in prose and verse—they are all, of course, in autograph. Here are Harold Prospect, Richard Lewis Cameron, Helen Newsome, George Reeves and many others writing in honour of Paul Frederick Southman. (*He holds out the book to* PAUL.)

PAUL: I was a real Turtle once, wasn't I? (*He takes the book.*)

STELLA: Don't be silly, Grandpa.

ROBERT: Now, Mrs Heberden—

STELLA: Yes?

ROBERT: I don't want to bother Mr Southman—so may I tell you about the arrangements I have made for today?

STELLA: Certainly.

ROBERT: Well, Mr Southman will have to walk to the car, I'm afraid—that is possible, isn't it?

STELLA: He has a little cart we sometimes pull him around in—he could use that.

ROBERT: Excellent. Now, we should start from here about four-thirty. (*He looks at the clock—then at his watch.*) Surely your clock is exactly an hour fast.

STELLA: Yes. Yes, it is. It's broken.

ROBERT: We should get to London by seven o'clock giving Mr Southman time for a short rest before the dinner.

   PAUL *and* CHARLES *have been whispering over the book of appreciation. Suddenly* PAUL'S *voice is raised.*

PAUL: No, no, Charles! A very nice young man.

   ROBERT *smiles at* STELLA *and continues.*

ROBERT: The dinner will be a formal affair. Many people wish to meet Mr Southman—I hope it won't tire him—he must say immediately if it does. There will be some speeches—we are hoping that he is going to speak—

STELLA: I think he will—but he's very frightened, you know. (*Very distantly the trumpet sounds.*) It is a fear that he is no longer—

ROBERT: What was that?

STELLA: I heard nothing.

PAUL: There it is again, Stella.

ROBERT: What is it, sir? A barracks?

CHARLES: No. We've no ideas about it, have we, Paul?

PAUL *and* CHARLES *grin at each other.*

ROBERT: A train, perhaps.

CHARLES: There are no trains round here.

There is a pause. Then ROBERT *laughs, and continues to speak to* STELLA.

ROBERT: I should tell you, Mrs Heberden, that there will be the presentation of a cheque to Mr Southman tonight. A certain sum of money has been collected by—What did you say?

STELLA: I said I'd like to speak to you about that.

ROBERT: Certainly.

STELLA: Later. You're leaving at half-past four, Grandpa. (*To* ROBERT.) His man, John Winter, will travel with him. That's all right, isn't it?

ROBERT: Quite all right.

STELLA: So you'll be ready, won't you, Grandpa?

PAUL: Stella!

STELLA: Yes? (*She moves to him.*) It's all right, darling! It's all right. (*She puts her arms around him.*) You see, Mr Procathren did come after all. (*To* ROBERT.) He was so frightened—so afraid that you weren't coming. Weren't you, darling? (*She kisses* PAUL.)

ROBERT (*going to the mural painting*): This is your work, Mr Heberden?

CHARLES: Yes.

ROBERT: Interesting. I can't recall seeing anything of yours since the famous show—when was it?—four years ago.

CHARLES: Five.

ROBERT: Five, was it? Anyway, when you were the infant prodigy startling the country with your engravings to the 'Purgatorio'.

CHARLES: That exhibition was a mistake.

ROBERT: For one so young? Perhaps.

CHARLES: I meant otherwise.

ROBERT: If you have any other new work I should be most interested to see it.

CHARLES: For recognition in your literary reviews?

ROBERT: I assure you—

CHARLES: I have nothing. I have ceased to comment upon a society I have forsaken.

ROBERT: But surely, Mr Heberden, the essence—

CHARLES: Did you have a good journey from London, Mr Procathren?

ROBERT: I didn't come from London. I came from Oxford.

CHARLES: I see.

ROBERT: I live there.

STELLA: Did you come through the village?

ROBERT: Yes.

STELLA: It was quiet?

ROBERT: There seemed to be no one about—but I drove through very quickly. Why?

STELLA: No reason.

ROBERT: As a matter of fact, I had intended to start earlier and stop in the village to call on the rector. The Reverend Giles Aldus. Do you know him? (*They are silent.*) He has a library—it has been left in his care—a small collection, but it sounds most interesting. You've heard of it, no doubt.

STELLA: No.

ROBERT: No? I was going to call and ask him if I might see it. They are books of a religious nature—almost legendary as they've never been catalogued. Aldus has never allowed it. I'm told he lives with his mother, and both she and the books he keeps from contact with the world. I'm not particularly interested in his mother, but I'd have liked to have seen the books. However, there was time to see neither. By the way, Mrs Heberden, I must apologize for walking into the house as I did, but I could find no bell or knocker.

CHARLES: We have very few callers.

ROBERT (*He laughs*): I nearly fell over a dog in the doorway. I meant to mention this before. There's a—

STELLA: Oh dear! I hope he didn't annoy you.

ROBERT: No, he didn't annoy me.

PAUL: He doesn't annoy people.

ROBERT: How could he? He's dead. (*There is a pause.* ROBERT *laughs.*) Is that your dog? I didn't know. I thought—
    PAUL *has risen to his feet. He shouts.*

PAUL: John Winter!

STELLA: Paul—Paul!

PAUL (*to* CHARLES): Get John Winter! (CHARLES *is about to move to the stairs when* JOHN WINTER *comes down into the room.*) John Winter!

WINTER: Yes?

PAUL: John Winter, this man says my dog is dead.

WINTER: Where—?

PAUL: This man says my dog is dead.

WINTER: Where is it?

ROBERT: In the doorway—down— (*He points.*)
    JOHN WINTER *runs from the room.*

PAUL: Help me—Charles, you fool—help me!

STELLA: Paul, you're not to—
    CHARLES *has taken* PAUL'S *arm and is assisting him across the room.*

PAUL: I must go down—I must go down! (*He shouts down the stairs.*) John Winter! Is it true? John Winter, is it true?
    PAUL *and* CHARLES *go from the room to descend the stairs.*

STELLA: O God! O dear Christ! (*She has moved to the table and, unseeing, beats down with her fist on the presentation book.*)

ROBERT: Be careful of that book, please!

STELLA: What?

ROBERT: The book. Please be careful. (*He removes the book from under her hand.*) I am most distressed, Mrs Heberden. I had no idea that the dog—you see, I tripped over the carcase and—I thought —well, I really don't know what I thought—the thing was still warm. I must apologize but at the time—

STELLA: —you had something very much more important to think about?

ROBERT: Well, yes.

STELLA: The presentation to Mr Southman.

ROBERT: Exactly.

STELLA: And I agree, Mr Procathren.

ROBERT: What? That—

STELLA: That the presentation was more important than a dead dog.

ROBERT: Thank you.

During this conversation between ROBERT *and* STELLA *there is heard from the foot of the stairs at the main door:*

CHARLES (*his voice rising to audibility*): —and we need proof. We don't know anything.

PAUL: Proof! I want no more proof of their intentions. Look at it —look at it—it lies there—dead! Dead!

CHARLES: Paul—Paul! Stop it! (*There is the sound of some heavy object being thrown to the ground.*) Paul—come here! Stop him, John Winter!

The main door of the house is thrown open and PAUL *can be heard shouting.*

PAUL: Come out! Come out, you toads! Why do you hide? You were not afraid of an old dog—why be afraid of an old man? Come out and let me see you! (*His last words become a long howl of grief.*)

STELLA: We must hope—we must pray that—

There is a pause.

STELLA: —that he will go with you this afternoon. I promise he shall go with you. This will make no difference at all. He shall go with you to London, and he will be all right. He will be all right.

ROBERT: We must hope so. Please don't be upset, Mrs Heberden. I can understand this. An old man—an animal beloved of him—

STELLA: But we must get him away from here soon. You said half-past four—

ROBERT: Yes.

STELLA: It must be before that. As soon as possible. At once!

ROBERT: Very well.

STELLA: He'll arrive early in London, but there must be somewhere he can go, surely.

ROBERT: My flat.

STELLA: He can wait there?

ROBERT: With pleasure.

STELLA: Good.

ROBERT: He'll be all right there, I can assure you. He can rest and during that time—

STELLA: Mr Procathren.

ROBERT: Yes.

STELLA: Help me.

ROBERT: How?

STELLA: Help me.

ROBERT: In what way?

STELLA: Please!

ROBERT: In what way can I help you?

STELLA: I had prepared what I was going to say to you.

ROBERT: Then please say it.

STELLA: You will help me?

ROBERT: In any way I can, but—

STELLA: There's very little time.

ROBERT: Before they return? I promise to look after the old gentleman, if that's what you mean.

STELLA: Yes. Yes, of course, you must look after him.

ROBERT: I will.

STELLA: Sir! Sir, our future is in your hands.

ROBERT: You must forgive me, I—

STELLA: Our future is in your most beautiful delicate hands.

ROBERT: You must forgive me but I don't understand you.

STELLA: You are young, you are famous and powerful, you are talented and you can do as I ask.

ROBERT (*he laughs*): I am a minor poet—nothing more.

STELLA: Why do you laugh?

ROBERT: I don't know.

STELLA: At this moment—why do you laugh?

ROBERT: Shyness, I suppose. I am shy.

STELLA: I'm sorry but there's no time for the courtesies and formalities as between strangers. You mustn't expect them from me. But please don't withdraw. A moment ago you were willing to help me.

ROBERT: I don't understand what you want.

STELLA: This! This is what I want! I want Paul to be restored to his former greatness. In that way there can be a future for my child.

ROBERT: Your child?

STELLA: I'm pregnant. The child Paul. Innocent, you will admit—in no way responsible. For this child's sake old Paul must be restored to greatness in the world.

ROBERT: But he is a great man now. No restoration is necessary.

STELLA: No, he is not a great man now, but—

ROBERT: I came here today to see a great man.

STELLA: —we can restore him. And this is the way. Listen—this is the way.

ROBERT: There is nothing I can do.

STELLA: Nothing can be done today, certainly. Nothing, beyond our having you take him to London. But in the future we can act. You promised to help me—

ROBERT: Really, I—

STELLA: You promised to help me! And you can help me in this way: until you can get us away from this place keep in touch with me—by letter, in person—I'll get away to London to see you if you wish—but by some means—by any means—we must retain contact.

ROBERT: I can see no point in this.

STELLA: Such a small thing to ask. Be gracious, sir—you have so much—be gracious to the poor. (*There is a pause.* ROBERT *turns away.*) What can I offer you?

ROBERT: Nothing.

STELLA: You can be godfather to my child.

ROBERT: I am an atheist.

Footsteps can be heard coming up the stairs.

STELLA: Together we can do so much for Paul. Apart we—

ROBERT (*He has heard the footsteps*): All right!

STELLA: You will help me?

ROBERT: Yes.

STELLA: God bless you!

ROBERT: I'll keep in touch with you by letter but you must instruct me. I've no idea what you intend. They're coming back.

STELLA: I will instruct you, as you put it, in our first letters. It is decided then—you and I can go together now. But I must have a token from you.

ROBERT: A token?

STELLA: A material token. That will do. (*She indicates the signet ring* ROBERT *is wearing.*)

ROBERT: This?

STELLA: Yes. (*She holds out her hand to him. He removes the ring and puts it on a finger of her left hand. As he is doing this* PAUL *comes in the room from below. He moves quickly and breathlessly across the room to the farther stairs.* STELLA *calls to him.*) Paul! (*He does not answer but continues up the stairs to the upper floor.* STELLA *speaks again to* ROBERT.) You mentioned a cheque to be presented.

ROBERT: Yes.

STELLA: It must come to me.

ROBERT: I don't think I can do that.

STELLA: You can contrive some trick.

ROBERT *still holds* STELLA'S *left hand from the giving of the ring.*

ROBERT: Some trick. Is that what you're up to, Mrs Heberden?

CHARLES *enters from below.*

CHARLES: Where is he?

STELLA: He's gone to his room. Is the dog dead?

CHARLES: Yes.

STELLA: How is he going to take it?

CHARLES: In anger. Listen! (*There is silence.*) I thought I heard him. (*He smiles at* ROBERT *and* STELLA.) Have you two settled the future?

STELLA: Yes, we have. (*To* ROBERT.) Haven't we?

ROBERT, *in an agony of embarrassment, moves away from her.*

CHARLES: Excellent! (*He laughs.*)

STELLA: I'm going to call Paul.

CHARLES: No, Stella—no, let him come down in his own time.

STELLA: You said he was angry. Did you say that?

CHARLES: I did.

STELLA: But why? Why anger?

CHARLES: He's convinced that the villagers poisoned the dog.

STELLA: Did they?

CHARLES: No, I don't think so. It must have died of old age.

STELLA: What a day to choose to die! (CHARLES *is laughing at her.*) It should have waited until tomorrow. (*Suddenly she laughs too, and, continuing to laugh, she speaks.*) It should have waited until tomorrow, when Paul would have been away. However, we must deal with this—this catastrophe. (*She goes to* CHARLES *and puts her hand on his shoulders.*) It will take more than the death of a dog to deter me. You see, Charles, I'm no longer alone. I now have an ally who is prepared with me. Mr Procathren has promised to help me.

ROBERT: One moment, Mrs Heberden. I feel I must define the limits of my obligations. They are these: to come here today not only on my own behalf but also on behalf of my committee: to present Mr Southman with the book of appreciations and our congratulations on his birthday: to drive him to London for the dinner tonight and during that time to accept personal responsibility for his safety: to return him to this house tomorrow. Those are the limits of my formal obligations—but—I have promised one thing further—to keep in touch with you by letter

in future. I will do that—but it does not mean, Mrs Heberden—
(*his voice becomes uncontrolled*)—it does not mean that I am prepared
to become engaged in a partisan way in any family feud or intrigue.
What you are attempting to do, and how you are attempting to
entangle me—indeed, why—I do not understand. But kindly
remember I have stated my obligations and I am not going beyond
them.

 PAUL *is coming down the stairs into the room.*

CHARLES (*to* STELLA): As an ally I prefer a dead dog.

 PAUL *comes into the room. Beneath his arm he carries a large automatic
pistol; he has removed the clip and is loading it with cartridges. There is a
change in his manner. Towards* ROBERT *he is friendly, almost familiar,
and no longer afraid. He speaks with a clear and forceful articulation.*

PAUL: I must admit that even with my daily care of this weapon I
have always looked upon it as being for defence, never for
revenge.

STELLA: What are you going to do?

PAUL: You must forgive me, Mr Procathren—Robert—I may call
you Robert, may I not?—

ROBERT: Certainly.

PAUL: You must forgive us, Robert, for engaging you in this
business. (*He inserts the magazine into the pistol.*) I trust your
sympathies are with us.

ROBERT: I know nothing of the circumstances, sir.

STELLA: What are you going to do, Grandpa?

PAUL: Whatever I do it will be with this! (*He lays the pistol down
heavily on the table.*) The circumstances, Robert, are these. For many
years past now the occupants of this house have suffered victimiza-
tion by the villagers. The reason has never been clear to me.
Perhaps it is based on some delusion with regard to our social
standing. Perhaps our being artists—I don't know. But I no
longer require reasons. The act—the act of poisoning my dog—
is enough.

STELLA: The dog died of old age.

PAUL: Don't be silly, child. This, Robert, is the first direct move
they have made. For years the threat has existed—but, although
very real, it was no more than a threat. It lasted so long without
action that it became a family joke—eh, Charles?—Stella?—but
this is an act and must be answered by as direct and cruel an act.
Where is John Winter?

STELLA: I want to know what you are intending to do. Are you forgetting that you go to London today?

PAUL: No, I am not forgetting that—and I shall go.

STELLA: You will?

PAUL: Most certainly. Where is John Winter?

STELLA: He hasn't come up yet. And are you going to London?

PAUL: Don't worry, darling—I shall go. At about four o'clock you said, Robert?

ROBERT: Yes, sir. We should start by then.

PAUL: In that case, I must hurry. Now then—we are one—two—three—four men with John Winter and one woman. With the three soldiers we shall be seven men.

STELLA: Soldiers?

PAUL: The soldiers that have escaped from prison. John Winter mentioned them. The soldiers that have anticipated us in their attack on the village. I propose to form an alliance with them. But, first of all, we must find them. I want you, Charles, to do that—and perhaps you, Robert, would care—

ROBERT: I don't wish to be involved in this, sir.

There is silence. PAUL *stares at* ROBERT, *his hand going out to touch the pistol. He withdraws and turns to* CHARLES.

PAUL: Then you will go with John Winter, Charles. Bring these soldiers back here. I want to talk to them.

ROBERT: Mr Southman! (PAUL *turns to* ROBERT.) You must understand my position. I cannot—dare not become engaged in something that is of no personal—no personal—

PAUL: Advantage, Mr Procathren?

ROBERT: No, sir! Not advantage, but—

PAUL: I have explained the circumstances to you. You are an intelligent man—you have undoubtedly understood. Will you or will you not help me?

ROBERT: My personal position—

PAUL: I don't understand your doubt and hesitation. With your admiration of myself surely you believe what I have told you to be true.

ROBERT: Of course.

PAUL: We need your help.

ROBERT: I will help you in any indirect way that I can—

PAUL: No qualifications! Will you or will you not help me? I shall not ask again.

There is a pause.

ROBERT: I will.

STELLA: You are being untrue to me!

ROBERT: What can I do? What else can I do?

STELLA (*she cries out*): Then what is going to happen? (*There is a complete cessation of activity whilst* STELLA *speaks. She is swept by a sudden storm of fore-knowledge, awful in its clarity. The men, silent and unmoving, watch her.*) Careful! We are approaching the point of deviation. At one moment there is laughter and conversation and a progression: people move and speak smoothly and casually, their breathing is controlled and they know what they do. Then there occurs a call from another room, the realization that a member of the assembly is missing, the sudden shout into the dream and the waking to find the body with the failing heart lying in the corridor—with the twisted limbs at the foot of the stairs— the man hanging from the beam, or the child floating drowned in the garden pool. Careful! Be careful! We are approaching that point. The moment of the call from another room. (*She pauses.*) Give me another of your cigarettes, Paul.

PAUL: What was it, my darling?

STELLA: Give me a cigarette.

PAUL *takes the box from his pocket and hands it to* STELLA.

PAUL: We are aware, my dear—stop it! you're trembling—yes, we are aware—

STELLA: Damn! (*She throws away the match with which she is attempting to light her cigarette.* ROBERT *steps forward and lights it for her as* PAUL *continues to speak.*)

PAUL: —very much aware of the menace of the point of deviation. We are eagerly awaiting the shout from another room for we know from whom it will come and to whom it will be directed. Also we are aware of the discovery—the destruction of the village —and so we have nothing to fear. All we have to do is to wait a little while—(JOHN WINTER *comes into the room from below*)— but apparently, not long. Yes, John Winter?

WINTER: There's a gentleman to see you, sir.

PAUL: The whole world is calling on us today. Who is it?

WINTER: From the village.

PAUL: Ah, well?

WINTER: The Reverend Aldus.

PAUL: The holy book-worm, eh? Tell him to come up. (JOHN

WINTER *turns and shouts down the stairs, 'Will you come up, please.')*
What does this mean? If they think I can't attack clerics they
should remember my history. Now for it.

The REVEREND ALDUS *comes into the room.* JOHN WINTER
goes out.

ALDUS: Good afternoon. (PAUL *inclines his head but is silent. The others*
whisper, 'Good afternoon.') My name is Aldus.

PAUL: I am Southman. This is my grand-daughter, Stella, her
husband, Charles Heberden, and a friend and sympathizer,
Mr Robert Procathren. (ALDUS *nods to each in turn.)* Please sit
down.

ALDUS: Thank you.

PAUL: You will notice, my dears, first of all, the general attitude.
That of humility bordering on servility. It is dangerous to the
unwary. It has been used by the Church for hundreds of years to
gain advantage in a situation such as this. Next, notice the facial
expression. A cursory examination and one might take it to be
shyness, perhaps idiocy. It is neither. The clothes, notice the
clothes. And the posture—neat, precise. if you were to go near
him you would smell not sanctity but intrigue. But don't go near
him. I forbid it.

There is a pause.

ALDUS (*he has a marked impediment in his speech*): May I speak?

PAUL. Certainly.

ALDUS: You have finished your attack?

PAUL: I have not yet begun.

ALDUS: It is evident, Mr Southman, that I cannot match your
fluency in this conversation. I am forced, by my disability to
select only certain words for my use.

PAUL (*he laughs*): You're doing very well. Carry on.

ALDUS: I have a proposal.

PAUL: Concerning the soldiers?

ALDUS: Yes. You've heard—?

PAUL: Partly. Tell us—in well-selected words—what has happened
—and what you propose.

ALDUS: Late last night these three men came to see me at the
Rectory. I was alone. Their leader— (*The trumpet sounds from the*
middle distance.) Listen!

PAUL: Yes, we've heard it. Is that the soldiers?

ALDUS: Yes.

PAUL: Apparently we were mistaken. We thought it was your people fooling about.

ALDUS: No, it is the soldiers. I will tell you. These men came to me —they were honest in that they explained the true position—their escape from criminal detention—it was I who practised dishonesty —and by that I have brought—

PAUL: Get on man! There's little time. Certainly no time for self-examination.

ALDUS: Forgive me. Their leader asked one thing of me—shelter for the night. I agreed, and told them that they could sleep in the church hall. They went there. They trusted me. In the early hours of the morning I got up and—moved by some sense of justice outside my province—I— (*He is in tears.*)

PAUL: Come along. What is it?

ALDUS: I say, forgive me. My mother—

PAUL: Never mind your mother now. Tell us about the soldiers.

ALDUS: I got up and went to the hall and locked them in. I locked the soldiers in.

Very sharply and suddenly, but shortly PAUL *and* CHARLES *laugh.*

PAUL: What happened then?

ALDUS: They broke out of the hall just before daylight. One of them had stolen a trumpet from among some band instruments that were stored there. That is the trumpet you can hear. With that they are advertising their presence. (*He has risen from his chair.*) They are marauding through the countryside. The village is terrorised. They attacked the baker—

PAUL: Why the baker?

ALDUS: There seems to be no reason for their acts. They are madmen. I do not understand! I do not understand! (*He is shouting and stammering incoherently.*)

PAUL: Be quiet! (*Then, in silence*) What do you expect of me?

ALDUS: Come to—come to ask your help, sir.

PAUL: You've what?

ALDUS: Come to ask your help, sir.

PAUL: Against the soldiers?

ALDUS: Yes, sir.

PAUL: I see. How long have you lived in the village, Mr Aldus?

ALDUS: Five years.

PAUL: Five years. Please sit down. Then you know the situation that exists—has always existed between the village and this house?

ALDUS: Yes, sir.

PAUL: You do?

ALDUS: Yes.

PAUL: And yet you come to ask my help?

ALDUS: I know the history of hatred, sir, and yet I appeal to you in my weakness to help us against these men.

PAUL: You turn in your weakness to me, Mr Aldus? You surprise me.

ALDUS: Mr Southman!

PAUL: Telephone for the police.

ALDUS: They destroyed the telephone lines last night.

PAUL: Send one of your young men as a runner.

ALDUS: You know we have no young men among us.

PAUL: And I have two.

ALDUS: Yes.

PAUL: And one of them has a car. Have you tried prayer?

ALDUS: Sir! Sir, we cannot—

PAUL: Have you tried appeasement? Offer them—

ALDUS: We cannot—

PAUL: Have you tried preaching? Appeal to their better natures! (ALDUS *has foundered upon his incoherence. He is silent.*) And so you have come to me. Why?

ALDUS: Because, by reputation, you are a great and powerful man.

PAUL: Thank you.

ALDUS: A man—

PAUL: Would you say a good man, Mr Aldus? (ALDUS *is silent.*) Ah! then you would use evil to combat evil. A strange presumption for one of your ridiculous uniform.

ALDUS: I cannot engage in polemics with you.

PAUL: Very well. You ask me to lead you against these men to achieve—what?

ALDUS: To uphold law and order; to protect the people of my village.

PAUL: Are you not thinking more of your books? Of the danger to your precious books.

ALDUS: No.

PAUL: Are you sure? I heard what Robert said—he didn't think I was listening, but I heard of all your books about God. Think, Mr Aldus! Perhaps you now love the books more than you love God.

ALDUS: No.

PAUL: That would be very wrong, Mr Aldus. Very wrong indeed.

ALDUS: I am thinking of the villagers—of the people. I am thinking—

PAUL: You are? I just thought it might not be so. It is for them you want help?

ALDUS: Yes.

PAUL: Ask me.

ALDUS: What?

PAUL: To help you.

ALDUS: Help us.

PAUL: Properly.

ALDUS: Will you help us?

PAUL: No.

ALDUS: There could only—

PAUL: Again!

ALDUS: What?

PAUL: Ask again.

STELLA: Paul!

PAUL: Shut up! Ask again.

ALDUS: Will you help us?

PAUL: No! (*He has taken up the pistol. He goes to* ALDUS *and taps him on the chest with the barrel of the weapon.*) No! I will not help you. I shall form an alliance however—oh, yes, I shall do that—but it will be with the soldiers and with them I shall revenge myself upon you and your impudent mob. (*He turns away.*) Go! Leave us! Will someone show Mr Aldus to the door.

STELLA *moves to* ALDUS.

CHARLES: I'll go with him.

STELLA: No, I'll go. (*She takes* ALDUS *by the arm.*) Will you be able to get back all right?

ALDUS *nods. They reach the door when* ALDUS *turns.*

ALDUS: Mr Southman, I will dare to say to you—

But PAUL *who has been performing a little silent dance, interrupts* ALDUS *by pointing the pistol at him, squinting along the barrel, and saying:*

PAUL: Bang! (ALDUS *and* STELLA *go out.* PAUL *moves to a position between* ROBERT *and* CHARLES. *He puts his arms about them.*) Well, my dear Robert—and my very dear Charles, that pathetic creature has been sent us to represent our enemy. Not very flattering, is it?

CHARLES (*he is laughing*): What are you going to do?

PAUL: Charles, no! We must be serious. (CHARLES *is silent*.) We mustn't allow what we've just seen—an awful display of fear, non-comprehension and self-conscious pathos—we mustn't allow that to make us laugh or to make us pity. It is an old trick, and we are human. He wanted to tell us about his mother. She is dead —or dying—or doesn't love him any longer—is angry with him, perhaps, for his part in this business—but I wouldn't allow him to speak of it. It might be that there is really some tragedy, and we cannot allow ourselves to be diverted by sympathy for such things. No, Charles—even though they had sent us the whole circus instead of the solitary clown we must not be amused or allow our emotions to be touched in any way. (*He pauses.*) What am I going to do, you ask? What am I going to do? (*The action becomes centred on* ROBERT PROCATHREN—PAUL *and* CHARLES *towards* ROBERT. *The three men move and speak at extreme speed.* PAUL *savagely and in great exaltation:* CHARLES *amusedly and lightly, foreseeing towards what they are moving although not the actual event:* ROBERT *through fear, attempting to join in the fantastic jollity as he attempted to join in games and horseplay when a schoolboy.*) Can you fight, Robert?

ROBERT: Well, sir, I—

PAUL: If you can't—

CHARLES: —we haven't much time to teach you.

PAUL: No.

ROBERT: A little boxing when I was at school.

    PAUL *and* CHARLES *laugh with delight.*

CHARLES: Always the little boys, was it?

PAUL: The boys a little smaller than you—

CHARLES: —but not too obviously smaller.

PAUL: Poor little bastards! I bet you punished them. No, I meant—

CHARLES: I've been told there are rules to that sort of thing. (*He has jumped upon the table and taken up an attitude of defence.*)

PAUL: Shut up, Charles! No, Robert, I meant—

CHARLES: You mustn't kick, must you?

PAUL: I meant, Robert, fighting. With weapons. Such as this. (*He holds up the pistol.*)

ROBERT: No. I've had no experience of such things.

PAUL: Never?

ROBERT: Never.

CHARLES: But surely—

PAUL: Could you learn?
CHARLES: Surely you must have been engaged in some war—
ROBERT: No.
CHARLES: —at your age.
ROBERT: No. I was not fit.
CHARLES: Morally or physically?
ROBERT: Both.
CHARLES: You fought with your pen, eh?
PAUL: Have you never—
CHARLES: Poems of victory!
ROBERT: And defeat.
PAUL: Have you never been moved—
CHARLES: Bravo!
PAUL: —moved by hate or persecution—
CHARLES: Or love?
PAUL: —to contemplate physical violence?
ROBERT: Never.
CHARLES: It has always been unemotional, calm force—
PAUL: —in boxing rings—
CHARLES: —with rules—
PAUL: —and referees—
CHARLES: —against harmless little boys.
PAUL: Do you think you could use this? (*He holds out the pistol to* ROBERT.)
ROBERT: I've never handled one before. (*He takes the pistol from* PAUL.)
PAUL: Will you use it—
CHARLES: It is simple!
PAUL: —with us against the villagers?
CHARLES: Oh, so very simple!
ROBERT: Yes, I'll use it.
PAUL: Against the villagers?
ROBERT: Yes.
PAUL: It's loaded.

    ROBERT *raises the pistol to point at* PAUL *and* CHARLES.
CHARLES: Look out!

    PAUL *and* CHARLES *raise their hands above their heads in mock terror and then shout with laughter.*
ROBERT (*smiling*): Sorry. (*He turns away.*)
PAUL: There's a catch—

CHARLES: There's a catch in everything, Robert.

PAUL: —at the side of the butt.

CHARLES: Which is the bit you are now holding.

PAUL: You release the catch to fire.

CHARLES: Then slight pressure on the trigger—

PAUL: Face away, dear boy, face away!

CHARLES: That releases the striker which explodes the cap which ignites the powder which, expanding as gas, forces out the bullet—

PAUL: Which brings down the house that Paul built!

CHARLES: Isn't that better—

PAUL: Bang! Bang!

CHARLES: —and simpler—

PAUL: Bang!

CHARLES: —than your boxing with bare fists?

ROBERT: You must explain the method by which— (*The pistol goes off in his hand.* PAUL *and* CHARLES *shout with laughter again.* ROBERT, *dropping the pistol to the floor, stands holding his wrist.*) O God!

PAUL: Oh dear, no, Robert! Not that way at all.

CHARLES: No. You must be conscious of when you fire—

PAUL: —and of the direction in which you fire. Oh, yes, you must be much more careful. It is simple, but not as simple as that. The agency is human, not providential. But at least you can fire it— accuracy will come.

    CHARLES *has taken up the pistol from the floor. He removes the clip of remaining cartridges and holds out the pistol to* ROBERT.

CHARLES: There you are. Now you can play with it.

ROBERT: I don't want it! I don't want it!

PAUL: It's all right now. Unloaded.

CHARLES: Of course it is.

PAUL: Take hold of it and we'll have a little drill.

ROBERT: I don't want it!

CHARLES: But it's perfectly safe now. Look! (*He thrusts the pistol into* ROBERT'S *face and pulls the trigger. The striker clicks: nothing nothing more.* ROBERT *after a pause, takes the pistol from* CHARLES.)

PAUL: That's right. Now— (*From almost immediately below the windows, in the garden, there is a great blast blown on the trumpet.*) Listen! They're here—the soldiers! (*He runs to the window.*) Our allies. They're here. They'll know how to use that. (*He is laughing.*)

CHARLES: Can you see them?

PAUL: No. Perhaps my eyes—I can see nobody. (*He opens the*

window.) But they're here. (*He shouts*.) Don't be afraid. Come out
—come up here. You're welcome. You're welcome!

CHARLES: Can you see them?

PAUL: No. There's nobody. Nobody at all.

CHARLES: Shout again.

PAUL: Don't be afraid. We are friends. We are enemies to the
village. Come up—come up!

The three men listen in silence and into that silence comes the voice of
JOHN WINTER *shouting from the foot of the stairs at the main door*.

WINTER: Mr Southman—Mr Southman, sir!

PAUL (*shouting*): We are friends, I assure you. We wish you well.
Bless you, I say, bless oh bless you!

Again they listen and again JOHN WINTER *shouts: this time from
just beyond the door*.

WINTER: Mr Southman!

PAUL: What is it? What does John Winter want?

CHARLES: I don't know.

WINTER: Mr Southman!

ROBERT: Fools! You fools! Don't you understand? Don't you
understand—that is the shout from another room.

PAUL: What?

ROBERT: The shout from another room—that is it. That! Have you
forgotten?

CHARLES: Where's Stella?

PAUL: The shout from another room?—

CHARLES: Where's Stella?

ROBERT: Yes. Where is Stella?

CHARLES: She went to show Aldus out.

ROBERT: She should be back, shouldn't she?

CHARLES: Yes.

ROBERT: Well, where is she now? Where is she now?

CHARLES: Stella! (*He runs to the door—for a moment he pauses and then,
decided, he begins to open the door. It opens a few inches but that is all:
there is some obstruction at the other side*.)

PAUL (*shouting to the soldiers*): Gentlemen, I assure you that we are
friends. Come up here and let us talk—

CHARLES: Paul—what is wrong? Why won't the door open?
John Winter!

PAUL *leaves the window and comes back into the room*.

PAUL: What is it? What are you doing?

CHARLES: Why won't the door open? The door—what is the matter with the door? Help me!

But in the moment's pause when neither PAUL *nor* ROBERT *move* CHARLES *has thrown the full weight of his body against the door. The door opens fully and* CHARLES, *still within the room, stands looking down at the stairs. He cries out then again, the second time the sound resolving itself into the name,* Stella.

PAUL: What? What? (CHARLES *runs from the room on to the stairs.* PAUL *stands plucking at* ROBERT'S *sleeve.*) What is it? What is wrong, Robert? What has gone wrong?

ROBERT *motionless, does not answer him.* CHARLES *calls from the stairs.*

CHARLES: Help me! Help me!

PAUL *goes from the room on to the stairs.* ROBERT *left alone, holding the empty pistol, does not move. He does not look towards the door.* PAUL, *looking down at the stairs, backs into the room.* CHARLES *and* JOHN WINTER *come in carrying* STELLA: *she is dead. For a time the group is still and silent then* JOHN WINTER *speaks.*

WINTER: Put her down, sir. (CHARLES *does not move. He stares down into* STELLA'S *face.*) Mr Heberden. Put her down, sir. We must see—

PAUL: Stella. Stella. Stella.

WINTER: Put her down, sir.

They lay the body on the floor.

PAUL: Robert—Stella's hurt.

WINTER: May I—? Mr Heberden, may I look at her?

CHARLES *nods his head. He moves quickly to the door. He finds the bullet-hole.*

PAUL: Or is it a joke? They've played jokes on me before. (JOHN WINTER *opens the bodice of* STELLA'S *dress, exposing her breasts.*) You wouldn't play jokes on me, Robert. That would be cruel. You wouldn't ridicule me. No, she's playing the joke on me. Stella—Stella darling, stop it. It's not a very good joke.

WINTER: There is a bullet wound—here.

PAUL: Stella!

WINTER: It has, I think, passed through her heart.

PAUL: What do you say, John Winter?

WINTER: There is no pulse.

PAUL: John Winter! You dare to enter into this joke?

WINTER: She is dead.

CHARLES: Dead.

PAUL: Dead! You go too far, sir. Leave the room!

CHARLES: John Winter says she is dead. Shot dead.

PAUL: Dead. Dead. The doors are shutting in the empty house. Dead. Dead.

WINTER: Who was it? I heard the shot. (CHARLES *without turning his head, points to* ROBERT *who, with the empty pistol half-raised has not moved.*) But why? Why?

PAUL: Won't any of you speak to me? I am at fault, I suppose. Listen—I'll confess. You've frightened me. There—I've admitted it. You've frightened me with your joke. Now speak to me.

WINTER (*to* CHARLES): Shall we take her upstairs, sir?

PAUL: Speak to me.

WINTER (*to* CHARLES): Shall we take her upstairs, sir? Nothing can be done.

PAUL: Nothing can be done. (CHARLES *and* JOHN WINTER *lift* STELLA'S *body from the floor. They begin to carry her to the stairs leading to the upper floor.*) Nothing can be done. (PAUL *follows* CHARLES *and* JOHN WINTER.) Don't go, Robert. I'll be down in a minute when I've settled this and then I'll show you how to use the pistol properly. A fine business, indeed. (CHARLES *and* JOHN WINTER *are going up the stairs.*) Wait for me. Where are you taking my darling? Wait for me.

CHARLES *and* JOHN WINTER, *carrying* STELLA'S *body between them, have gone up the stairs from the room. From the foot of the iron steps leading from the balcony to the garden comes a piercing human whistle piping a popular tune. It does not disturb* ROBERT *who remains motionless, and* PAUL *has followed* CHARLES *and* JOHN WINTER *from the room. There is the sound of heavy boots on the iron steps. On to the balcony and so into the room by the window come three soldiers—* WALTER KILLEEN, HENRY CHATER *and their leader* CHRISTIAN MELROSE. HENRY CHATER *carries a trumpet. It is* WALTER KILLEEN *who is whistling, but he stops as they enter the room to stand a little inside the window.* ROBERT, *unmoving, has his back to them.*

MELROSE: Good afternoon. I hear we're welcome in this house. That'll be a change. (ROBERT *does not move.* MELROSE *raises his voice.* Good afternoon. (*It is when* ROBERT *turns that* MELROSE *sees the pistol in his nand.*) A nice welcome. A very nice welcome, indeed! (*To* CHATER *and* KILLEEN.) Don't move. (*To* ROBERT.) And what are you going to do with that?

ROBERT: What?

MELROSE: You have a pistol in your hand.

ROBERT: What do you say?

MELROSE: Are you deaf? I said, You have a pistol in your hand.

ROBERT: Oh, yes. It's not loaded—now.

MELROSE: I'm very happy to hear that. Very happy, indeed. (*He takes the pistol from* ROBERT, *examines it and puts it on the table.*) I thought—just for a minute, you know—I thought we weren't welcome here. (*To* KILLEEN *and* CHATER.) Come in—sit down—don't fool about. Keep quiet. You can sit there, and you sit there, where I can see you. (KILLEEN *and* CHATER *come into the room and sit down.* MELROSE *turns back to* ROBERT.) Who are you? What's your name?

ROBERT: Procathren.

MELROSE: What?

ROBERT: Procathren. Robert Procathren.

MELROSE: Robert, is it? I'll call you Bob—or perhaps Bobby would be better. I'm Melrose—1535380 Christian—my name not my faith. This is Killeen, and this, Chater. Stand up! (KILLEEN *and* CHATER *stand up and perform magnificent mock bows to* ROBERT.) That's better. Once upon a time, although you wouldn't think it to look at us, we were soldiers.

ROBERT: Yes, I've heard about you.

MELROSE: Oh, you've heard about us. Then that saves a lot of explaining, doesn't it? About why we're here and—

ROBERT: Yes. You needn't explain.

MELROSE: Thank you very much. But you can explain something to me. Why are you all dressed up?

ROBERT: I was on an errand.

MELROSE: Do you always put on your best clothes to run errands? What's your job?

ROBERT: I'm a poet.

MELROSE: A poet. (*To* KILLEEN *and* CHATER.) He's a poet. (MELROSE *is about to speak but* KILLEEN *has risen and recites.*)

KILLEEN: Oh it was down by the river
                That I made her quiver
                Oh, you should have seen her belly
                It was shaking like a jelly
                Oh, you should have seen her—

MELROSE: That's enough! (KILLEEN *sits down.*) Give us your professional opinion, Bobby. Isn't that lovely poetry? Well—(*he laughs*)—never mind. Do you live here?

ROBERT: No.

MELROSE: What are you doing here, then? You don't look right. You don't— (CHATER *blows softly on the trumpet.* MELROSE *turns on him.*) Listen! I've told you about blowing on it when I'm talking. So shut up or I'll take it away from you. Do you hear? I'll take it right away from you—so shut it! (*To* ROBERT.) Who lives here, then?

ROBERT: The Southman family.

MELROSE: I see. Who was it called to us from the window?

ROBERT: Paul—the old man.

MELROSE: What is he?

ROBERT: A poet.

MELROSE: Birds of a feather, eh?

ROBERT: No!

MELROSE: Well, don't shout. (*He has taken out a packet of cigarettes.*) Have one?

ROBERT: No, thank you.

MELROSE: Well, Bobby, I'm afraid we must be getting on.

ROBERT: No, don't go! Don't go!

MELROSE: What?

KILLEEN: Hey, Christy? (*He has been staring at the painting on the wall.*)

MELROSE: Wait a minute. Why don't you want us to go, Bobby? Come on, tell me—I'm interested. People usually want us to move on as quickly as possible. But you want us to stay. Now, why is that?

KILLEEN: Hey, Christy!

MELROSE: Well, what is it?

KILLEEN: Look! (*He points to the painting.*)

MELROSE: Well, what about it? It's a painting—done with brushes, you know.

KILLEEN: Hey, but Christy—look, look!

MELROSE: I'm looking.

KILLEEN: What is it?

MELROSE *and* KILLEEN *move to stand before the painting.*

MELROSE: Well, what's your guess?

KILLEEN: It's as good as yours. Look! (*He extends a finger.*)

MELROSE: Don't touch!

KILLEEN: All right.

MELROSE: Well, don't touch. It isn't finished. Look—(*he rubs his fingers into the paint*)—here. It isn't finished.

KILLEEN: There's some paint—let's finish it.

MELROSE: No! (*They stand looking up at the painting. Then* MELROSE, *without turning, asks:*) Are there any women here? (ROBERT, *unaware that he cannot be seen, shakes his head.*) I said, Are there any women here?

ROBERT: There was one.

MELROSE: Oh?

ROBERT: I killed her.

MELROSE: What?

ROBERT: I killed her.

MELROSE: Wasn't that rather a silly thing to do?—when there was only one, I mean.

ROBERT: She was horrible—she was pregnant—

MELROSE: I see

ROBERT: —but it was an accident.

MELROSE: Is that why you asked us not to go?

ROBERT: Yes. (*There is a silence as the* THREE SOLDIERS *stare at* ROBERT. *Then* ROBERT, *stretching out his hands before him, seems to be about to fall.*) What have they made me do?

    MELROSE *goes to him and holds him.*

MELROSE: Hold up! Hold up, you're all right. Killeen, get the cure-all. (KILLEEN *goes to a small haversack he has been carrying and takes out a bottle of whisky.*) Now, come along, Bobby, you're all right.

ROBERT: Oh, what have they made me do?

    MELROSE *takes the whisky from* KILLEEN.

MELROSE: Here—have some of this. Spoils of war.

ROBERT: No.

MELROSE: Oh, don't be an old woman! Go on. (ROBERT *drinks from the bottle.*) Careful! You're dribbling it. Better? Nothing like it, is there? What are you afraid of, Bobby?

ROBERT: Of what is going to happen.

MELROSE: We won't let anything happen to you. Will we? (*He turns to* CHATER *who, with the trumpet across his knees, is peaceably picking his nose.*) Happy?

    CHATER *grins.*

ROBERT: You'll help me?

MELROSE: Of course. (*He holds out the bottle of whisky.*) Have some more. We've got another bottle. (*He winks at* KILLEEN *and* CHATER.)

ROBERT: You will help me?

MELROSE: I've said, yes. Go on, drink up.

ROBERT: Oh, my dear friend, they have made me do dreadful things. But you will help me?

MELROSE: Yes.

ROBERT: Thank God for you!

MELROSE: Yes, indeed.

ROBERT: We must plan what we shall do.

MELROSE: Yes, we will—we will.

ROBERT: Then let us go.

MELROSE: You're going to run away?

ROBERT: No, my friend, I'm going to run towards the event. A thing I have never done before—but now I have the authority. Let us go.

MELROSE: Where to?

ROBERT: First, the village.

MELROSE: All right.

    PAUL *calls from an upper room.* Then nothing can be done! Nothing! And it is no joke—no joke!

ROBERT (*whispers*): No joke.

MELROSE: The old man?

ROBERT: Yes.

MELROSE: With the woman?

ROBERT: Yes.

MELROSE: Should I go up?

ROBERT: No! No!

MELROSE: All right.

ROBERT: You can trust me.

MELROSE: I'm sure I can.

ROBERT: It will all be for the best.

MELROSE: I'm sure it will. (*He looks at* KILLEEN *and puts his finger to his forehead. They laugh.*)

ROBERT: Let us go.

    MELROSE *picks up the pistol from the table.*

MELROSE: I'll take this.

ROBERT (*to* CHATER): Sound the trumpet! (CHATER, *standing, raises the trumpet smartly and blows a single sustained note.* ROBERT *looks towards the stairs.*) Ready?

MELROSE: Ready. (MELROSE, CHATER *and* KILLEEN *move to the window, out on to the balcony and so down into the garden.* ROBERT *is about to follow them and has reached the window when* PAUL *comes down the stairs.*)

PAUL: Robert!

ROBERT: I am here.

PAUL: It's no joke.

ROBERT: Indeed, it is no joke. No joke at all. (*He is crouched by the window, one arm outstretched to support himself.*)

PAUL: She's dead.

ROBERT: Yes. Quite, quite dead.

PAUL: You killed her.

ROBERT: I did.

PAUL: Why, Robert?

    ROBERT *is staring at* PAUL.

ROBERT: Beast-face!

PAUL: Robert!

ROBERT: Beast-face!

PAUL: Robert!

ROBERT: Satisfied? Satisfied by the shift of responsibility, eh?

PAUL: Robert!

ROBERT: Shan't step from under it this time. Surprised, eh?

PAUL: Robert! (*But* ROBERT *has gone, running down the steps to the garden after the soldiers.* PAUL *moves to the window.*) Robert, come back! I have forgiven you—I have forgiven you! (*But* PAUL *can no longer be seen or heard by* ROBERT. PAUL *turns back into the room.*) I have forgiven him. (*Then, alone and old, he is seized by a terrible paroxysm of grief and fear. His eyes are closed: from his mouth comes a thin sound: his hands go up and tear the scarf from his neck. It is as if he would do himself great physical violence but his strength fails him—he can only stand exhausted.*)

CURTAIN

ACT THREE

The scene is the same.

The time is six hours later: it is night.

CHARLES *is working on the mural painting. He has gathered the lamps of the room around him and light is so concentrated on his work. His model is the body of Stella which lies on an improvised bier on the rostrum before the painting. The body is draped but for the face and head. On the floor, at the foot of the bier, lies a collection of human and animal bones. The painting on the wall is almost complete for* CHARLES *has added the figure of Stella as she lies in death. The other figures now look down at her and the dog stands at her head.*

At the other side of the room about the fireplace and in darkness but for the firelight are five women and a child. HANNAH TREWIN, MARGARET BANT, EDITH TINSON *and* FLORA BALDON *are old. The other woman, who is young, is* JUDITH WARDEN—*mother of the* CHILD *who stands at her side. This* CHILD, *a girl, is ten years of age. She is dressed, fortuitously, as though for some celebration; although she wears a large pair of boots and a pair of boy's long trousers she also wears a short white embroidered frock of satin. A gay scarf is tied about her head to frame her face and also on her head is a yellow straw hat decorated with tiny artificial flowers. Each of the women in this group carries, wears, or has placed on the floor by her feet some of the surprising objects taken by those flying from a catastrophe. In this case there is a large shining china jug, a gramophone, an oleograph of a scene from 'Romeo and Juliet' and various nondescript bundles.* EDITH TINSON *has two pairs of shoes slung round her neck by a length of string.* MARGARET BANT *carries an ornate parasol, and is hung about with an excessive amount of cheap jewellery.* HANNAH TREWIN *appears to be wearing at least three hats These things, quite worthless to these people in their present predicament, were snatched up in the last desperate moment. The group is silent and motionless but for the* CHILD *who bounces a rubber ball against the door.*

Through the windows the visible expanse of sky is red: the village is burning.

It is this fire that JOHN WINTER *stands by the window to watch. The tolling of church bells can be heard.*

WINTER: It doesn't look as if he'll be able to sound the bells much longer.

CHARLES: Why?

WINTER: I can see the tower now—very black against the fire—very near—not much longer.

CHARLES: The sooner the better—damned noise.

The CHILD *is restrained by her* MOTHER *from bouncing the ball.*

WINTER: What do they hope to gain by ringing the bells?

CHARLES: Help, I suppose.

WINTER: From God?

CHARLES: God alone knows! (*They smile at each other.*) Where's Paul?

WINTER: Upstairs, sir. Packing.

CHARLES: Packing?

WINTER: Packing his bag.

CHARLES: Does he think he's still expected to go?

WINTER: He seems to have no doubt, sir. I'm afraid he's very ill.

CHARLES: Oh, don't put it like that. Say he's going mad, nuts, bats, potty but not that he's very ill

WINTER: I'm sorry, sir. I tried to explain that he's no longer expected to go to London today and that Procathren may—

CHARLES: What did Procathren say to the old man before he went? That's what I'd like to know.

PAUL *calls from an upper room:*

PAUL: The village is burning away. There'll be nothing left as far as I can see—nothing at all.

CHARLES: Why isn't there more light?

WINTER: Shall I get you candles?

CHARLES: No! Don't leave the room. I can see. I can see. (JOHN WINTER *begins to make a rearrangement of the lamps.*) There's someone out there!

WINTER: Where?

CHARLES: Out on the balcony.

JOHN WINTER *turns to stare out of the window.*

WINTER: Yes. (*He raps on the window and then, opening it, calls:*) Come along! Come along in here. It's all right—don't be frightened.

CHARLES: Who is it?

WINTER (*he laughs*): Old Cowper, the postman. Chk-chk-chk-chk-chk! (*He says as if calling an animal.*) Come on. Come on. Come on.

THOMAS COWPER *appears at the window. He is in the uniform of a country postman and carries his mail delivery bag.*

COWPER: What do you mean, chk-chk-chk-chk-chk, indeed. Do you think I'm afraid to come in here? If so, let me say I'm as good as any that lives in this damned house and what's more, I'm here in the course of my duty and you are at the moment impeding that duty. Get out of the way! (JOHN WINTER *steps aside and* COWPER *marches into the room and goes to* JUDITH WARDEN *holding out a letter to her*.) For you, Mrs Warden, my dear. I've been looking for you all evening—your house has quite gone so I couldn't leave it there. But they told me you'd come this way. It's from your husband, my dear. Well, that's the last one. (*He takes off his cap and turns to* CHARLES.) Now then, young man. Stop that— whatever it is you're doing. I want a few details from you.

CHARLES: Details?

COWPER: Yes. (*He has taken a notebook from his pocket and has a pencil ready.*)

CHARLES: What about?

COWPER: About the disaster, of course.

CHARLES: The fire?

COWPER: Yes. Now leave that dummy alone for a few minutes, there's a good boy.

CHARLES: In what capacity do you want these details? As a postman?

COWPER: As an officer of the law. Police-Constable Pogson is engaged with the fire.

CHARLES: I see.

COWPER: When he heard that I was coming this way he asked me to take any particulars from you. I should like to say that as a civil official I have never taken either side in the quarrel that has gone on between this family and the villagers. You may speak quite freely to me.

CHARLES: Thank you.

COWPER: Not at all.

CHARLES: But I have nothing to say.

COWPER: Haven't you?

CHARLES: No.

There is a pause.

COWPER (*to* JOHN WINTER): Have you anything to say?

WINTER: No.

COWPER: Oh. (*He puts the notebook and pencil back in his pocket.*)

Well, that's all, then. You can carry on with whatever you were doing. (*He speaks to the villagers.*) I don't know what to do with you. I suppose you can stay here tonight. (*He turns to* CHARLES.) Can they—? What are you laughing at?

CHARLES: You.

COWPER: Is it a laughing matter that the village is destroyed, that the people are wandering homeless, and that the Reverend Mr Aldus is trapped at the top of the church tower and is roasting like a potato?

CHARLES: Is that why he's ringing the bells?

COWPER: I can tell you, young man, this terrible accident is no laughing matter.

CHARLES: Accident? Was it an accident?

COWPER: Of course. You don't think anybody would do such a thing on purpose?

CHARLES: They might.

COWPER: Don't be silly. Of course it was an accident. I should know—I was there when it started. Complete accident, it was. Just after six o'clock—I was delivering the last post—I was late, I'll admit it, I was late. A letter has just gone into Mr Aldus's box, and as I was turning away from the door I saw three soldiers coming to the house. The soldiers—you've heard about them?— bit of trouble from them today—nothing that couldn't have been handled with understanding—old soldier myself—but still—there you are. The soldiers had another man with them—a towny fellow, toffed up like. While they passed I hid in the bushes— didn't want to expose myself to any insults while I was in uniform. Anyway, they went straight into Mr Aldus's house. Just like that —as if they owned it. I could see the four of them talking to Mr Aldus in his drawing-room—I could see it by the light—by the light of the room. It was the dandy fellow who spoke—talked for about twenty minutes he did and then they came away. I was still hiding as they passed me. The big soldier had his arm around the dandy fellow—and the dandy fellow was talking and talking. I was going to wait until they got from sight before I came out to get on with my round. Then Mr Aldus came to the door of his house and he must have seen me because he called out, 'Cowper, come here.' By the time I'd got to the house he'd gone inside and so I sounded the knocker. He didn't come to the door again, so after a few minutes I went inside. He was in the room with the books and he was carrying armfuls of those books from the shelves and throwing them on the open fire. They were tumbling out from the fireplace into the middle of the room and they were burning, burning away. When I went into the room he stood there for a moment pointing at them and trying to say something, but he couldn't get it out—that stutter of his, you know—and he was crying—crying noisily like a baby. I suppose he wanted me to help him—I don't know really. Anyway, then he went back to carrying more books off the shelves and throwing them on the fire. I was taken aback, I don't mind admitting it. When I'd gathered myself together I ran into the street and began shouting but nobody would come out—they've been hiding from the soldiers all day. I ran through the empty streets but there was no one. When I got back to Mr Aldus's house the place was afire and then I heard the bells—he'd gone into the church and was ringing the bells. The fire spread and nobody would help me—nobody came out—not even P.C. Pogson—until they were forced out by the fire. And now the whole village is destroyed—burned right away. (*He pauses.*) I hope you think I acted for the best, sir.

CHARLES: What? Yes, I'm sure you did.

COWPER: Thank you, sir. (*He puts on his cap and touches the peak to* CHARLES.) But what am I doing? I oughtn't to be here talking. I must get back. Will you let me out, please?

JOHN WINTER *opens the window and* THOMAS COWPER *goes out by the way he came. There is a murmuring, a whispering, from the four old women:* HANNAH TREWIN, MARGARET BANT, EDITH TINSON *and* FLORA BALDON.

CHARLES: What is it?

EDITH ⎫ (*together*): We saw him.
HANNAH ⎭ We know about the man—

EDITH: You speak, my dear.

HANNAH: No. You speak, my dear.

EDITH: Very well. We saw him.

CHARLES: Who?

HANNAH: The man with the soldiers.

MARGARET: The man who talked so much.

HANNAH: Yes, we saw him.

EDITH: We saw him spoil his beautiful clothes by walking through the burning streets.

MARGARET: The soldiers followed him—they were laughing, but he didn't laugh.

EDITH: They came towards us as we ran from the fire.

HANNAH: His white face frightened us.

MARGARET: Yes, it did.

HANNAH: His voice frightened us, too.

MARGARET: Yes.

HANNAH: Long after he'd passed us we could hear it through the sound of the fire.

EDITH: And through the cries of the people.

HANNAH: Even though the bells were ringing.

There is a pause.

FLORA: He spoke to me.

EDITH: No!

HANNAH: Never!

FLORA: Yes, he did.

CHARLES: What did he say? (*She does not answer.*) Well, what did he say?

FLORA: I didn't understand him—I didn't understand what he said —but he spoke to me.

CHARLES: Somewhere here there is a link— (*He strikes his forehead.*) Think, John Winter, think! (*He leaves the painting and moves about the room.*) What did he say to Paul? What did he say to the old woman? Is it contained in that? I don't know. Perhaps so simple. No, we've missed the moment for discovery. It was when she— (*he points to* FLORA BALDON)—said, 'He spoke to me.' Gone now. Never mind. Doesn't matter. (*He returns to the painting, but as an afterthought, says:*) But you, John Winter—would you like to get away? You've time. I'll look after the old man.

WINTER: I'll stay.

CHARLES: All right.

PAUL *has come down the stairs into the room. He is wearing his cloak and carries a hat, a stick and a small case.*

PAUL: John Winter tells me you have given sanctuary to some women of the village.

CHARLES: Yes.

PAUL (*to the villagers*): You are welcome. (*The church bells stop ringing there is a single bell, then silence. To* CHARLES.) The village is on fire.

CHARLES: Yes.

PAUL: I've been watching the fire from my room.

CHARLES: Have you?

PAUL: It's burning right up—right up into the sky.

CHARLES: Yes.

PAUL: Who is responsible?

CHARLES: It was an accident.

PAUL: There is always the responsibility—it must rest with someone.

WINTER: Mr Aldus, sir.

PAUL: I remember him.

WINTER: He was burning his books—

PAUL: What's the time?

CHARLES: We don't know. The clock has stopped.

PAUL: I must go soon. I'll wait here. (*He sits down.*) Have you got the cigarettes, John Winter?

WINTER: No, sir. Aren't they in your pocket?

PAUL: I haven't looked. (*He makes no move to do so.*) I just thought I'd like a cigarette whilst I'm waiting. Have you finished the picture, Charles?

CHARLES: Not yet.

PAUL: How long will you be?

CHARLES: I shall work until the last moment.

PAUL: What?

CHARLES: Nothing. I shan't be long.

WINTER: Do you want a cigarette, Mr Southman?

PAUL: It doesn't matter, John Winter, it doesn't matter. I just thought it would pass the time until I go.

CHARLES: Paul, my dear, listen to me. You must try to remember. You're not going now. Stella is dead—

PAUL: Poor Stella.

CHARLES: —yes, poor Stella—and Procathren has run away and so you are not going to London after all.

PAUL: An excellent statement on the situation, sonny. Very good.

CHARLES: Well you must try to help John Winter and me by remembering these things.

PAUL: I will.

CHARLES: Good. (*He looks down at* STELLA.) Why is her face all sunken? She looks monstrous. Give me that lamp, John Winter.

PAUL: Is it dark out tonight?

WINTER: There's the fire.

PAUL: Of course, the fire. Good. Go and get the axe, John Winter. Also a saw, spades and some rope—we shall want some rope.

WINTER: What are you going to do?

PAUL: Cut down those two trees. Those in front of the house. I told you about them.

WINTER: Yes, you told me, but—

PAUL: What did she call them? She had pet names for them. What were they? I've forgotten. Never mind. We'll have them down—down they shall come. It'll give me something to do—something to occupy me whilst I'm waiting. You think I'm not strong enough. Is that what you think? (*He stands up and strikes* JOHN WINTER *across the face.*) Am I strong enough? Am I? I think so. Get the tools.

CHARLES: Yes, go along, John Winter.

PAUL: Yes, go along. And remember you're a servant. The rope must be strong.

> JOHN WINTER *goes out.*

CHARLES: You'd be better employed digging a grave.

PAUL: That's a very unkind thing to say, Charles. Very unkind, indeed. She must be buried, but surely you can't expect a man of my age to go out at night and dig a grave. You must do it with John Winter. I can't do it. You can't expect me to do it—not at my age.

CHARLES: I meant a grave for the dog.

PAUL: Anyway, she can't be buried until you've finished with her. (*He is staring at* STELLA.) Is that blood on her face?

CHARLES: What? No. Paint.

PAUL: Wipe it away.

CHARLES: We mustn't touch her.

PAUL: It disfigures her.

CHARLES: It is the death that disfigures her.

PAUL: She would have been glad to know I still intend to go tonight. It was her wish—she was most insistent.

CHARLES: Listen!

PAUL: I'd want to please her, poor dead thing.

CHARLES: Listen to me!

PAUL: I'm going, Stella, just as you wished. (*He laughs.*) Shame on me! Talking to the dead.

CHARLES: Listen to me, Paul.

PAUL: Yes, sonny.

CHARLES: You're not going.

PAUL: No?

CHARLES: Do you hear me? You're not going.

PAUL: Am I not?

CHARLES: No. Procathren's run away. The dinner in your honour has all been eaten up and the guests gone home by now. Whilst they chatted and wondered why you were absent—do you remember what you did?

PAUL: What did I do?

CHARLES: You wandered about this house, a crazy old man, talking of your hey-day.

PAUL: Did I really?

CHARLES: Yes. So you can take off your cloak and put away your hat—you are too late now. It is never going to be.

PAUL: How you run on. Get along with your painting, sonny. (*He calls to the* CHILD). Come here, little girl. Or are you a little boy? (*The* CHILD *goes slowly to him.*) And what are you called?

CHARLES: Damn you, Paul! God damn you for the beastliness—the selfishness of shutting yourself up in your tower of senility and lunacy at this moment—at this moment!

PAUL: Hush, Charles! You'll frighten the child.

CHARLES: If only I could take refuge in madness as you have done. If only I could convince myself, as you have done, that I am an artist, that the world waited to honour me, that the fires out there were a display for a victory, that these brushes I hold were sceptres and these people princes. Then I might face the future! You have the belief and the refuge—but it is not for me. I cannot go so far. I am not mad. I am not mad. God help me! I can touch the reality and know that I am nothing, that the world censures me, that the fires burn without reason, that these brushes are instruments of torture and these people miserable, frightened clods!

PAUL: Charles, I command you to be quiet! You're frightening this child. (CHARLES *stands quite humbled before the* CHILD'S *penetrating stare.*) Get on with your painting.

CHARLES: Well, try to remember. If you love me, try to remember. Don't pretend. (CHARLES *returns to the painting.* PAUL *speaks to the* CHILD.)

PAUL: Don't let him frighten you. He's afraid—always has been. Poor Charles! Now then—are you going to talk to me for a little while before I go? What shall we talk about? You can talk, can't you? Well, come along, say something to me. Say, 'Hullo.' Say my name. Say 'Paul'. No? Very well, then, you tell me your name. Haven't you a name? You must have a name. Everyone has a name. Tell it to me for a penny. For twopence, then. Won't you talk to me? Not even for a little while? It can only be for a little while because, you see, I'm going away. Look! I've got my hat—and a stick because I'm very old, and a little case packed with all the things I shall need. Perhaps I should be going now or I shall be late. I wonder what the time is? Ah! you have a watch. What does it say? Let me see. But it has no hands on the face—it's no use at all. Pretty, though. Is that why you wear it? Because it's pretty? I expect so. We don't have pretty things here. I'm sorry. I'd like pretty things and children around me again. Darling, there is one thing I must tell you: I have forgiven you—I have forgiven you. I'm not sad—not really. I'm happy—quite happy. O darling. darling Stella, it's a very great day for me this birthday of mine, There you are—there's something for you to say. Say, 'Many happy returns of the day.' (*After a pause the* CHILD *says with great clarity*, Many happy returns of the day.) There! I knew you could speak. Well done! 'Many happy returns of the day', you said. And that is what they will say when I arrive—the great and famous people receiving me—they will say— (*And the little crowd speaking together, say*, Many happy returns of the day—*and then, possessed by quite a tiny fever of excitement they cry out separately*, Happy birthday—God bless you—Much happiness to you *and* Good men are rewarded. PAUL *standing and holding the hand of the* CHILD *at his side speaks to her.*) Can you sing? Can you dance? Dance for me! Dance for me in your lovely gay clothes—as a birthday gift. Not much to ask. Don't be shy. Look at me. I'm very old—oh, very old but I can dance and sing. (*And he does so as the* VILLAGERS *laugh and clap their hands.* CHRISTIAN MELROSE *has come up the stairs and stands inside the doorway.* PAUL, *turning and looking beyond the* CHILD, *sees* MELROSE *and stops his singing and dancing: the* VILLAGERS *stop their laughter and clapping.*) Have you come for me?

MELROSE: That's right.

PAUL: I'm ready. Look, I'm quite ready.

MELROSE: Were you expecting me?

PAUL: Oh yes. (*To the* CHILD.) No more dancing now.

MELROSE *comes fully into the room. The group of women give a short scream in unison and gather even closer together. The* CHILD *runs to her*

MOTHER. *After* MELROSE *has entered* KILLEEN *and* CHATER *come in.*

MELROSE: How did you know?

PAUL: I knew.

MELROSE: Who told you I was coming here?

CHARLES: Don't take any notice of him.

MELROSE: Oh, hullo, over there. And why shouldn't I take any notice of him?

CHARLES: Because he's mad—lunatic.

MELROSE: Is he?

CHARLES: Yes.

MELROSE: Well, mad or not, he's got hold of the right end of the stick.

CHARLES: About going away?

MELROSE (*yawning*): Yes. God! I'm tired.

CHARLES: Who are you?

MELROSE: That doesn't matter. KILLEEN *and* CHATER *are clowning and fighting in the doorway.* MELROSE *turns on them.*) Stop that! You're Charles Heberden.

CHARLES: Yes.

MELROSE: And that. That's your late, lamented wife?

CHARLES: Yes.

MELROSE: I see. Where's the servant?

CHARLES: Downstairs.

MELROSE: Call him.

CHARLES: I refuse.

MELROSE: Oh, all right. (*To* KILLEEN.) Call him. His name's Winter. (KILLEEN *goes to the door and calls down the stairs in a mincing and effeminate way*, Oh, Winter; Winter, come up, please. Your master wants you.) What are these? (*He indicates the crowd of villagers.*)

CHARLES: They're from the village. From the fire. We've given them shelter.

MELROSE: Quite right, too. I'd better not make a mistake. This is Paul Southman, isn't it?

CHARLES: Yes.

MELROSE: I shouldn't think there could be two of him. (JOHN WINTER *comes into the room from below. He is carrying a coil of rope.*) Ah! Winter?

WINTER: Yes.

MELROSE: Come in. What have you got there?

WINTER: Rope.

MELROSE: I see. Rope.

WINTER: Mr Southman asked for it.

MELROSE: Asked for it, eh? Chater—Chater, wake up! Take that. You know what we want. (CHATER *takes the rope from* JOHN WINTER *and squatting on the floor begins his work. To* CHARLES.) We thought we'd have to look for rope. (*He calls to* JOHN WINTER *who is about to go from the room.*) Hey, you! Winter! Stay here. (*And to* PAUL.) And you sit down, old man. You're not going yet.

PAUL: Not yet?

MELROSE: No, not for a little while. (PAUL *hesitant, sits—his hat on his head, and the small bag clutched on his knees.*) Now, Mr Heberden—

PAUL: May I talk to the child?

MELROSE: What child? Yes, if you want to. (*He calls to the* CHILD.) Come here, you, and talk to the old man.

The CHILD *comes forward to stand beside* PAUL.

PAUL: I'm not going yet.

MELROSE *has moved to before the painting on the wall.*

MELROSE: Your work, Mr Heberden?

CHARLES: Yes.

PAUL (*to the* CHILD): Won't you talk to me?

MELROSE: It's very beautiful. I suppose I can call it that, can I?

CHARLES: Certainly.

PAUL (*to the* CHILD): Shall we play a game?

MELROSE: Very beautiful.

PAUL: Shall we?

MELROSE: Should be in a church.

CHARLES (*he laughs*): Thank you.

MELROSE: What does that mean? Laughing, like that.

CHARLES: Nothing.

PAUL: Crocodiles. (*He has taken his spectacles case from his pocket and, removing the spectacles, begins snapping the case at the* CHILD'S *nose.*)

MELROSE: Is it finished?

CHARLES: No.

MELROSE: Pity.

CHARLES: Yes.

MELROSE: Because it'll never be finished, now, will it?

CHARLES: I suppose not.

MELROSE: Why not?

CHARLES: There won't be time, will there?

MELROSE: That's better—much better! You're beginning to understand. Now we can talk. (*To* CHATER.) How long will you be? (CHATER *stopping his work for a moment, holds up his hand with spread fingers.*) Five minutes? Right. If you'd rather spend those five minutes on your painting, Mr Heberden—

CHARLES: It doesn't matter.

MELROSE: Sure? O.K.

CHARLES: I should need more than five minutes.

MELROSE: Sorry. Can't give you longer than that. Bobby Procathren should be here by then. I don't know where he's got to. Sit down, Mr Heberden. (CHARLES *and* MELROSE *sit on the edge of the rostrum: the* VILLAGERS *are grouped together:* PAUL *plays with the* CHILD: CHATER, *sitting cross-legged on the floor, the trumpet at his side, is cutting the rope into lengths:* WINTER *and* KILLEEN *stand alone.*) Have a cigarette.

CHARLES: Thank you, I will. (*They light cigarettes.*)

PAUL: And it comes along—along—along and snap!

MELROSE: And have some of this. (*He brings out a bottle of whisky.*)

CHARLES: No, thank you.

MELROSE: No? Oh, well— (*He drinks from the bottle throughout the following conversation with* CHARLES.) Are you afraid?

CHARLES: Of course.

MELROSE: You're very young to die. How old are you?

CHARLES: Nearly twenty-one.

MELROSE: I'm thirty-three—but I look older, don't I?

CHARLES: Yes.

MELROSE: I do. I know I do. (*He sees* KILLEEN *among the* VILLAGERS.) Killeen—what are you doing there?

KILLEEN: Nothing! Nothing at all.

MELROSE: Well, come out of it, there's a good boy.

KILLEEN: I wanted to know if they'd got anything to eat.

MELROSE: You can't be hungry. You can't possibly be hungry! You've just had a bloody great meal. (*To* CHARLES.) I don't know, really. Like animals. (*He laughs.*) Perhaps I shouldn't say that. Your cigarette's gone out. Here—let me light it.

CHARLES: Thank you.

PAUL (*to the* CHILD): I was a real Turtle once.

CHARLES: Why are you going to kill us?

MELROSE: Ssh! Keep your voice down. There's no need to frighten the old boy.

CHARLES: You won't do that now. Why are you—you, especially, of all people—going to kill us?

MELROSE: Don't you think I'm capable.

CHARLES: Certainly. I should think so, anyway.

MELROSE: You do?

CHARLES: Yes.

MELROSE: Good. Bobby doesn't think I'm capable. He's dared me to do it. (*He stands up, smiling.*) That's a silly thing to do, isn't it? What does he think I am? What does he think I shall feel? You're nothing to me—neither's the old man. Nobody's anything to me —because there is nobody—hasn't been for years. I care for nothing. They put it right when they said I was an 'incorrigible'. Look at me. What do you see?

CHARLES: A monster.

MELROSE: That's through your eyes—and quite natural. I don't take offence. But Bobby can't see me that way. And why? Because he's lived in the world where people—well, where they behave. Where they do this and that for this and that reason—and they do this and that for this and that reason because they have a life to live—a life to plan—and they've got to be careful. That's how he's judging me—that's how he judged you. Silly, isn't it? (*He laughs.*) What am I doing standing up talking like this? I must look a perfect fool! (*He sits down again beside* CHARLES.)

CHARLES: Why should he judge me—or Paul—at all? The fool!

MELROSE: You shouldn't have done it, you know. You've brought this on yourselves. People like us shouldn't do such things to people like that—people who live away out there with women and music. You've struck him very deep. He's talked to me about it and my God! can't he talk. He told me about it, all right. I didn't understand one word in ten about his guilt and the way you've destroyed his innocence—but I understood a little. Poor Bobby!

CHARLES: Why?

MELROSE. He's afraid. Afraid of—what do they call it out these in the world?—hell! it's called by a short, sweet name—I know it as well as my own name—what do they call it?—

CHARLES: I don't know.

MELROSE: Got it! They call it 'death'. That's what they call it—death. And that's what he's afraid of.

CHARLES: So that's the corruption beneath the splendour: the maggot in the peacock.

MELROSE: He told Aldus—you know, the clergyman down in the village.

CHARLES: Of course. You went to see Aldus.

MELROSE (*he laughs*): Yes, we saw him. Then he began to burn all his books.

CHARLES: Why?

MELROSE: What?

CHARLES: I asked why he began to burn his books.

MELROSE: Because of what Bobby said to him, I suppose—I don't know.

CHARLES: What did he say?

MELROSE: I've told you—I couldn't understand a blind word. He talked nineteen to the dozen, though. Not only in English but in foreign languages. He took down books and read things out of them. Whatever he said must have been very convincing because he made the padre cry—sat their crying like a baby, he did. I don't wonder. Bobby talked to me—talked until I was drunk with it. I'm so bloody tired as well—we've been on the run for eight days. (MELROSE *sees that the door from below is slowly opening. He calls.*) Who's there? Oh, it's you, Bobby. Come in. We've been waiting for you. (*The door opens fully and* ROBERT PROCATHREN *stands there. His clothes are filthy and torn, his face and hands blackened by the fire.*) Come in. (ROBERT *steps into the room.*) What's the matter? Did you get lost?

ROBERT: I've been sick.

MELROSE: I should say you have. Look, it's all over your coat. Have you eaten too much—

ROBERT: Probably.

MELROSE: —or is it the exercise? Killeen, have you got a hand-kerchief? Wipe him down.

KILLEEN: I'm a nursemaid—that's what I am.

MELROSE (*to* CHARLES): Bit of a change in him, isn't there? (MELROSE *is exultant, excited by* ROBERT'S *appearance, his degradation.*) Not so beautiful as he was—as we remember him, eh? (*To* ROBERT.) Better now?

ROBERT: Yes. All right, now.

MELROSE: Oh, he's lost that beautiful tie. You've lost your tie, Bobby.

KILLEEN: He gave it to me. (KILLEEN *is wearing the tie loosely round the neck of his uniform.*)

MELROSE: He gave it to you?

KILLEEN: Yes.

MELROSE: Gave it to you?

KILLEEN: Yes!

MELROSE (*laughing*): All right—I'll believe you.

KILLEEN: Well, it's true.

ROBERT: Yes, I gave it to him—as a token.

MELROSE: It's your business.

ROBERT: Melrose.

MELROSE: Yes?

ROBERT: You're not—not 'putting it off', as they say, are you?

MELROSE: No, Bobby, I'm not 'putting it off'.

ROBERT: Don't 'put it off', Melrose.

MELROSE *goes to* ROBERT *and takes* ROBERT'S *face in his hands.*

MELROSE: You think I won't do it, I know. But I'm going to do it.

ROBERT: And what is it you're going to do? Tell me.

MELROSE: You tell me. Ha! It's like a kid's game, isn't it? Who tells who, eh? No, but seriously, Bobby, you tell me. You're the boss from now, you know. You can't get away from it now. If you want to order people like me around you've got to take the responsibility—you've got to. It's always been like that. But it makes me laugh sometimes. 'Melrose do such-and-such!' 'Yes, sir!'—and then I look down and see their eyes and their eyes are asking me, 'Melrose you think that decision is right, don't you? If you think I'm wrong for God's sake don't do it.' But I do whatever I think—if I can be bothered to think. What is it I can do for you, Bobby?

ROBERT: Kill the old man and the boy for me.

MELROSE: Just for you. (*There is a pause and then* EDITH TINSON *begins to give short repeated screams.*) What are you doing there, Killeen?

KILLEEN: I'm not doing a thing. I'm not near her. It's not me—it's what he said.

MELROSE: Well, shut her up!

KILLEEN *goes to the woman and her screams stop. It is then a human voice can be heard humming a polite little tune. It is* CHATER *singing as he works. Now it is apparent what he is doing: from the rope he is constructing two nooses.*

ROBERT: How long?

MELROSE: Not long. (*He grips* ROBERT *by the shoulder: his voice is strong and clear but without anger.*) What have I got to lose in this? Tell me that. Nothing! You're a fool to doubt me, Bobby—a fool! (*Turning, he runs into* KILLEEN.) Get out of the way!

KILLEEN: Hey!

MELROSE: What?

KILLEEN: Do you think there's any food in the place?

MELROSE: For God's sake!—

KILLEEN: Well, some biscuits or something.

MELROSE: There must be something the matter with you.

KILLEEN: I'm thirsty too.

> ROBERT *has moved to stand before* PAUL. *He speaks to him.*

ROBERT: Southman—Southman, can you hear? You're not asleep —you're pretending. Come alone, look up. Look up!

MELROSE: Listen! He's beginning to talk to the old man. Quiet, everyone!

ROBERT: Please let me speak.

MELROSE: Carry on, Bobby. Let anyone try to stop you.

ROBERT: You must look at me, Southman.

> PAUL *turns his head.* ROBERT *is now crouched beside him and* PAUL *looks into his face without recognition, without comprehension.*

CHARLES: Leave him alone.

MELROSE (*shouting*): Quiet!

ROBERT: Southman—I thought the power invested was for good. I believed we were here to do well by each other. It isn't so. We are here—all of us—to die. Nothing more than that. We live for that alone. You've known all along, haven't you? Why didn't you tell me—why did you have to teach me in such a dreadful way? For now—(*he cries out*)—I have wasted my inheritance! All these years trying to learn how to live leaving myself such a little time to learn how to die. (*He turns to speak to the* CHILD.) Afraid of the dark? But it is more than the dark. It is that which lies beyond, not within, the dark—the fear of the revelation by light. We are told by our fairy-tale books that we should not fear but the darkness is around us, and our fear is that the unknown hand is already at the switch. I tell you, do not fear, for there is no light and the way is from darkness to darkness to darkness. (PAUL *takes*

ROBERT'S *hand and holds fast to it.* ROBERT *again speaks to him.*) You old rascal! Knowing it is not a question of finding but of losing the pieties, the allegiances, the loves. You should tell. I've been talking to Aldus. Told him I lost faith in God years ago and never felt its passing. But man—oh, take faith in man from me and the meaning becomes clear by the agony we suffer. What a cost it is. Clear—not for all immediately—no, Aldus is out there at the moment chasing his lost God like a rat down a culvert. But for myself—I am well. (*He moves from* PAUL.) Perhaps I should have understood before coming here. There are many signs out in the world offering themselves for man's comprehension. The flowers in the sky, the sound of their blossoming too acute for our ears leaving us to hear nothing but the clamour of voices protesting, crying out against the end—'It's not fair!'—as they fasten to the walls of life—and the storm is of their own making— it is the howling appeal for tenderness, for love. Only now I see the thing's played out and compassion—arid as an hour-glass— run through. Such matters need not concern us here in this— (*for a moment he is silent*)—in this place. For we have our own flowers to give us understanding. (*He points to* STELLA.) The rose she wears beneath her heart. There, released, is the flowers within us all—the bloom that will leap from the breast or drop from the mouth. It shall be my conceit that a flower is our last passport. Who wears it shall go free. Free, Southman!

There is a shrill whistle from CHATER. *He has finished his work and points to two nooses lying coiled on the floor before him.* MELROSE *leaps forward and snatches up the ropes.*

PAUL: John Winter!

ROBERT: Wait!

MELROSE: Ready!

ROBERT: Wait!

PAUL: Let us go.

MELROSE: Yes, come along, old man.

PAUL: I intend to cut down the trees—

ROBERT: Wait!

PAUL: —that stand before the house. They are a danger.

MELROSE: Quite right.

PAUL: You'll help me?

MELROSE: Yes.

PAUL: Are the tools there, John Winter?

MELROSE: Let him believe it. Come on, let him believe it!

WINTER: The tools are at the door, sir.

PAUL: I see you have the rope.

MELROSE: Yes, I have the rope.

PAUL: Good.

MELROSE: Killeen, take Mr Southman down.

KILLEEN: Right-o.

PAUL: Thank you. (PAUL *and* KILLEEN *go out and down the stairs.*)

MELROSE: Chater, bring Mr Heberden. (CHATER *takes* CHARLES'S *arm.*) Oh, by the way, you're not a religious man or anything?

CHARLES: No.

MELROSE: What I mean is, do you want to say goodbye to your wife?

CHARLES: No.

MELROSE: Go along, then. (CHATER *and* CHARLES *go out and down the stairs.*) What are you going to do, Winter?

WINTER: I don't know.

MELROSE: Any ideas?

WINTER: Go away, I suppose.

MELROSE: Have you anywhere to go?

WINTER: No.

> MELROSE *takes some bank-notes from his pocket. He separates several and holds them out to* JOHN WINTER.

MELROSE: Here, take this.

WINTER: Oh, thank you, sir. Thank you.

MELROSE: That's all right. (JOHN WINTER *takes the money and hurries away by the stairs to the upper part of the house.* ROBERT *moves to* STELLA'S *body and stands looking down at her. There is silence. Suddenly* MELROSE *speaks.*) Ready?

ROBERT (*immediately*): Ready.

> MELROSE *and* ROBERT *go out and down the stairs. When they have gone there is a pause and then the* CHILD, *detaching herself from the group of* VILLAGERS, *moves across the room to where* STELLA'S *body lies. The* CHILD *stares from above at the dead face and, extending a finger, touches for a moment the closed eyes. It is then the* MOTHER *calls to the* CHILD.

JUDITH: Stella! (*Startled by the call the* CHILD *stumbles among the bones and so moves from the body. In doing so she accidentally knocks against the table and cries out in pain.*) Stella, dear child! (*But the* CHILD *moves on and seeing the green scarf,* CHARLES'S *present to*

PAUL, *lying on the floor, she picks it up and puts it around her neck.*)
Stella! We are strangers here, Stella.

The CHILD *takes up the copy of 'Alice in Wonderland' from the table. The trumpet suddenly sounds from the garden: a raucous tune. The* CHILD, *with the book in her hand, performs a grave dance to the music. As abruptly as it began the trumpet stops. The* CHILD'S *dance continues for a little but she hesitates, listening. There is no sound. Dropping the book to the floor she runs to her* MOTHER *and hides her face in the woman's lap. There is no sound and everything is still: quite still.*

CURTAIN

A PENNY FOR A SONG

INTRODUCTORY NOTE

WRITTEN IN 1949, *A Penny for a Song* was staged before *Saint's Day* in March 1951, when Tennent Productions Ltd presented Peter Brook's production of it at the Haymarket, with designs by Emmett and with Alan Webb as Sir Timothy, Ronald Squire as Hallam, Marie Lohr as Hester and the nineteen-year-old Virginia McKenna making her London début as Dorcas. Ronald Howard played Edward and Basil Radford was Selincourt.

The critics were unenthusiastic and patronizing and several were fatuous.

The Times:

> Unfortunately he lacks M. Anouilh as a collaborator, and if we had to rename *A Penny for a Song,* the new title would not be *Ring Round the Moon* but *A Penny for a Good Try*.

Alan Dent in the *News Chronicle*:

> We could forgive this play being a joke and no play at all if it were a good joke or even a well-sustained bad joke.
> It is neither.
> It is largely an excuse for the director (Peter Brook) and the designer to have lots of fun all to themselves.

Cecil Wilson in the *Daily Mail*:

> He has written a so-called farcical comedy which, for all its fuss, remains stubbornly static.

Beverley Baxter, M.P. in the *Evening Standard*:

> The humour is never cheap, nor is it easily discernible. . . . Mr Whiting is full of fun but unfortunately he is not full of wit. Nothing can be so depressing as high spirits. This is not a play, a comedy or even a farce. It is a superbly mounted and well-acted rag—fifth form without the excuse of adolescence.

Ivor Brown in the *Observer*:

> At times I thought I was watching a Napoleonic sequel to *1066 and All That*.

T. C. Worsley in the *New Statesman*:

> No it's no use, I'm afraid: it won't do. There isn't, in fact—that's the sad conclusion—a play here; a series of charades no more. Some of the comic ones are made quite funny in themselves, but none of the serious ones are within a mile of success.

It only had thirty-six performances, running from 1 March to the end of the month.

In August 1953 it was televised by the B.B.C. in a production by Barbara Burnham with Hugh Burden, Godfrey Kenton, Judith Stott and Geoffrey Sumner.

A German translation under the title *Wo wir fröhlich gewesen sind* was staged at Berlin's Schlosspark Theater in February 1955 in a production by Boleslaw Barlog.

For the revival in 1962, Whiting rewrote it drastically. What follows is the earlier version, which is much the better, but I have added some notes about the changes made for the new version which Colin Graham directed at the Aldwych with Marius Goring as Sir Timothy, Gwen Ffrangcon-Davies as Hester, Michael Gwynn as Hallam, Judi Dench as Dorcas, Mark Eden as Edward and Clive Morton as Selincourt.

Colin Graham also directed the opera version with music by Richard Rodney Bennett at Sadlers Wells in 1967.

Hey, nonny no!
Men are fools that wish to die!
Is't not fine to dance and sing
When the bells of death do ring?

ANONYMOUS

For oure tyme is a very shadow that passeth away,
and after our ende there is no returnynge, for it
is fast sealed, so that no man commeth agayne.
Come on therefore, let us enjoye the pleasures
that there are, and let us soone use the creature
like as in youth. . . . Let us leave some token of
oure pleasure in every place, for that is oure
porcion, els gett we nothinge.

THE BOKE OF WYSDOME

All things can tempt me from this craft of verse:
One time it was a woman's face, or worse--
The seeming needs of my fool-driven land;
Now nothing but comes readier to the hand
Than this accustomed toil.   When I was young,
I had not given a penny for a song
Did not the poet sing it with such airs
That one believed he had a sword upstairs;
Yet would be now, could I but have my wish,
Colder and dumber and deafer than a fish.

W. B. YEATS

PERSONS

SIR TIMOTHY BELLBOYS
HALLAM MATTHEWS
EDWARD STERNE
JONATHAN WATKINS
LAMPRETT BELLBOYS
GEORGE SELINCOURT
WILLIAM HUMPAGE
SAMUEL BREEZE
JOSEPH BROTHERHOOD
JAMES GIDDY
RUFUS PIGGOTT
DORCAS BELLBOYS
HESTER BELLBOYS
A MAIDSERVANT

The scene is the garden before Sir Timothy Bellboys's house in Dorset, on a summer's day in 1804.

ACT I. Morning.
ACT II. Later in the Day.

ACT ONE

The scene is the garden before Sir Timothy Bellboys' house in Dorset. The time is morning of a day in the summer of the year 1804.

The garden is bounded on one side by the house: on a second side by a low wall in which there is a gate leading to an orchard and on the third side it is open to the sea and sky.

At the moment the curtains of the house are drawn but when, later in the day, they are withdrawn a view is given into a parlour and a dining-room on the ground floor and of three bedrooms on the first floor. There is a front door surmounted by an elegant fanlight. Set about the lawn are various articles of garden furniture.

A little apart there is an alcove—a small retreat. This place is cloistered, self-contained—out of sight of the house and garden. There is a well: it is fully equipped with windlass and bucket.

The door of the house is closed and the garden is empty but for WILLIAM HUMPAGE *who reclines at a point of vantage in a tree above the orchard wall. He is asleep and the sun shines down on his ugly and scarlet face reflecting also in the metal buttons of his strange uniform: satin knee-breeches with worsted stockings and boots all surmounted by a gay tunic which is, perhaps, of some long-forgotten militia. A brass telescope hangs from his hand and about his wrist is tied a silver whistle. He is surrounded by an apparatus the purpose of which is not immediately apparent. It consists of two large wooden flaps or signals—one red, one green and both movable—the green flap being prominently displayed at the moment. Also to hand is a great brass bell very highly polished. It is a fine morning and the sky promises a clear, hot day.*

Suddenly the curtains of a room on the first floor are torn apart and the window is thrown open. SIR TIMOTHY BELLBOYS, *in a state of partial undress, leans out. After a racking yawn he surveys the garden and beyond with interest. Then, in a frightening voice, he shouts:*

TIMOTHY: Humpage!

    HUMPAGE *awakes with a start scattering several small cakes and the remains of an alfresco meal to the ground. He raises the telescope, in reverse, and putting it to his eye begins to scan seawards with an alarming intensity.*

  TIMOTHY *calls again.*

TIMOTHY: Humpage!

HUMPAGE: Sir!

TIMOTHY: Anything to report?

HUMPAGE: No, sir.

TIMOTHY: Nothing in sight?

HUMPAGE: No, sir.

TIMOTHY: No ships?

HUMPAGE: No, sir.

TIMOTHY: No troops?

HUMPAGE: No, sir.

TIMOTHY: Nothing suspicious?

HUMPAGE: No, sir.

  TIMOTHY *is about to withdraw.*

TIMOTHY: Were you asleep?

HUMPAGE: No, sir.

  TIMOTHY *withdraws to the bedroom and closes the window but does not draw the curtains. He can be seen moving about the room. By this time* SAMUEL BREEZE *has entered the garden. He is a servant, neatly dressed: a Londoner by birth. He looks up at* HUMPAGE *who by this time has relaxed.*

BREEZE: 'Morning.

HUMPAGE: 'Morning.

BREEZE: Now this isn't right. I can't seem to find my way around this place at all. I'm looking for the outhouses. (HUMPAGE *points to the back of the house.*) But I've just come that way.

HUMPAGE: Then you must have passed them.

BREEZE: If you say so. I'm a stranger here. However— (BREEZE *turns to go back by the way he came and meets* LAMPRETT BELLBOYS.) Good morning, sir.

LAMPRETT: Good morning. (BREEZE *goes out. At the sight of* LAMPRETT, HUMPAGE *is again galvanized into action. He snatches up the telescope and views the countryside.* LAMPRETT *speaks to him.*) Humpage!

HUMPAGE: Sir?

LAMPRETT: Attention! Anything to report?

HUMPAGE: No, sir.

LAMPRETT: Nothing in the night?

HUMPAGE: No, sir.

LAMPRETT: No smoke?

HUMPAGE: No, sir.

LAMPRETT: Oh. (*After a pause.*) Not even a gorse bush?

HUMPAGE: No, sir.

LAMPRETT: Very well, Humpage. Keep your eyes open. Good morning, my love. (*He speaks to his wife,* HESTER, *who is now standing in the open doorway of the house. She is dressed in clothes of a former period.*)

HESTER: Good morning, Lamprett. Have you seen our daughter?

LAMPRETT: No, my dear, I have not.

HESTER (*calls*): Dorcas!

LAMPRETT: Humpage!

HUMPAGE: Sir?

LAMPRETT: Any sight of Miss Bellboys?

HUMPAGE *views about.*

HUMPAGE: No, sir.

HESTER: Tiresome child. Lamprett!

LAMPRETT: My dear?

HESTER: You have on odd shoes. Change them. (*She goes into the house.* LAMPRETT *sits, removes his shoes and stares at them.*)

HUMPAGE: Report, sir!

LAMPRETT (*leaping up*): What's that?

HUMPAGE: Miss Bellboys approaching, sir.

LAMPRETT: Oh. (*He sits again.* DORCAS BELLBOYS, *his daughter, runs into the garden.*) Your mother is looking for you, Dorcas.

DORCAS: Why?

LAMPRETT: I don't know. Where have you been?

DORCAS: Swimming.

LAMPRETT: Absurd habit. Your mother tells me my shoes are odd, but I cannot see it. Can you? (*Together they examine the shoes.*)

DORCAS: They seem to be a pair.

LAMPRETT: I think so. However, I'd better change them—you never know. (*He goes into the house.* DORCAS, *who is barefoot, sits and begins to rub the dry sand from her feet with a handful of grass. Suddenly and simultaneously two bedroom windows are thrown up and* TIMOTHY *and* HESTER *appear.*)

HESTER: Dorcas!

TIMOTHY: Humpage!

HESTER: Good morning, Timothy.

TIMOTHY: Good morning, Hester. One moment, please, Humpage!

HUMPAGE: Sir?

TIMOTHY: Which way does the wind blow? (HUMPAGE *produces a small portable wind-vane which he holds in the air.* TIMOTHY *observes this.*) That's bad. (*He withdraws.*)

DORCAS: What is it, Mama?

HESTER: How old are you?

DORCAS: Seventeen last birthday.

     TIMOTHY *again appears at his window.*

TIMOTHY: Humpage, according to my calculations the wind cannot be blowing from that direction today. (*For answer* HUMPAGE *again dumbly holds up the vane.*) I see. Then we can expect some excitement. (*He withdraws.*)

HESTER: Seventeen. It has occurred to me that now is the time to put off your childish ways.

DORCAS: Yes, Mama.

HESTER: We must all grow up.

DORCAS: Yes, Mama.

HESTER: Good girl.

     HALLAM MATTHEWS *has come from the house.* HALLAM, *a giant of a man, is an exquisite, a dandy par excellence. His clothes are magnificent in their sobriety.*

HALLAM: May I wish you a very good day, Hester?

HESTER: Good morning, Hallam. You're up from your bed, I see.

HALLAM: Indeed, yes. Some time ago.

HESTER: You're recovered from your journey?

HALLAM: Fully. You must forgive my petulance on arrival last night.

HESTER: You must forgive our complete ignorance of your visit. Timothy forgot to tell anyone that you were expected. Have you seen him yet?

HALLAM: I've seen no one but you. Even my man, Breeze, has quite disappeared. Perhaps it had better be known at once—I require peace here but not complete indifference to my welfare. There was a touch of asperity in that remark, wasn't there? Please forget it.

HESTER: I've done so.

HALLAM: For today I feel that nothing shall deter me from fully enjoying this charming occupation known as life.

HESTER: How is London?

HALLAM: In uproar. This invitation was god-sent. I asked myself, 'Shall it be a few days in the country with my old friends?' and a few days in the country it is. I shall return to London well able to withstand all assaults on my character and reputation. Only two things could have saved me after the past few weeks' activity —death or a visit. I've chosen this visit.

HESTER: Rightly, I'm sure.

HALLAM: But I'm keeping you from some important duty with my chatter.

HESTER: Good gracious! So you are. (HESTER *goes into the house.* HALLAM *looks about him with appreciation. He sees* HUMPAGE *and decides:*)

HALLAM: I think it best, in the circumstances, to ignore you. (*And so, speaks to* DORCAS.) And who are you?

DORCAS: My name is Dorcas.

HALLAM: Ah, yes. The daughter of the house.

DORCAS: Yes.

HALLAM: charming!

BREEZE *in a confused state, has wandered into the garden.*

BREEZE: Oh, there you are, Mr Matthews.

HALLAM: Oh, there *you* are, Sam. I think I'm a little angry with you.

BREEZE: Why, sir?

HALLAM: Recall: you left me over an hour ago. In that time I have risen, shaved myself, dressed myself and breakfasted. All this without your usual assistance. Is it right, Sam, is it right?

BREEZE: No, sir. Forgive me.

HALLAM: What have you been doing?

BREEZE: Getting very lost.

HALLAM: Why? The place is simplicity itself—there is the charm.

BREEZE: Have you been that way? (*He indicates the way he has come.*)

HALLAM: Not yet.

BREEZE: I beg of you, sir—don't go that way.

HALLAM: You must not expect every thoroughfare to be as straight as St James's Street. The way about here may be tortuous but the occupants are innocent, honest and homely. Let us absorb these unusual qualities and begin the day. What have you for me this morning?

BREEZE *takes a book from his pocket.*

BREEZE: Mr William Wordsworth, sir.

HALLAM: Oh, dear! Not a happy choice perhaps, but we must persevere, must we not? And better to have him today in the sunshine than to have him when it is raining. Where shall we take him?

BREEZE: I wouldn't dare to advise you, sir.

HALLAM: In that case we must consult a native of the place. (*He turns to* DORCAS.) Tell me, Dorcas, do you know of a secluded place in the vicinity of this house to which I can retire for a while?

DORCAS: For what purpose?

HALLAM: For the purpose of performing my usual literary chores of the day: which is to have Samuel here read to me from contemporary works. Your expression leads me to understand that you are not fully in sympathy with such an occupation. However, do you know of a suitable place?

DORCAS: I'm trying to think.

HALLAM: Thank you.

DORCAS: There is a ruined cottage on the cliffs.

HALLAM: Excellent! I'd contemplated a field. I'd not dared to hope for a roof.

DORCAS: It has no roof.

HALLAM: No roof. Well, four walls—

DORCAS: Three walls. (*She laughs.*)

HALLAM: I think you are a very nasty little girl. Come, Samuel.
    TIMOTHY *appears at the bedroom window.*

TIMOTHY: Hallam! There you are.

HALLAM: Yes, Timothy. Here I am.

TIMOTHY: I shall be down soon to greet you.

HALLAM: That will be very pleasant.

TIMOTHY: Your visit here is secret. (*He puts a finger to his lips.*) Ssh! (HALLAM *replies in the same way.*) Where are you going now?

HALLAM: Just a very little way off, Timothy, for a very little while. Samuel is going to read something new by Mr—what's the fellow's name?

BREEZE: Wordsworth, sir.

HALLAM: By Mr Wordsworth—and I didn't wish to alarm or distress anyone in the house.

TIMOTHY: Well, don't be long. I want to talk to you. (*He is about to withdraw, when:*) Keep your eyes to the south!

HALLAM: I will, indeed. (TIMOTHY *disappears.*) Come, Sam. (HALLAM *goes from the garden followed by* BREEZE. *A diminutive*

MAIDSERVANT *can be seen going about within the house withdrawing the curtains of various rooms.* LAMPRETT *comes from the house.*)

LAMPRETT: Who was that?

DORCAS: Old Matthews and his servant, Sammy.

LAMPRETT: Don't be familiar.

DORCAS: Sorry, Papa.

LAMPRETT: Mr Matthews is a guest here. (*He looks down at his shoes.*) I've changed them.

DORCAS: Have you?

LAMPRETT. Yes. They look better, don't they? This is the uncomfortable pair. Oh, well—to work! Don't dream away the day.

    LAMPRETT *hobbles out.* DORCAS *is now lying full length on the grass.* HUMPAGE *has gone to sleep again. From within the house* HESTER *calls sharply,* Lamprett— Lamprett! *From her recumbent position* DORCAS *slowly raises her legs before her. She regards her feet, flexing her toes, and then, continuing the movement proceeds to perform a slow backward somersault. This brings her to an inverted view of the orchard gate where now stand a man and a small boy.*

EDWARD: There's someone here, I think. (JONATHAN *pulls at his hand, and bending down,* EDWARD *listens to the boy's whispering.*) Jonathan tells me that we are in a garden speaking to a young lady.

DORCAS: That is true.

EDWARD: We have broken our journey for a moment to ask if we might have a drink of water.

DORCAS: Of course. (*She moves towards the house, and then turns.*) There's milk if you prefer it.

EDWARD: Jonathan?

    The BOY *nods his head.*

DORCAS: It shall be milk then. Something to eat? (*The* BOY *shakes his head.*) Please sit down. DORCAS *goes into the house.* JONATHAN *leads* EDWARD *to a chair and he sits. The* BOY *squats on the ground beside him.* TIMOTHY' *bedroom window is thrown up and* TIMOTHY *leans out.*)

TIMOTHY: Humpage!

HUMPAGE (*awakened*): Sir?

TIMOTHY: The portents are ominous. (HUMPAGE *crosses himself.*) Keep your eyes to the south!

HUMPAGE: Yes, sir.

TIMOTHY: Always to the south. (*He notices* EDWARD *and* JONATHAN.) Good morning to you.

EDWARD: Good morning.

TIMOTHY: A fine morning.

EDWARD: Yes.

TIMOTHY: For a battle, I mean. (*He withdraws, closing the window.*)

DORCAS *comes from the house carrying a tray with two tankards of milk and some apples. For a moment she stands silent before* EDWARD. *Then, very quietly, she speaks:*

DORCAS: I am here.

EDWARD: Yes.

DORCAS: I didn't wish to startle you.

EDWARD: Thank you.

DORCAS: Because you are blind.

EDWARD: What's that?

DORCAS: Because you are blind. Why, what's the matter? It's true, is it not? Now I've startled you—why?

EDWARD: To hear it spoken in that way. Blind! Without pity, as you did. Never, since I returned—

DORCAS: I'm sorry.

EDWARD: No, indeed. Let it be spoken in such a way. (DORCAS *puts the tankard of milk into his hand.*) This was meant for the boy —it was he who was thirsty.

DORCAS: There's one for him. He has it.

EDWARD: Then, thank you. (*He takes the milk.*)

DORCAS: And I thought you would like these.

EDWARD: What are they?

DORCAS: Apples.

EDWARD: For the journey. Thank you.

DORCAS *gives the apples to* JONATHAN, *who stores them away in various pockets.* DORCAS *sits on the ground beside* EDWARD. JONATHAN *respectfully rises.*

DORCAS: Sit down, please—Jonathan, isn't it?

EDWARD: Yes. My name is Edward Sterne.

DORCAS: I am Dorcas Bellboys.

EDWARD: How do you do.

DORCAS: How do you do. (*And they laugh at themselves.*) You say you are on a journey.

EDWARD: Yes. I am going to London. And Jonathan, here— Jonathan Watkins—is on his way to a distant village in a holy land. (*He pauses, drinking the milk.* JONATHAN, *who has drunk his milk at a draught, has taken from his pocket a length of twine and formed upon his hands a cat's cradle.*) We may yet turn back.

DORCAS: Why do you go to London?

EDWARD: I'm going to see the King.

DORCAS: King George?

EDWARD: Yes. I have a request to make of him. (*He pauses.*) I'm going to ask him to stop this war. You're laughing at me.

DORCAS: No!

EDWARD: You may if you wish. (JONATHAN *holds out the cat's cradle to* EDWARD, *who feeling his hands, takes it and by touch converts it.*) But you must not laugh at my friend here. That I cannot allow. My friend who is on his way to Bethlehem. The BOY *takes back the cat's cradle.*) You think us absurd?

DORCAS: Why should I? My uncle Timothy believes he can defeat the entire French fleet and army single-handed.

EDWARD (*he laughs*): A man after my own heart. He lives here.

DORCAS: Oh, yes. This is his house.

EDWARD: Was it he who called to me a moment ago? Saying it was a fine day for a battle.

DORCAS: That would be him.

EDWARD: And how is he going to defeat the French army—to say nothing of the fleet?

DORCAS: Perhaps in the way that you are going to convince the King that it is necessary to end the war. How are you going to do that?

EDWARD: Show myself to him.

> *There is a pause.*
>
> DORCAS *puts her hand out to* EDWARD'S *arm, hesitates, and withdraws without touching him.* TIMOTHY *appears at his window.*

TIMOTHY: Dorcas!

DORCAS: Yes?

TIMOTHY: Is Mr Matthews back?

DORCAS: No.

TIMOTHY: Request him to come up to me when he returns.

DORCAS: Very well.

TIMOTHY: And remember—

DORCAS: To keep my eyes to the south.

TIMOTHY: That's right. (*To* EDWARD.) And you, sir—all eyes to the south.

TIMOTHY *withdraws.* EDWARD *turns his blind eyes towards*
DORCAS. *She immediately takes his hand, saying:*

DORCAS: Please! He doesn't know! Please!

EDWARD: Why to the south?

DORCAS: Because it is from that way Bonaparte will come. They
say he will come with his armies any day now. He has been preparing for months and—well, look at the weather.

EDWARD: I can feel the heat of the sun. Yes, I should say it is a
very good day for a battle, although from my experience almost
any kind of day will do. Are you an orphan?

DORCAS: No. Why?

EDWARD: I thought—living here alone with your uncle—

DORCAS: I don't live here alone with him. Good gracious no!
There is Mama and Papa. Mama orders the house for Uncle
Timothy and Papa—well, Papa looks after his fire engine and—

LAMPRETT *appears from behind the house.*

LAMPRETT: Dorcas.

DORCAS: Yes, Papa?

LAMPRETT: I beg your pardon. Do I disturb you? Good morning.

EDWARD: Good morning, sir.

LAMPRETT (*seeing* JONATHAN): Ah! Little boy. You'll do. Come
with me.

JONATHAN *hesitates.*

DORCAS: Go with him. He won't harm you. He is my father.

JONATHAN *rises and slowly crosses the garden to* LAMPRETT, *who
takes him by the arm: together they go out.*

EDWARD: Did he hesitate?

DORCAS: Jonathan? For a moment.

EDWARD: He doesn't fully understand about fathers and mothers:
he is an orphan.

DORCAS: How did you come together?

EDWARD: Four days ago a warm dry hand was placed in mine. It
has guided me since.

DORCAS: You were travelling—

EDWARD: —alone. Alone. Hoping to find and make my way by
charity. I was singing for my supper outside an empty house when
Jonathan came to me. I told him I was on my way to see the
King and he explained that he could take me there incidental to
his own journey.

DORCAS: Why is he going to Bethlehem?

EDWARD: Last Christmas he was told the story of the birth of a child in Bethlehem. From that story Jonathan recognized his brother. But the story ended and the storyteller forgot to say that the birth was over eighteen hundred years ago, and that the boy has long since been dead. (HUMPAGE *stirs in his sleep.*) Aren't we alone—now—at this moment.

DORCAS: It's no one. And you—Edward—where do you come from?

EDWARD: I was sent home—(*He raises his hands to his useless eyes.*)— three months ago. They landed us at Plymouth and then, to return, took on a cargo of men with arms and legs, with eyes and honest minds. I have been alone since I returned. Now I am going to see the King to ask him to stop the war. Do you understand or do you think I am mad? (*He rises.*) Where are you? You have moved from me?

DORCAS: I am here.

EDWARD: Then tell me: Jonathan goes to Bethlehem not knowing that Christ is dead—do I go to London not knowing—not knowing that—

DORCAS *has risen to stand by* EDWARD'S *side; she takes his hand.* HESTER *within the house, calls:* Dorcas—Dorcas. *The girl, looking up into* EDWARD'S *face, says:*

DORCAS: I did not know that blind eyes could cry. Come away! It is my mother calling me. Come. (*She leads* EDWARD *out to the orchard. Immediately* HESTER *comes from the house. She looks about the garden and then calls.*)

HESTER: Lamprett!

HUMPAGE *awakes and views the horizon through his telescope.* LAMPRETT *comes into the garden.*

LAMPRETT: I've changed them, my dear.

HESTER: Changed what?

LAMPRETT: My shoes.

HESTER: Never mind that now. What are you doing?

LAMPRETT: Cleaning the engine.

HESTER: Again?

LAMPRETT: Well, my dear—

HESTER: You cleaned it only yesterday.

LAMPRETT: We must be prepared.

HESTER: Ridiculous! (LAMPRETT *prepares to go.*) Lamprett!

LAMPRETT: My dear?

HESTER: Do I bully you?

LAMPRETT (*he smiles*): A little.

HESTER (*she smiles*): Forgive me. I must a little or belie my appearance.

LAMPRETT: Of course.

HESTER: Have you seen Dorcas?

LAMPRETT: A moment ago.

HESTER: Where?

LAMPRETT: I really can't remember.

HESTER: She's growing up, Lamprett.

LAMPRETT: Yes, with a young man.

HESTER: What's that?

LAMPRETT: I saw her with a young man.

HESTER: You see! (*She turns to go into the house.*)

LAMPRETT: Hester—

HESTER: Yes?

LAMPRETT: Did you wish to speak to me?

HESTER: I don't think so.

LAMPRETT: You called me as if you wished to speak to me.

HESTER: Then what can I say? (*She pauses.*) God bless you. (*She goes into the house.*)

LAMPRETT: Humpage!

HUMPAGE: Sir!

LAMPRETT: If this fellow, Napoleon Bonaparte, does come over with an army I expect there will be work to do. The battle is sure to start a few fires. Murder, rapine, looting—that sort of thing, you know.

HUMPAGE: Yes, sir.

LAMPRETT: It will, however—(*As* LAMPRETT *continues to speak,* JONATHAN *comes in to hand him a polishing rag.*)—be more difficult than usual—thank you, my dear—(JONATHAN *returns to his duties.*)—considerably more difficult. For while we must extinguish our own fires we must be careful to foster those of the enemy.

HUMPAGE: That's right, sir.

LAMPRETT: There our duty as Englishmen must precede our duty as firemen. But knowing how against the grain it will be to foster—indeed, positively encourage!—any fire, friend's or enemy's, I've been considering the advisability of using some combustible mixture in certain hoses. Have you anything to suggest?

HUMPAGE: Brandy.

LAMPRETT: Well, yes—

HALLAM MATTHEWS, *followed by* BREEZE, *enters the garden.*

HALLAM: Take those things to my room, Samuel. I shall sit here for a while. (BREEZE *goes into the house.* HALLAM *sits down, fanning himself.*) Good morning, Lamprett.

LAMPRETT: Good morning, Hallam.

HALLAM, Inflammatory weather.

LAMPRETT: Yes, thank God. Have you been walking?

HALLAM: Yes. Your daughter—

BREEZE *re-enters the garden. He carries a small jewelled box which he hands to* HALLAM.

BREEZE: Your lozenges, sir.

HALLAM: Oh, thank you, Sam. (BREEZE *goes back into the house.*) For my voice, you know. Have one—delicious.

LAMPRETT: No thank you. Been walking, have you?

HALLAM: Yes. Your daughter advised me of a secluded place to which I could retire for the purpose of reading.

LAMPRETT: Excellent!

HALLAM: It was far from excellent. The premises themselves had little to commend them other than an overpowering smell of decaying seaweed, a complete exposure to the sky, and the fact that they were situated on a sheer precipice of several hundred feet. You must know, my dear Lamprett, that nothing is so necessary to a reading of Mr Wordsworth's work than a sense of security.

LAMPRETT: Reading that fellow, eh?

HALLAM: It was my intention. I must attempt to know something of the forces that are conspiring the destruction of my kind.

LAMPRETT: Where was this place?

HALLAM: A ruined cottage—in that direction.

LAMPRETT: Oh, that place.

HALLAM: You know it?

LAMPRETT: Yes. It was burnt out two years ago—a magnificent conflagration!—the only occasion on which my brigade became sea-borne. An unfortunate legend credits me with firing the place —it was the first time my brigade was called out under my captaincy—but I can assure you it is nothing more than a legend. (*He points to* HUMPAGE.) He used to live there.

HALLAM: Now he lives up there?

LAMPRETT: Yes. He's the look-out.

HALLAM: And what does he look out for?

LAMPRETT: Fires. Any spark, flash, flame or cloud of smoke as small as a man's hand and I am instantly informed. The engine stands ready—the signals and bell are summons to the members of my brigade. We should proceed within seconds.

HALLAM: Excellent!

LAMPRETT: I believe Timothy also employs Humpage as a look-out for any sign of this threatened invasion but that is a secondary consideration. Have you seen Timothy yet?

HALLAM: For a moment. He called to me from his window.

LAMPRETT: I think I should tell you, Hallam, that you will find him strange—very strange. God forbid that I should speak ill of my brother—

HALLAM: God forbid!

LAMPRETT: —but this threatened invasion by Bonaparte seems to have unhinged him completely. His behaviour has become eccentric in the extreme. (HUMPAGE, *in his active viewing of the surrounding countryside, turns and lightly strikes the brass bell with the telescope.* LAMPRETT *leaps to his feet.*) Action!

HUMPAGE: An accident, sir. It was an accident. (*He demonstrates.*) I was viewing about as is my duty, and the bell being in this position—here—my arm raised—so—I accidentally struck the bell —so! (*He does so.*) An accident, sir. See? If my arm is raised—so— and I am viewing—so—I am able— (*He again strikes the bell. Then there is silence. At last* LAMPRETT *speaks.*)

LAMPRETT: A false alarm.

HUMPAGE: Yes, sir.

LAMPRETT: No fire.

HUMPAGE: No, sir.

LAMPRETT: No smoke.

HUMPAGE: No, sir.

LAMPRETT: In fact, nothing.

HUMPAGE: Nothing, sir.

LAMPRETT (*shouting*): That is no excuse for relaxation! Attention! (HUMPAGE *again takes up the telescope and begins to view with an insane concentration.*) You were saying, Hallam?—

HALLAM: I wasn't saying anything. You were speaking of Timothy.

LAMPRETT: Of course. Quite unhinged, poor fellow. Given to the most extraordinary outbursts and madcap schemes. Very sad to see a man of his capabilities with his reason overthrown. My brother—very sad.

HALLAM: Yes, indeed. But the cause surely is not—

LAMPRETT: Nothing more than this absurd invasion by the French. He has no trust in the official precautions in hand against Bonaparte.

HALLAM: By that he shows his sanity.

LAMPRETT: You mean—

HALLAM: I mean that any system of national defence is non-existent.

LAMPRETT: God bless my soul!

HALLAM: However, what is Timothy proposing to do?

LAMPRETT: I thought you must know. I had imagined you were in his confidence.

HALLAM: I know nothing more than this: that I am arrived from London by Timothy's wish and bring him a box of clothes and a French phrase book.

LAMPRETT: A box of clothes and a French phrase book! My God, what can he be up to?

HALLAM: We shall just have to wait and see, my dear Lamprett, just wait and see.

LAMPRETT: That is a notion to which I have never subscribed. I find out, my dear Hallam, I find out!

HALLAM: Then pray tell me—what have you found out?

LAMPRETT: Nothing.

HALLAM: Nothing. I see.

LAMPRETT: Except that his room is hung with maps and reports of the weather—that he has set four mantraps in the orchard— that I was awakened three nights ago by his calling out words of command in a foreign language—except for these things I know nothing.

At this moment TIMOTHY *appears in the doorway of the house. He is now fully dressed and carries a pistol. This he raises and aims at the brass bell. He fires and the bell chimes under the impact of the bullet.*

TIMOTHY: Good shot, sir! Sit down, Lamprett. (*He exhibits the pistol.*) Hit a penny at ten paces last night. Pretended it was Boney's belly-button. Good morning, Hallam.

HALLAM: Good morning, Timothy.

TIMOTHY: A brisk and beautiful day!

HALLAM: Indeed, yes.

TIMOTHY: Have a good journey?

HALLAM: Very fair.

TIMOTHY: Sorry I was not available to welcome you. What time did you arrive?

HALLAM: A little past midnight.

TIMOTHY: Sleep well?

HALLAM: Thank you, yes.

TIMOTHY: Breakfasted?

HALLAM: Yes.

TIMOTHY: Well, that's done.

HALLAM: What, pray, is done?

TIMOTHY: The conventional enquiries as to your general welfare. Tedious, eh? Now, I want to talk to you. Off with you, Lamprett.

LAMPRETT: What's that?

TIMOTHY: I say, off with you. I want to speak to Hallam privately.

LAMPRETT: Oh, very well.

TIMOTHY: Now, Hallam, I wish to tell you about a little plan. That is, when Lamprett has had the decency to absent himself. (*He glares at* LAMPRETT *who is hanging about the house.*)

LAMPRETT: Timothy.

TIMOTHY: Yes.

LAMPRETT: Where can I go? What can I do?

TIMOTHY: God bless my soul! Our very existence is threatened by Napoleon Bonaparte, and the man asks where he can go and what he can do. Prepare, my dear brother, prepare for the worst in whatever way you please—but prepare.

LAMPRETT: I think you are a very foolish fellow, Tim. (*He leaves the garden with a certain dignity.* TIMOTHY *stares after him.*)

TIMOTHY: I am being made to understand with increasing force the impossibility of expecting Lamprett to take his life with the smallest degree of seriousness. He has, I'm afraid, an incontrovertibly frivolous nature. Father, had he lived, would have found an even deeper dissatisfaction with his younger son, I feel. During his lifetime he found Lamprett a sore trial. We cannot deny that the affair of Hester whilst Lamprett was at Oxford—

HALLAM: Hester! His wife!

TIMOTHY: Oh, yes, he married her. Father insisted upon it—and quite rightly—after the disgraceful business of the warden's breeches. Hester was his niece, you know.

HALLAM: I didn't know.

TIMOTHY: Lamprett, of course, has lived in complete retirement ever since. His passions must be controlled.

HALLAM: Lamprett's passions!

TIMOTHY: No, no! You misunderstand me. I mean, of course, his passion for lost causes. That is how the disgrace came upon us. Instead of attending to his studies when he was at Oxford he became convinced that women should be admitted to the Colleges. To prove their worth he prevailed upon Hester—with whom he was friendly, both of them playing the bass fiddle—to dress in her uncle's second-best ceremonial breeches and coat. So dressed, she attended lectures for three weeks and might never have been discovered had not Lamprett then insisted that to complete the illusion she should begin to smoke. One evening, in his rooms, with Horace Walpole as his guest, Hester was standing before the fire, pipe in hand, when the breeches caught alight. She would have been burnt to the ground had not Lamprett extinguished the fire manually. (*He demonstrates.*) So, of course, he married her, and he's been fighting fires ever since. As for the present—I can only enjoin you to the greatest secrecy.

HALLAM: We are not alone. (*He indicates* HUMPAGE.)

TIMOTHY: Very true. Humpage!

HUMPAGE: Sir!

TIMOTHY: You are not to listen to my conversation for the next few minutes. Do you understand?

HUMPAGE: Very good, sir. (*He covers his ears with his hands.*)

TIMOTHY: No, no, no! You must keep your ears open for other sounds! The approach of danger may be heralded by nothing more than a whisper, the advance of an army may be borne on the gentlest breeze. Take down your hands! (HUMPAGE *remains covering his ears: he grins.*) Take down your hands! (HUMPAGE *does not move.*) God grant me patience! (TIMOTHY *shouts.*) Listen, you blockhead! Listen! (*He then stands silent and at a complete loss until, in a moment of inspiration, he snatches off his hat and throws it to* HUMPAGE *who, with an automatic reaction, catches it.* TIMOTHY *seizes the opportunity.*) Listen! You are to keep your eyes open for other sounds, but you are not to listen to me. Do you understand?

HUMPAGE: Yes, sir.

TIMOTHY: Keep your eyes to the south—and give me back my hat. (HUMPAGE *does so. To* HALLAM.) Sorry about that. To continue, I must as I say, enjoin you to the greatest secrecy. It is a well-known fact that this part of the coast is alive with French spies and Bonaparte's personal agents. Now, have I your solemn word that you will not tell a single living soul?

HALLAM: I can give you my word on that with the greatest assurance.

TIMOTHY: Thank you. You have brought me some things from London.

HALLAM: Yes.

TIMOTHY: What are they?

HALLAM: A large black box which you asked me to collect from Drury Lane Theatre—

TIMOTHY: Where is it?

HALLAM: Upstairs in my room.

TIMOTHY: Hidden?

HALLAM: Under the bed.

TIMOTHY: Locked?

HALLAM: Locked.

TIMOTHY: And the second article?

HALLAM: This book—(*He takes it from his pocket.*)—which appears to be—

TIMOTHY: Excellent! (*He takes the book from* HALLAM *and reads in execrable French.*) 'Sautons à bas du lit, j'entends la bonne qui monte.' Dear me! I'm not sure this is the sort of thing I want at all. (*He turns a few pages.*) Ah! this is better. (*He reads.*) 'Retirez! Je connais le dessous des cartes!'

HALLAM: What does that mean?

TIMOTHY *consults the book.*

TIMOTHY: 'Retreat! I know what's what!' Oh, yes—I think I shall find what I want in here. It will repay a few hours quiet study. Good. (*He puts the book away in his pocket.*) Now, Hallam. The situation is roughly this: myself, versus one hundred and seventy-five thousand Frenchmen.

HALLAM: An epic situation, no less. Go on.

TIMOTHY: That is the popular estimate of the number of Bonaparte's troops assembled on the French coast at this moment, and preparing for the final assault. They will make the crossing in two thousand Shallops, despatch boats, caiques, bomb-ships, praams—

HALLAM: Praams?

TIMOTHY: —yes, praams and transports. That crossing may be made at any moment now. What is to be done?

HALLAM: What, indeed?

TIMOTHY: I'll tell you in a moment. But first let us consider the arrangements made by the country as a whole to deal with this menace. Are they daring, brilliant and worthy of the English in such a situation? Are they?

HALLAM: I should say, no.

TIMOTHY: And you would be right. Shall I tell you why they are not daring, brilliant and worthy of the English?

HALLAM: If you please.

TIMOTHY: Because they do not exist. No arrangements for dealing with this menace exists.

HALLAM: Astounding!

TIMOTHY: Disgraceful! A national disgrace! But you will agree that something must be done.

HALLAM: I should think so.

TIMOTHY: Well, what?

HALLAM: You are aching to tell me, Timothy.

TIMOTHY: My first plan was to raise a private army under my command. I actually put this plan into action. Two months ago I raised a force of one hundred and twenty-seven men—eight children: the Bellboys Fencibles. All was prepared, the corps was in being, when I received a communication from some central office in Dorchester informing me that the raising of an army for a private purpose—my God! a private purpose—was illegal. More than that. I was also informed that owing to the national emergency my corps—the Bellboys Fencibles—would be taken over intact. I applied, very naturally, for their command. It was refused. Can you credit that?

HALLAM: With difficulty.

TIMOTHY: Yes, refused. But—and this will strain your credulity to breaking point—I was informed that an officer was being sent from Taunton to take up the command and that they wished me —my God! I can hardly tell you—they wished me to give him any advice and information on the corps and local terrain that he desired.

HALLAM: Which you have undoubtedly done.

TIMOTHY: Nothing of the kind. I refused even to meet the fellow. I withdrew my support and every material object associating me with the corps—including the banners bearing the corps inscription—'Tintinabulum pueri'. I washed my hands of them.

HALLAM: Understandably.

TIMOTHY: This Taunton fellow—what's his name?—George Selincourt has had them in training now for almost two months, and if you should chance upon a ragged band of scruffy, drunken, ill-disciplined, noisy louts rampaging the countryside you will be viewing our sole defence against Bonaparte.

HALLAM: Alarming!

TIMOTHY: Something, however, must be done. You agree?

HALLAM: Yes.

TIMOTHY: It will be done. Never fear.

HALLAM: You have a plan.

TIMOTHY: I have. (*He smiles in anticipation.*) You will understand that in such a situation a gesture of defiance is useless. The odds are great.

HALLAM: One hundred and seventy-five thousand to one, you said.

TIMOTHY: Yes.

HALLAM: I think those odds may be considered as lunatic.

TIMOTHY: Quite. Therefore, as I say, a direct conflict must be avoided. Yet I contemplate engaging the French single-handed using but a single weapon.

HALLAM: The jawbone of an ass, I presume.

TIMOTHY *rises to stand a little apart from* HALLAM. *He pulls a lock of hair down over his forehead and stands squeezing his cheek with his right hand.*

TIMOTHY: I am a certain person making a grand decision of policy?

HALLAM: How many guesses am I allowed?

TIMOTHY: Oh, come, come! Only one should be necessary. (HALLAM *is silent.*) I'll give you a clue. (*He then says, in his very individual French.*) Mettez bas les armes! Vive la France!

HALLAM: Comme vous écorchez cette lange!

TIMOTHY: I beg your pardon?

HALLAM: Nothing.

TIMOTHY: You understand who I am?

HALLAM: You know, I'm very much afraid that I do. But I don't see—

TIMOTHY: You must see! The resemblance is remarkable, you will admit. I can look very like Napoleon Bonaparte, and there lies the basis of my scheme of defeat for the French. At the moment the likeness is possibly remote but when I am dressed—

HALLAM: Dressed?

TIMOTHY: Exactly! The box that you have brought for me contains a uniform of the French National Guard.

HALLAM: My God!

TIMOTHY: And here is my plan. (*Very quietly he asks.*) Humpage, are you listening?

HUMPAGE: No, sir.

TIMOTHY: Now, Hallam, this is my plan. I shall be informed of the approach of the French fleet, the moment of imminent invasion. At that moment I shall do nothing—nothing! I shall allow the army to disembark, to land on the coast out there. I shall not make the slightest effort to prevent them from doing so. When their landing is almost complete I shall dress in the National Guard uniform and assume my impersonation of Bonaparte. I shall then descend the well. I shall have to be lowered in the bucket. Perhaps you would be so good as to oblige me— (HALLAM *inclines his head in assent.*) I shall then make my way along the tunnel at the bottom of the well which leads to the cliffs, and I shall make an appearance behind—mark this!—I shall come up in the rear of the French army. They will, of course, recognize me as their Emperor and consent to be led by me.

HALLAM: And where, pray, do you intend to lead them?

TIMOTHY: To confusion and ultimate damnation!

HALLAM: How?

TIMOTHY: I shall give orders. Inform them that all is lost: that there is nothing but retreat.

HALLAM: In their own language?

TIMOTHY: Certainly. That is why I required this little book. (*He pats his pocket.*) I know a certain amount, of course. Je suis l'avant coureur! Je suis l'Empereur!—and that sort of thing. (*For a moment he regards* HALLAM *with a smile—then:*) Well, what do you think of it?

HALLAM: I am really at a loss for words to express my admiration or my—

TIMOTHY: The charm—the essential charm of the plan is its simplicity, eh?

HALLAM: Yes—yes.

TIMOTHY: I will admit to you, Hallam, that I am more than a little nervous—I might also say frightened—of what I am about to do. It is, after all, no small thing.

HALLAM: Timothy—(He *appears to be suffering from some difficulty in expressing himself.*) Timothy, I—(*His head bowed and the words scarcely audible.*)—God bless you! (*Turning away from* TIMOTHY, *he is shaken by laughter.* TIMOTHY, *unaware of this, and deeply moved, puts a hand on* HALLAM'S *shoulder.*)

TIMOTHY: Thank you, Hallam, thank you. But you must not distress yourself. (*A pause.*) Can I have the key to the box of clothes?

HALLAM: In my room, on the dressing-table.

TIMOTHY: Thank you. (*He turns to go into the house.*) May I say that your deep emotion proves to be the complete justification of my scheme. I may fail—but what of that? It is what we attempt that matters. I know by your sympathetic reception that I am right at least in the attempt. I can even forgive the desperate foolishness of my fellow-countrymen. Alas! They cannot comprehend what is almost upon them. But I will stand for them. I will be England. (*He again turns to go into the house.*)

HALLAM: Timothy!

TIMOTHY: Yes?

HALLAM: Forgive me.

TIMOTHY (*very puzzled*): Of course, my dear fellow, of course. I shall now retire for a while. A little study, you know. (*He puts the book in his pocket, laughs, and then goes into the house.* HALLAM *turns to* DORCAS *and* EDWARD, *who are now standing at the gateway of the orchard.*)

HALLAM: Hullo, horrid child.

DORCAS: Mr Matthews. (*A deep curtsey.*)

HALLAM: I wish I could rid myself of the feeling that you are making mock of me.

DORCAS: May I introduce Mr Edward Sterne to your acquaintance. Mr Hallam Matthews.

EDWARD: How do you do, sir.

HALLAM: Can I give you my arm to a chair?

EDWARD: Thank you.

> HALLAM *sits beside* EDWARD.

HALLAM: Travelling, Mr Sterne?

EDWARD: Yes, Mr Matthews. I'm on my way to London. Miss Bellboys kindly provided me and my companion with refreshment, and has also pleasurably detained me with her conversation.

HALLAM: Tell me, does she make fun of you?

EDWARD (*he laughs*): I've not noticed it.

HALLAM: She does of me. I'm sure of it. Not directly, you understand. If it was direct I should be justified in spanking her.

    DORCAS, *who for a moment has stepped into the house, puts her head round the doorway.*

DORCAS: Are you talking about me?

HALLAM: Bless my soul. Why should we talk about you?

DORCAS: I thought you might have nothing better to do.

HALLAM: Nothing better to do. (*To* EDWARD.) You see? Or is it that I am too sensitive. I don't know. (*To* DORCAS.) Come here. (*The girl moves to* HALLAM.) Now sit down. (*She does so.*) You, in your youth, regard us as your clowns, do you not? The world, spinning about the centre of your untouched heart, somersaults for your amusement. Very well, but you must remember—

DORCAS: Mr Matthews—

HALLAM: Don't interrupt! But you must remember that there are some days when the clowns must sit together in the sun and talk of clownish things. (EDWARD *laughs.*) Even if they sit together for no other reason than to think up new ways of distracting you, eh, Mr Sterne. And so, sir, to continue our conversation. I was about to say—

DORCAS: Nothing—nothing—nothing—nothing! (*She rolls on to her back on the grass and, laughing, says:*) Isn't it a lovely day? Too fine and sweet for fighting. Look up, Mr Matthews, look up! (HALLAM *stares doubtfully at the sky.*) Do they look as though they are about to fall?

HALLAM: What?

DORCAS: The heavens. That is what they tell us, you know. That is what they tell innocent people—simple people—like you and me—

HALLAM: Eh?

DORCAS: That the heavens are about to fall. Mr Matthews, you wished to be serious. Then answer me this. Why do men fight each other?

    There is a long pause.

HALLAM: Any suggestions, Mr Sterne?

EDWARD: Where are you, Dorcas?

DORCAS: Here! (*She kneels before him.*)

EDWARD: Why do men fight each other?

DORCAS: That is what I asked.

EDWARD: Perhaps because there is a long-wished-for home they

seek, and they are too frail to take upon themselves the responsibility for the journey. Did you never, when you were a baby,
know of something you desired but of which—oh, so humanly—
you were ashamed? And did you not, perhaps—shall we say—
engineer that thing to come about—oh, so sinfully—through the
fault of another? (*He smiles.*) You see, my life-loving darling, the
dark journey to the dark home is sometimes sweeter than the
summer's day.

DORCAS: I think you must be a very serious and unhappy man to
speak like that.

EDWARD: Not unhappy, no. A journeying man, that's what I am.

HALLAM: Don't, please, talk of such things. I feel, somehow, as if
the sun has gone in.

DORCAS: Why not talk?

HALLAM: Has it?

DORCAS: The sun has gone in for him for all time!

EDWARD: No! You mustn't say such things, Dorcas. Forgive her,
sir. I comprehend your distress. We will talk of other things.

HALLAM: Thank you.

DORCAS (*in a sudden rage*): I wish to talk! I want to know—to
understand—why men do such terrible things to each other. I
want to know!

EDWARD: Then come away. (*He rises.*) Mr Matthews will forgive us.

HALLAM: Certainly. I don't wish to think— (*He pauses.*)

EDWARD: Yes?

HALLAM: I don't wish you to think that I—how shall I put it?
Odd, very odd—you two creatures take every word—and God
knows there are many—from my head.

EDWARD: I'm sorry, sir. You have lived a sheltered life?

HALLAM: I like to think I have. But you break into my idyll like a
sword-thrust.

DORCAS: Come along, Edward. (*She takes his hand.*) Can you find
something to amuse you, Mr Matthews?

HALLAM: Don't make fun of me at the moment, please. You have a
most unfair advantage.

DORCAS: What's that?

HALLAM: Your age. You are young. You have no past.

DORCAS: One day—alas!—

HALLAM: Yes! Try then to reconcile the ambitions and pure
designs of youth with the failures and confusions of middle age:

the morning, sweet as a nut, with the early evening, sad as a mustard pot: reconcile the loves of boyhood with the friendships and harsh passions of *nel mezzo del cammin di nostra vita*. (*He pauses.*) I think I'm going to cry.

DORCAS: We distress you, Mr Matthews. Shall we go away.

HALLAM: If you please.

DORCAS: Come along, Edward. (DORCAS *and* EDWARD *go leaving* HALLAM *staring after them.* HESTER *comes from the house.*)

HESTER (*to* HALLAM): Don't sit in the sun. (HESTER *returns to the house passing* BREEZE *who is coming out into the garden.* HALLAM *sees* BREEZE.)

HALLAM: Ah, Sam.

BREEZE: You seem very relieved to see me, sir. Anything the matter?

HALLAM: I'm a little upset, Sam, a little upset. You're happy, I see. Enjoying yourself?

BREEZE: Very much, thank you, sir. Nothing like a few days in the country, is there?

HALLAM: Nothing like it in the whole wide world, I should think.

BREEZE: You are in a state.

HALLAM: Thank you. I couldn't have put it better myself. I am, quite decidedly, 'in a state'.

BREEZE: I don't like to see you in such a way. I leave you contentedly talking about yourself. I come back to find you in a state. From past experience I'd say that people here are either paying too much attention to you, or too little. Has someone suggested that you're either too young or too old? Tell me, sir, is that the way they've been getting at you?

HALLAM: You must teach me your vocabulary, Sam. You express everything so much more accurately than I am able. 'Getting at you'! Oh, yes—yes indeed! The young people speak, and I am revealed—a magnificent ruin.

BREEZE: Then if I may say so, sir, it's not going to do you any good walking up and down like that.

HALLAM: Am I walking up and down? Good gracious me! (*He sinks into a chair.*)

BREEZE: I think we can find you something more comfortable than that, Mr Matthews. (*He looks around the garden and sees the alcove.*) Ah! What about this? (*He goes into the alcove.*) It feels to be dry and warm. You need not necessarily sleep, sir. Will you go in?

HALLAM: I am tempted, I confess. (*Suddenly they smile at each other.*)

BREEZE: Come along, sir. (HALLAM *goes into the alcove.*) Put your feet up. (HALLAM *sitting, does so.*) I think it would be wise to remove your hat. Ah! This is useful. (*He has discovered a shawl.*) Put it round your shoulders. (HALLAM *drapes himself.*) Is the light going to bother you? It's rather strong. (HALLAM *looks doubtful.*) Cover your face, sir. (*He takes* HALLAM'S *handkerchief and puts it over his face.*)

HALLAM: Is it necessary?

BREEZE: Let it be a little curtain between you and the world. Out here, vulgar mankind—behind there, Boodles. How's that? Now you can forget your troubles, can't you? (*He begins to tiptoe away.*)

HALLAM: Where are you going?

BREEZE: To the orchard, sir.

HALLAM: What have you got in that orchard?

BREEZE: Some apples—

HALLAM: Yes?

BREEZE: A pint of cider—

HALLAM: Yes?

BREEZE: And a young woman named Chastity Meadows.

HALLAM: Off you go.

BREEZE: Thank you, sir. (*He goes out to the orchard.* HALLAM *turns restlessly beneath the handkerchief and shawl.* HUMPAGE *has again fallen asleep.* LAMPRETT *and* JONATHAN *enter in earnest conversation.* JONATHAN *carries a large home-made firework of complicated design.*)

LAMPRETT: —and I cannot impress upon you enough the vital necessity of placing that apparatus under—mark that! under—the object. The reason for this is the blow-back which might— and this is no exaggeration—decapitate you. (*He crouches beside* JONATHAN *over the firework.*) My experiments with fire-fighting by explosives are in a primitive state as yet, but we progress. This is the fuzee with which I set it off—this is a linstock. Both technical terms you will learn in due course. Now—ready? When I have lit it we will retire to a safe distance. (*He applies the fuzee to the firework and then cries:*) Right! (*He and the* BOY *rush from the garden. For a time there is stillness, then the firework goes off. It is dazzling, but quite silent.* JONATHAN *and* LAMPRETT *return.* LAMPRETT *explains.*) I am putting the sound in it later. In my opinion, the only way of extinguishing a fire is to blow up—well, everything that is burning if necessary. The loss of life would probably be considerable, but we must keep in mind the main object—and that is, to put out the fire. (LAMPRETT *and* JONATHAN *go out to the orchard.* GEORGE SELINCOURT *enters with considerable energy. He is a little upset at finding the garden apparently deserted. Suddenly, from within a room on the first floor of the house,* TIMOTHY *shouts.*)

TIMOTHY: Bravo! Cours, cours et cours encore!

SELINCOURT: Foreigners!

HUMPAGE (*he is asleep*): Yes.

SELINCOURT: Bless me! (*Looking up at* HUMPAGE, *he moves across the garden until he comes to rest, at a complete loss, just above the alcove where* HALLAM MATTHEWS *lies. After a moment,* HALLAM *speaks.*)

HALLAM: Are you by any chance a French spy?

SELINCOURT: Good God! (*He discovers* HALLAM.) What did you say?

HALLAM: I asked if, by any chance, you were a French spy?

SELINCOURT: Certainly not!

HALLAM: Not?

SELINCOURT: No. (*During the following conversation* HALLAM *does not move or take the handkerchief from his face.*) Excuse me—

HALLAM: Yes?

SELINCOURT: Would you be Sir Timothy Bellboys?

HALLAM: My dear sir, I wouldn't be Sir Timothy Bellboys for all the tea in China.

SELINCOURT: No, no! You misunderstand me. I mean, of course, are your Sir Timothy Bellboys?

HALLAM: No.

SELINCOURT: Not?

HALLAM: No.

SELINCOURT: That is a pity.

HALLAM: On the contrary, sir, it is a stroke of fortune for which I have never ceased to thank Providence.

SELINCOURT: My name is George Selincourt. (*There is silence.*) Selincourt. (*He spells it.*)

HALLAM: Matthews. (*He spells it.*)

SELINCOURT: I've come to advise you not to be alarmed.

HALLAM: Extremely civil of you.

SELINCOURT: The conflict you will hear and see in a few minutes is merely an exercise, a mock battle, a prank of my own, designed to introduce my local defence Volunteers to the conditions they

must expect in the forthcoming engagement with the Beast of the
Apocalypse.

HALLAM: I beg your pardon?

SELINCOURT: The Fiend of the Bottomless Pit.

HALLAM: I still don't quite—

SELINCOURT: The Serpent of Corsica.

HALLAM: Oh, you mean—

SELINCOURT: Napoleon Bonaparte.

HALLAM: The heat—I think it must be the heat. Very hot today, is
it not?

SELINCOURT: More than warm—more than warm.

HALLAM: Then that is undoubtedly the reason for my incapacity to
make head or tail of anything that is said to me today. Your name,
you say, is—

SELINCOURT: Selincourt. I am commander of the local forces—
alas! so small—ranged against Bonaparte.

HALLAM: Yes, yes! I remember. I am with you. Continue.

SELINCOURT: It is my intention to begin a mock battle on, if I
may put it so—(*He giggles.*)—your doorstep. The noise may be
considerable, not to say alarming. I have walked up to advise you
of this. Would you be so kind as to warn Sir Timothy and other
members of this household?

HALLAM: Delighted.

SELINCOURT: Thank you. Well, well! I must be off to see to the
final disposal of my forces. Are you concerned with military
matters, sir? But, of course, you must be.

HALLAM: Why?

SELINCOURT: Everyone must be in this hour of England's peril.
Rather interesting: I have retained one-third of my forces under
my command. The remaining two-thirds I am using as the enemy
—a larger proportion, you notice, as will be the case. This 'enemy'
will land from the sea—we have commandeered the local fishing
fleet for the occasion—and I shall repulse them. Care to come
along and watch?

HALLAM: No, thank you.

SELINCOURT: Ah! Conserving your energy for the real thing, eh?

HALLAM: Yes.

SELINCOURT: What will be your precise duties when the great
moment comes? Have you any special qualifications?

HALLAM: I can run very fast.

SELINCOURT (*delighted*): Can you really? Then you may be the very man I'm looking for. My word, this is lucky!

HALLAM: In what way?

SELINCOURT: Well, as a commander of the local forces it is one of my responsibilities to arrange that at the moment of invasion someone runs through the countryside putting up, at certain points, a poster bearing the information. This must be done quickly and efficiently. Perhaps, for the sake of your country, you would care to take on the job. I have a specimen poster here. (*He takes out the poster which he proceeds to unfold. It bears the single word, in large, staring type*, 'INVASION'.) The price is twopence each, one and eight the dozen, or one hundred for twelve shillings.

HALLAM: Am I expected to pay for them?

SELINCOURT: That's very good of you. Then I should advise you to purchase them by the hundred. The simplest arithmetic will show that you save four and eightpence on each hundred bought. No need to make up your mind immediately. Think it over. I'll leave this with you so that you can keep it in mind. (*He pins the poster on the alcove beside* HALLAM.) I've also borrowed a balloon from the local fair to give a further touch of reality to the proceedings. That goes up in half an hour. Now I really must be off. Goodbye.

HALLAM: Goodbye.

SELINCOURT *goes as* DORCAS *and* EDWARD *come into the garden.*

EDWARD: That's what laughter is, nothing more—

DORCAS: Nothing more than that? Good gracious!

EDWARD: Anyone here?

DORCAS *looks about the garden, but does not see* HALLAM *reclining in the alcove.*

DORCAS: No. No one here. Let's sit down.

EDWARD: There now—I've told you about war, and I've told you about laughter. Anything else?

DORCAS: Yes.

EDWARD: Well?

DORCAS: Love. Tell me—

EDWARD: What?

DORCAS: Tell me—can you love if you cannot see?

EDWARD: I can. (*He laughs.*) Bless me—

DORCAS: No! No, wait a moment and I'll explain what I mean. I can see— (*She pauses.*)

EDWARD: Yes?

DORCAS: I can see—oh, a thing or a person—and seeing I can say I love. But you—

EDWARD: You think that when I lost my sight I lost the power to love.

DORCAS: Yes. No! No, I don't think that. But I cannot understand how you can love anything new—unseen. Something that you didn't love before. How can you fall in love? As I have with you. *There is a pause.*

EDWARD: What did you say?

DORCAS: That I love you, Edward. (*There is a pause then she says quickly.*) I don't seem to be able to help it. I don't want to help it, anyway.

EDWARD: You love me?

DORCAS: Yes.

EDWARD: I love you, Dorcas.

DORCAS: Edward.

EDWARD: Dorcas. Where does your name come from, Dorcas?

DORCAS: I don't know. Timothy does. He sometimes calls me Tabitha. He says it's the same name but I hate it. But, Edward—no, stop laughing!—Edward, listen—I can *see you*. How can you love me when you don't know what I look like? I might be very ugly—I'm not!—but I might be.

EDWARD (*he laughs*): I know you're not.

DORCAS: But you can't know, Edward—you can't!

EDWARD: It is now the one thing in the whole world that I do know surely. That you are beautiful and I love you. (*He pauses.*) You don't love me.

DORCAS: I do!

EDWARD: Would you love me had you never seen me?

DORCAS: I think I've always loved you, Edward.

EDWARD: You see!

DORCAS (*she is laughing*): Yes, I see.

EDWARD: That is all you need. You don't need to know things like —well, where my nose is. Tell me, is your nose in the right place?

DORCAS: What do you mean?

EDWARD: In the middle of your face.

DORCAS: Of course.

  EDWARD *stretches out and takes her nose between his finger and thumb.*

EDWARD: So it is.

DORCAS: You're laughing at me!

EDWARD: Just a little. Mind you, it's very nice to know these things. What colour are your eyes?

DORCAS: Now, that's rather difficult to say. Let me think about it for a moment for I don't want to mislead you. (*She sits in silence.*) Hazel. Do you know the colour?

EDWARD: Yes. I remember what hazel looks like.

DORCAS: I should like to kiss you, Edward. (EDWARD *moves to her and very gently they kiss each other on the mouth.*) Oh, you look happy! You look—

EDWARD: I am happy. I love you.

DORCAS: I love you so I expect I look happy too. (*She kisses him.*) Are you going away from here?

EDWARD: Yes. To London, as I told you.

DORCAS: I don't think I want you to go away from here now. Will you return to me? I want you to return to me. Of course you must go.

EDWARD: You understand that?

DORCAS: Oh, yes—but come back. (*She pauses.*) Now I feel sad, is that love?

EDWARD: Yes.

> *Very faintly there is a bugle call from the beaches.* HESTER *comes from the house.*

HESTER: Ah, Dorcas. I never seem to be able to find you. What have you been doing?

DORCAS: Putting off childish ways.

HESTER: I see. (*To* EDWARD.) I'm Dorcas's mother. Don't be frightened. It is only my looks that are against me. Ask Dorcas. I'm afraid I'm not so imposing as I look, Mr

EDWARD: Sterne.

HESTER: Mr Sterne. Nature endowed me with the appearance of a frigate, so what you see you must necessarily admire if not immediately love.

DORCAS: Mr Sterne is blind, Mama.

HESTER: I'm sorry to hear that. Sit down, Mr Sterne. Is Dorcas making you happy?

EDWARD: Very happy, thank you.

DORCAS: I've something to tell you, Mama.

HESTER: And I've something to tell you. Is your news important?

DORCAS: Yes.

HESTER: So is mine. Now listen carefully. I have just heard from Lady Jerningham. She wants me to go and join the Amazon Corps she is forming in East Anglia. I am to command a Platoon. This means that—(LAMPRETT *and* JONATHAN *have wandered in from the orchard*.) Ah! Lamprett—

LAMPRETT: My dear?

HESTER: I am telling Dorcas—(TIMOTHY *comes from the house*.)—that I have heard from Lady Jerningham.

LAMPRETT: Such a pleasant woman.

HESTER: She wishes me to go up to East Anglia to command a Platoon in what she calls her Amazon Corps. It is being formed so that the women of England may exercise their natural power of command. I am to be a Sergeant-Major. Stand up straight, Lamprett.

LAMPRETT: Sorry, my dear.

HESTER: I shall be leaving almost immediately, this evening at the latest. I understand that there are recruits to be disciplined. Dorcas will look after the house in my absence. You understand, Dorcas?

DORCAS: Yes, Mama.

TIMOTHY: Are you going to wear uniform?

HESTER: Certainly.

TIMOTHY: Breeches, I suppose! Eh, Lamprett? (*He is seized by quite immoderate laughter*.)

HESTER: I understand that Lady Jerningham has designed the undress uniform herself. An undergarment in the shade of *fumée de Londres* with a cloak and cap of *grisantique*. In action, of course, we shall wear something very different.

LAMPRETT: And I'm sure you'll look very handsome.

BREEZE *comes in from the orchard*.

TIMOTHY: I wish something would happen. It distresses me to see everyone standing about like this when we might be getting on with the job of throwing the French into the sea. (LAMPRETT *is examining the poster bearing the stark word* 'INVASION'.) What's that? Another cattle sale?

LAMPRETT: No.

TIMOTHY *comes to beside* LAMPRETT *and sees the wording of the poster*.

TIMOTHY: Lamprett! (*He turns from the poster: then, spinning round, again transfixes it*.) It remains! Lamprett, can I believe my eyes?

LAMPRETT: You can.

TIMOTHY: But that's it, man!

LAMPRETT: Yes.

TIMOTHY: What I've been waiting for.

LAMPRETT: Yes.

TIMOTHY: The official instructions—I remember them well. Part Four, Section VIII: At the landing of enemy troops runners will pass through the countryside liberally distributing bills bearing the single word, INVASION. These bills may be purchased, price twopence each— (*He breaks off, removing his hat.*) Ladies and gentlemen, it is upon us. Like a thief in the night in broad daylight it is upon us. (*All stand in a reverent silence. Distantly from the direction of the coast, a bugle sounds a military call.* TIMOTHY *at the top of his voice shouts.*) Humpage!

HUMPAGE (*awake*): Sir!

TIMOTHY: Anything to report? Was that man asleep, can anyone tell me? Was he? Anything to report, Humpage?

HUMPAGE: Yes, sir.

TIMOTHY: Something in sight?

HUMPAGE: Yes, sir.

TIMOTHY: Something suspicious?

HUMPAGE: Oh, yes, sir!

TIMOTHY: Ships of war?

HUMPAGE: Oh, yes, yes, sir!

TIMOTHY: Troops?

HUMPAGE: Oh, sir—oh, sir—yes, yes, yes, sir! One, two, three, four, five— (*He continues to count aloud in a growing agony and panic as the scene proceeds.*)

TIMOTHY: Every man for himself!

LAMPRETT: What's that?

TIMOTHY: Every man for himself! (*He rushes into the house.*)

HUMPAGE: —thirty-seven, thirty-eight, thirty-nine, forty. Oh, God! Forty, forty-one, forty-two—

The action within the garden becomes confused. From the general activity the following can be heard.

LAMPRETT: Humpage!

HUMPAGE: —fifty-seven, fifty-eight—yes, sir?—fifty-nine, sixty—

LAMPRETT: You must on no account, allow this diversion to distract you from your primary duty.

HUMPAGE: No, sir—sixty-five, sixty-six, sixty-seven—

LAMPRETT: Fires, Humpage, fires!

HUMPAGE: Yes, sir. Seventy, seventy-one—

    BREEZE *speaks to* HUMPAGE.

BREEZE: You want to be careful up there, you know.

LAMPRETT: Don't distract him, if you please.

BREEZE: Sorry, sir.

LAMPRETT: No point in alarming him. We must all take our chance. What are you going to do?

BREEZE: I shall have to look after Mr Matthews.

LAMPRETT: Well, if you'll take my advice—

    HESTER *is speaking to* JONATHAN.

HESTER: Are you prepared to fight for your life, little boy? If we meet the enemy squarely, my dear, will he run away? Bless your innocent face, you're laughing! Is it at me? Or do you laugh at all of us? Let me confide something to you—

    DORCAS *is speaking to* EDWARD.

DORCAS ⎫
EDWARD ⎭ (*together*): Don't be frightened. (*They laugh.*)

DORCAS: Perhaps this will stop you from going away. I hope so.

EDWARD: You'd even have a battle to keep me with you?

DORCAS: Anything—anything! What is a battle!

EDWARD: The people here—what are they going to do?

DORCAS: Talk, I expect. We always do, every one of us.

    And indeed they are. HESTER *to* JONATHAN.

HESTER: —for that's what the old song tells us, and it is true, believe me. (*And, turning to* LAMPRETT.) Lamprett, what are your intentions?

LAMPRETT: What's that, my dear?

HESTER: Your intentions. What are they in this emergency?

LAMPRETT: To stand by, my dear, until required.

HESTER: And when will that be?

LAMPRETT: It will be when the first spark, flash, flame, scintillation, blaze or conflagration is reported. And then—

BREEZE: Excuse me, sir.

LAMPRETT: What is it?

BREEZE: Do you think it would be wise to wake Mr Matthews now?

LAMPRETT: Wake him?

BREEZE: He's sleeping at the moment and he does so dislike being woken. Could you again advise me, Mr Bellboys? Does the emergency warrant so grave a liberty?

LAMPRETT: As waking him? I should say so. Wouldn't you, my dear?

HESTER: Yes, Breeze. I think you may wake him.

BREEZE: Thank you, ma'am. (*He crosses to* HALLAM *and stands looking down at him.*)

HESTER: This will make it necessary for me to expedite my departure, Lamprett. At any moment you may be seeing the last of me.

LAMPRETT: I hope not, my dear.

HESTER: Temporarily, I mean.

LAMPRETT: I must have a word with Hallam. (*He goes to* HALLAM, *who, gently shaken by* BREEZE, *is coming to consciousness.*)

BREEZE: Excuse me, sir. The invasion.

HALLAM: Thank you, Sam. (*He discovers* LAMPRETT *standing over him.*)

LAMPRETT: Hallam!

HALLAM: My dear fellow?

LAMPRETT (*he holds out his hand*): Goodbye.

HALLAM: You're off?

LAMPRETT: Certainly not! I'm standing by.

HALLAM: Then why—?

LAMPRETT: The situation is grave.

HALLAM: Yes, yes! Goodbye.

LAMPRETT: The lieutenant of my brigade was burnt to a cinder two months ago in what was merely a civil conflagration. Don't tell the women.

HALLAM: About your lieutenant?

LAMPRETT: No, no. About the danger to me at the moment.

HALLAM: Of course. Not a word, I assure you.

LAMPRETT: Thank you.

> *They shake hands.* LAMPRETT *then salutes and marches away with* JONATHAN.

HUMPAGE: One hundred and fourteen—one hundred and fifteen!

HALLAM: What's that fellow doing?

BREEZE: Counting the enemy forces, I imagine.

HALLAM: Oh, dear!

BREEZE: Would you like to retire to a place of safety, sir?

HALLAM: I don't think so. I'm very comfortable here.

HESTER: What are you children going to do?

DORCAS: What do you suggest, Mama?

HESTER: I really don't know.

DORCAS: In that case we'll just sit here and wait for something to happen.

It does—in a tremendous cannonade from the beaches and, simultaneously, the appearance of TIMOTHY *in the doorway of the house. He is dressed for his impersonation of Bonaparte: the resemblance is very startling. Firmly grasped in his right hand is the French phrase book.*

TIMOTHY: Halte-là! Où est mon baton? Il n'est pas dans mon havresac! (*He roars with laughter.*) Good, eh? I'm really very pleased. But no nonsense! Humpage!

HUMPAGE: One hundred and sixteen.

TIMOTHY: One hundred and sixteen what?

HUMPAGE: Men, sir.

TIMOTHY: Nonsense! There are one hundred and seventy-five thousand men. You can't count, anyway—you know that. (*Again there is a bugle call from the beaches—followed this time by the rattle of musketry.*) Obviously no time to be lost. They are ashore. Humpage!

HUMPAGE: Sir!

TIMOTHY: You may ring the bell and put up the signals. I am ready.

HUMPAGE: Thank you, sir. (*He is galvanized into action.*)

The clangour of the great brass bell rings out. The signal flaps whirl and wave, finally coming to rest to show an ominous scarlet. LAMPRETT, *in uniform, rushes in with* JONATHAN.

LAMPRETT: No! Humpage! No! You'll call out the brigade! Ah! Damn the invasion.

HESTER: Lamprett!

LAMPRETT: Well, my dear, what shall I say to the men when they arrive?

TIMOTHY: If your men have any spirit they'll already be on the beaches fighting the French, and not waiting for you to show them some miserable little fire they can fight.

LAMPRETT: Oh, what a thing to say! My men are brave and good and true. Bless them! (*Then—very maliciously, he says:*) And if you, Timothy, think that by dressing yourself up as Lord Nelson—

TIMOTHY (*furious*): Lord Nelson!

LAMPRETT: —and running away—if you think by that you are helping your country, then I'm a Dutchman.

TIMOTHY: You're a damned ignorant fool, I know that. Anyway, I've no time for a row with you. Hallam!

LAMPRETT: Well, don't say horrid things about my brigade, then. (*He moves to* HESTER, *who consoles him.*)

TIMOTHY: Hallam!

HALLAM: Timothy?

TIMOTHY: You recall your promise?

HALLAM: My—

TIMOTHY (*he points to the well*): The initial part of the plan.

HALLAM: Yes, indeed.

TIMOTHY: I am quite ready. If you will take the handle, I will grasp the rope and stand in the bucket. On the command from me— lower! (HALLAM *has moved to the well and now miserably takes hold of the handle.*) Got it? (HALLAM *nods.*) Right! (TIMOTHY *puts both feet into the bucket and takes hold of the rope.* HALLAM *takes the strain of his weight.*) Am I clear?

HALLAM: I think so.

TIMOTHY: A last word to everyone. Should I not return there must be no tears. I go on this mission of my own free will, giving my services—

HALLAM: Timothy!

TIMOTHY: —to my country with a good heart. Those that have gone before me and those that will come after me—

HALLAM: Timothy!

TIMOTHY: What is it, Hallam?

HALLAM (*breathlessly*): Last words should be spoken before entering the bucket.

TIMOTHY: What? Oh, sorry! Well— (*He consults the phrase book.*) Au revoir, mes amis, au revoir. La! Descendons maintenant. (HALLAM *begins to lower.* TIMOTHY *and the bucket remain unmoving, the rope wreathing itself about* TIMOTHY.) Can you release me? I seem to be caught in something. (*In his little struggle,* TIMOTHY *glances at the sky. He is immediately transfixed.*) What's that?

   Everyone looks up: they are lost in wonder.

HUMPAGE: It's a balloon!

HESTER: Bless me! What a pretty thing!

DORCAS: Edward—an air-balloon—above us.

HUMPAGE: You'd never get me into one of them.

TIMOTHY: That's an idea. I like that (*He catches sight of* LAMPRETT: *he remembers.*) Lord Nelson! (*Suddenly he descends the well. There is a loud cry from everyone—followed by an explosion.*)

CURTAIN

ACT TWO

The scene is the same.

The time: later the same day.

The battle may have passed this way for there are sounds of military activity from a little way off. A drum rolls ominously and a voice shouts commands at intervals. Across the garden drifts a cloud of smoke and from an upper part of the house flies a tattered banner—a symbol of resistance it can only be supposed.

HUMPAGE *remains at his post.*

The garden is otherwise empty, but the fire-engine has been brought in. This stands at the ready, pulsating with the need for action. From the engine a length of hose runs out of the garden below the house.

After a moment LAMPRETT *appears rolling in the hose which he stores away on the engine. He adjusts a complication of valves: the engine becomes silent and still, and some kind of order is restored.* LAMPRETT *sits on the engine and looks hopefully at* HUMPAGE, *who shakes his head.*

LAMPRETT: Then we can but wait. For I'll not believe that this day —so-called Armageddon—can pass without our being needed. (JONATHAN *comes into the garden.* LAMPRETT *speaks to him.*) Nothing yet, I'm afraid. (JONATHAN *sits beside* LAMPRETT.) Could you grasp that lever there? Thank you. It controls something. I have to look after it like a child, you know. For example, the cold atmosphere makes the thing fret in a quite distressing manner. But today is very warm. (*He pauses.*) Ironic, isn't it, that the only place we have a fire is inside the engine. But I've long ceased to believe in the art of reasoning. When I was a young man at the university I studied logic and it lead to dreadful conclusions. Such fearful results came from attempting to arrange my thoughts. No, I cannot tell you! However, on some subjects my mind is clear. (*The* MAIDSERVANT *has come into the garden from the house carrying the necessities for a picnic meal, which she proceeds to lay out on the ground.*) I'm an example of the man of learning turned man of action by necessity. Yet, I will confess, there are times when I'm tempted to retire, put up my feet, draw my cap over my eyes and let the world burn away around me.

HESTER *comes from the house.*

HESTER: Pippin!

MAID: Yes, ma'am?

HESTER: As much food as possible, I think. We cannot tell how many we shall be called upon to feed and succour on a day like this.

MAID: Very good, ma'am.

HESTER: I thought, Lamprett, we'd eat out here. A fine, if rather noisy day. I don't want people tramping all over the house, you know.

LAMPRETT. Quite right.

HESTER: We should have eaten before this but the household arrangements are a little awry. Forgive me.

LAMPRETT: More than understandable in the circumstances.

HESTER: Thank you, my dear. (*She is looking at the fire-engine.*)

LAMPRETT: Is the engine in your way?

HESTER: Well, perhaps—

LAMPRETT: Yes, I can see you wish me to move it.

HESTER: We are all aware of its usefulness. But at meal times, do you think—

LAMPRETT: Very well. (LAMPRETT *and* JONATHAN *move the engine from the garden.*)

HESTER: Pippin, run into the house. You'll find some wine in the cooler. Bring it to me. (*The* MAID *goes into the house.* HESTER *sits on the ground beside the picnic meal.*) There is great comfort, I find, in resorting to good food during a crisis. Man's behaviour to man would be less ungenerous if everyone ate regular meals. For when conversation fails how much better to resort to the knife and fork than to the sword and trumpet.

HUMPAGE: Are you speaking to me?

HESTER: Not necessarily. (LAMPRETT *returns with* JONATHAN.) Come along. Everything is ready.

LAMPRETT: How charming! It would appear it takes a siege to return us to the pleasures of our youth.

HESTER: Indeed, it must be thirty years, Lamprett, since you and I sat together in the sun.

LAMPRETT: There has been much to do in that time. Come, little boy, don't be shy.

HESTER: Join us, please.

JONATHAN *joins them at the meal. The* MAID *comes from the house, carrying the wine.*

LAMPRETT: Ah! You anticipate my wishes. A glass of wine to rinse from me the staleness of approaching age. Have some, little boy—

HESTER: With water!

LAMPRETT: —but always remember—'Drink not the third glass—which thou canst not tame when once it is within thee.'

They laugh gently at the child. The MAID *returns to the house.*

HESTER: Tell me, Lamprett, is it reprehensible that we should enjoy a moment's peace?

LAMPRETT: I should say not, my dear. Let us enjoy it whilst we can. You may be assured we shall be brought to rude fact at any moment by some disgraceful incident.

HESTER: Which reminds me to ask you something. But first—I'll just take the merrythought from the chicken.

LAMPRETT: These bouches are delicious. What was it you wished to ask?

HESTER: Concerning rude fact, I fear.

LAMPRETT: Never mind. We must face it.

HUMPAGE: Excuse me.

HESTER: What was at the bottom of the well?

HUMPAGE: Excuse me.

LAMPRETT: What is it? (*To* HESTER.) Harsh reality, alas, is ever with us.

HUMPAGE: Might I have some form of protection?

LAMPRETT: Protection against what?

HUMPAGE: Missiles, I think they're called.

LAMPRETT: Are you being shot at? At this very moment—are you being shot at?

HUMPAGE: No, sir.

LAMPRETT: But you think it may happen soon?

HUMPAGE: Yes, sir. And I fear for my life.

LAMPRETT *takes a dish from among the picnic, empties it, and carries it to* HUMPAGE.

LAMPRETT: Try wearing this. It will afford you some kind of protection.

HUMPAGE: Yes, sir.

LAMPRETT: You cannot expect both to look handsome and be safe, can you?

HUMPAGE: No, sir.

LAMPRETT: Is it comfortable?

HUMPAGE: No, sir.

LAMPRETT: But you think it will do?

HUMPAGE: Yes, sir.

LAMPRETT: Good. (*An afterthought.*) It doesn't obscure your vision, does it?

HUMPAGE: No, sir.

LAMPRETT (*a second afterthought*): It is a saucepan, you know.

HUMPAGE: Yes, sir. (*He adjusts the headgear.*)

LAMPRETT: Must look after the servants in this business. Quite incapable of doing so themselves. You were saying, my dear—before that absurd interruption by Humpage complaining of the danger of his somewhat exposed position? (*He glances at* HUMPAGE *who is immediately suffused by shame.*) You were saying?—

HESTER: I asked—what was at the bottom of the well?

LAMPRETT: Darkness and dirt, and a most peculiar, rather interesting smell.

HESTER: No water?

LAMPRETT: Oh, dear no!

HESTER: And, as you said, no Timothy.

LAMPRETT: Not a sign of him.

HESTER: May I say, Lamprett, that I consider you showed the most admirable courage in volunteering to descend the well in search of Timothy.

LAMPRETT: Well, after all, he is my brother. And it provided an excuse for doing something I've always wanted to do.

HESTER: Descend the well?

LAMPRETT: Yes. Now I have, so to speak, broken the ice I may make it a regular habit.

HESTER: Have you any idea what Timothy is about?

LAMPRETT: No idea at all.

HESTER: What was the purpose of the uniform he was wearing?

LAMPRETT: Ah, that! Foolish of me to mistake it for an impersonation of Lord Nelson—it was obviously the uniform of the Consular Service. From that we can draw but one conclusion.

HESTER: Which is—?

LAMPRETT: That he is attempting to escape the country.

There is a loud explosion a little way off.

HESTER: Do you think we shall ever see him again?

LAMPRETT: I very much doubt that. It would appear that he was successful in getting away. I shall, of course, take over the administration of the estate from today and—(*Through the open orchard gate there rolls, very slowly, a cannon-ball. It traverses the garden and comes to rest at* LAMPRETT'S *feet.*)—I may say that under my direction—

HESTER: What is that?

LAMPRETT: A cannon-ball, my dear. Under my direction things here will be very different. I've never agreed to the subordination of certain public services, such as the fire brigade, to ephemeral activities such as agriculture. My views—(*There is a loud explosion.*)—will now be put into practice and I think we can look forward—(*Through the open gate a second cannon-ball comes fairly bounding into the garden. It comes to rest by the first.*)—to an era which will be without parallel—

HESTER: Lamprett!

LAMPRETT: My dear?

HESTER: Shut the gate.

He does so, saying:

LAMPRETT: —an era without parallel in the history of the county.

HESTER: Where is everyone?

LAMPRETT: Whom do you mean by everyone?

HESTER: Well, Dorcas and her blind soldier. And Hallam—Hallam Matthews, where is he?

LAMPRETT: The last I saw of him was when he was being led away by his servant after his regrettable behaviour with Timothy and the well. I've no idea where they were making for. (HALLAM *and* BREEZE *come into the garden from the orchard.*) But wherever it was, they are returned.

HALLAM: Hester. Lamprett.

HESTER: How are you, Hallam?

HALLAM: Shaken, but recovering.

HESTER: I'm pleased to hear that.

HALLAM: What is happening?

LAMPRETT: At the moment? Well, the battle—if it can be called such—appears to have moved somewhat to the west. With regards to the general situation it is fluid. Anything may happen.

HALLAM: Oh, dear!

LAMPRETT: Don't fret, my dear fellow. I am now in charge

HALLAM: Any sign of Timothy?

LAMPRETT: None. Apparently he was successful in his escape.

HALLAM: Escape! No, no, my dear Lamprett, you have mis-understood his intentions.

LAMPRETT: I think not—

HALLAM: But I can assure you—

LAMPRETT: No more, if you please! The subject is delicate. What I do not understand is this: an invasion in force but no fires. Not one. I cannot believe that Bonaparte and his Generals can have underestimated the effect upon a civil population of a good whole-some blaze. But that is apparently the case. Not a fire within sight. (*Shouting*.) Is there, Humpage?

HUMPAGE: No, sir.

LAMPRETT: Although how you should know with that pot crammed over your eyes in that preposterous fashion is beyond me! (HUMPAGE *prises the saucepan from his forehead*.) Better! Any-thing to report?

HUMPAGE: No, sir.

LAMPRETT (*to* HALLAM): You see?

HALLAM: I admit that things seem unnaturally quiet.

LAMPRETT: The lull, perhaps, before the storm.

HALLAM: Please don't say that!

DORCAS *and* EDWARD *come in from the orchard.*

DORCAS: Ah, Mama! Have you recovered Uncle Timothy yet?

HESTER: Don't be frivolous, my dear.

DORCAS: La! Descendons maintenant! Bump! (*She laughs*.)

HALLAM: Oh, horrid, horrid, heartless child.

DORCAS: Do the present remarkable and unforeseen circumstances upset your plans, dear Mama?

LAMPRETT: What's the child saying?

DORCAS: A simple question, Papa. Does the loss of Uncle Timothy prevent Mama from taking up her duties as Sergeant-Major to the Amazons of Norfolk? Or do we all, in that very English way, refuse to admit that 'Something has happened' and proceed to carry on as if nothing ever could—happen, I mean—that we didn't ourselves decree?

HESTER: Whatever is the matter with you, Dorcas?

DORCAS: I'm happy, Mama.

HESTER: That's no excuse for talking the most utter nonsense.

DORCAS: But there's no excuse for anything, Mama, is there, ever.

HALLAM: Hadn't you better lie down for a while?

DORCAS: A very immodest suggestion, Mr Matthews, in the circumstances. I'm in love.

HALLAM: God bless my soul!

LAMPRETT: This is no time to be falling in love, Dorcas. At any other time—yes, yes!—your mother and I would be only too pleased, but now there is much to be done. (*He speaks to* JONATHAN.) Come with me, little boy.

DORCAS: Where are you taking Jonathan?

LAMPRETT: I'm instructing him in the rudimentary principles of fire-fighting. He knows nothing about it. Quite ignorant. It is ridiculous this business of not letting children play with fire when they are babies. (*He goes out with* JONATHAN.)

HESTER: Hallam, I'm wondering if I might borrow your servant, Breeze, for a short while.

HALLAM: Most certainly, my dear Hester, but take care not to damage him.

HESTER: The reason is this: among the accoutrements Lady Jermingham has sent to me is a large brass breastplate. This is in a quite shockingly dilapidated condition. It occurred to me that Breeze might be the very person to refurbish it.

BREEZE: Certainly, ma'am.

HALLAM: That's right, Sam. Go with Mrs Bellboys and do your best. What is your experience with breastplates?

BREEZE: Very limited, sir.

HALLAM: Never mind. Do all you can.

HESTER: None of us can do more.

> BREEZE *follows* HESTER *into the house.*

HALLAM: I am contemplating the effect on my digestion of eating during a battle. (*He fusses over the little meal before him.*)

DORCAS: Mr Matthews—

HALLAM: Yes?

DORCAS: Mr Matthews, you're not really so deeply concerned about yourself, are you?

HALLAM (*he smiles*): No.

DORCAS: I know you're not. Then why—

HALLAM: Yes?

DORCAS: I mean to say—why pretend?

HALLAM: What an inquisitive child you are! You must learn to accept things—attitudes—especially if you're going to be in love. More important then than at any other time: for love itself is only

a delicious pose to gain for ourselves the comfort we all so deeply
need.

DORCAS: Oh, I know all about love—

HALLAM: You do?

DORCAS: —yes—but what has been puzzling me is why you play
the fool all the time.

HALLAM: Everyone does so.

DORCAS: Nonsense!

HALLAM: Everyone attempts to be other than they are.

DORCAS: I don't believe it. What about the saints?

HALLAM: Worse than any. It is clowning, you know. A most
consequent factor of life.

EDWARD (*he speaks to* DORCAS): He means, I think, that we find
the reality unbearable. That factor within us—ah!—the infrangible
burden to carry: self-knowledge. And so we escape, childlike, into
the illusion. We clown and posture but not to amuse others—no—
to comfort ourselves. The laughter is incidental to the tragic
spectacle of each man attempting to hide his intolerable self.

HALLAM: In arguments you treat me as a museum piece which
occasionally needs dusting, eh?

EDWARD (*he laughs*): Bless you! I may be wrong. What we call the
illusion—you and I—which is the laughter and the happiness and
the sudden flowering of love, perhaps that is the reality. Who
knows and—by God! today who cares? (*He swings* DORCAS *up in
his arms, laughing.*) Do you love me?

DORCAS: Yes.

EDWARD: How much?

DORCAS: That much.

EDWARD: Not enough.

DORCAS: No?

EDWARD: To defend me against myself.

HALLAM (*observing them*): We fight even our love from a catena of
unprepared positions retiring ever deeper upon ourselves. The
battle lost, we pretend the sacred citadel taken by the enemy is
nothing more than a paper palace.

DORCAS: Oh, do be quiet, Mr Matthews! (DORCAS *and* EDWARD,
their heads together begin to whisper and laugh. HALLAM *continues.*)

HALLAM: Rather than reveal our human imperfections we will turn
ourselves, even for the beloved, into a fair-booth from which we
offer for sale at extravagant cost the gayest and most useless toys.

We cry our wares hoping the naked baby cowering at the back of the booth will not be noticed. We never give up our rattles: our thumbs will go to our mouths on our death-beds. (*There is a pause:* DORCAS *and* EDWARD *still whisper together.*) Dorcas?

DORCAS: Yes?

HALLAM: Go a little way off.

DORCAS: Why?

HALLAM: Don't ask questions. Just go a little way off for a little while.

DORCAS: Something I shouldn't hear?

HALLAM: Yes. (*Then he smiles.*) Remember, I told you that the clowns must sometimes sit in the sun and gossip. Go, for a moment.

DORCAS: All right. (*She wanders away.*)

HALLAM: You will not think badly of me?

EDWARD: If you destroy my illusion? No, I am accustomed to destruction. Go on.

HALLAM: The King—

EDWARD: You know His Majesty?

HALLAM: Yes. He is not in London at the moment. He is, I understand, at Weymouth, sea-bathing.

EDWARD: I shall await his return.

HALLAM: If you do you will find him—how shall I put it?—oh, he will see you, my dear Sterne, he will see you. He will be, alas, his very kind and charming self. He will ask you innumerable questions every one of which he will answer for you. He will grant any request you may care to put to him, fully and without qualification. But it will be no good, Sterne, it will be no good.

EDWARD: Why not?

HALLAM: Because—dear, sweet, kindly soul—he is not quite right in the head. At the moment we refer to his eccentricity. In a few years we shall call it something else.

EDWARD: But he's the King of England!

HALLAM: Yes.

EDWARD: But, I say, he is the King of England.

HALLAM: Is the illusion so great?

EDWARD: I didn't know.

HALLAM: Very few do. (*There is a pause.*) She is waiting for you.

EDWARD: Dorcas?

HALLAM: Yes.

EDWARD: Why did you send her away?

HALLAM: Because, Mr Sterne, you will go to London, you will see His Majesty and you may—you may very well be the instrument that will stop this war.

EDWARD: In spite of what you have told me?

HALLAM: In spite of anything I might have told you. (*He calls.*) Dorcas!

She returns to EDWARD. JONATHAN *has come into the garden.*

DORCAS: Have you finished with my beloved?

HALLAM: Yes. Yes.

EDWARD: Thank you, Mr Matthews.

HALLAM: Off you go. You don't need me. (EDWARD *and* DORCAS *move across the garden.* JONATHAN, *standing beside them as they pass, for a moment, stretches out a hand towards them. But, of course, he is unseen by* EDWARD *and even, in her own blindness, by* DORCAS. *They go out by the gateway and the boy stares after them* HALLAM, *now by the alcove, speaks to him.*) What is it? Didn't they see you? (*The boy shakes his head.*) Well, you're really very small, you know. Hasn't that got anything to do with it? You're right, it hasn't. But you mustn't be hurt: upset. Come here. (*The boy, unmoving, again shakes his head.*) Now, why not? Do you think I'm going to talk to you? To try to tell you why—why—why things happen. Do I look like a great talker? I suppose I do: I am. But come here. We'll sit together in absolute silence. Or do you like music to pass the time? (HALLAM *takes from an inner pocket a tiny pipe—a recorder— ludicrously small in comparison with his bulk. He plays a snatch of a hornpipe. The child turns to him.*) An unexpected accomplishment, eh? (*He continues to play and then holds out the pipe to* JONATHAN.) Try. (JONATHAN, *taking the pipe, blows a single note.*) Were someone to overlook us now they would take it that Innocence conversed with Experience. In that latter part what can I say to you? I feel I should say something, don't you? The situation requires it. Very well, then: retain the defensive weapons of your childhood always, my dear. They are invaluable, these delights and amusements. They are many, too. And all so simple. Indeed, what is this? Only a wooden pipe with some holes in it. But thrust a current of air through it—there is a sound—and you smile and smile as you are smiling now. What is more—

GEORGE SELINCOURT, *accompanied by three of his fencibles—the Reverend* JOSEPH BROTHERHOOD, JAMES GIDDY *and* RUFUS

PIGGOTT—*marches into the garden. They are, each one of them, in a state of considerable alarm and confusion. Each is armed to a certain degree: there is not an element of uniformity about their clothes.* GEORGE SELINCOURT *shepherds them forward, crying out.*

SELINCOURT: Now, please, gentlemen, please! Sort yourselves out! The first principle of modern warfare is to accept an unexpected occurrence with equity, dignity and discipline. Discipline, Piggott! (PIGGOTT *is greeting* HUMPAGE *with enthusiasm.*) And we do not consort with members of other units. Now, then. (*The tiny Corps is lined up and now stands to attention.*) Oh, good! Very, very good! (SELINCOURT, *for only a moment, is lost in admiration.*) Your hat, Reverend Sir—(*He speaks to* BROTHERHOOD.)—perhaps just a trifle forward. (BROTHERHOOD *adjusts his hat.*) Excellent! Excellent! Now, gentlemen, the situation which has arisen has quite confounded my original plans for today. I have therefore rearranged my notions with speed and skill. The mark of the modern soldier, gentlemen. Giddy!

GIDDY: Sir!

SELINCOURT: You will mount guard over this gate. (GIDDY *falls out to take up his place.*) Piggott!

PIGGOTT: What?

SELINCOURT: You will mount guard on some object over there. (PIGGOTT *falls out to take up his place.*) And you, Reverend Sir, will you be so kind as to keep an eye on the front door of this house. (BROTHERHOOD *takes up this position.*) This, gentlemen, is to prevent any possible attack on my rear. Ever vulnerable according to the textbooks. (*He regards his men.*) Excellent—excellent!

From the alcove, whilst speaking to JONATHAN, HALLAM'S *voice is raised.*

HALLAM: —and there, my dear, you find the music of civilised conversation. The counter-point of voices, the fugue of argument, the bravura passage—in cadenza—myself, for example—the coda of peroration. Magnificent! We must guard—(SELINCOURT *has approached the alcove, but in his excessive wariness he now trips and tumbles headlong at* HALLAM'S *feet.* HALLAM *acknowledges his presence but continues to speak to* JONATHAN.)—we must guard our right to practise this. Will you remain such a silent boy, I wonder?

SELINCOURT: Excuse me—

HALLAM: Yes?

SELINCOURT: You are the gentleman I saw earlier today.

HALLAM: Am I?

SELINCOURT: You are.

HALLAM: You must forgive me but I cannot recall ever having seen you in my life before.

SELINCOURT: Come, come! Only a little time ago I saw you.

HALLAM: You did, sir?

SELINCOURT: And now I want to see you again.

HALLAM: And so you shall. Can I help you up?

SELINCOURT: No, no! I can manage. (*He gets up.*) First, I must ask you not to be afraid of, or intimidated by, my fencibles.

HALLAM: Certainly not. You may rest assured on that point. (*A pause.*) Where are they? (SELINCOURT *indicates* BROTHERHOOD, GIDDY *and* PIGGOTT. HALLAM *peers from the alcove.*) Ah, yes. Fencibles, eh? Is that all you have?

SELINCOURT: No, indeed not! There are ninety-six at the ready on the beaches and cliffs, every one alert, crafty and massively courageous. The gentlemen you see here are my personal body-guard. Mr Matthews—

HALLAM: That is my name.

SELINCOURT: Mr Matthews, at our previous meeting today I grievously misled you.

HALLAM: I'm very sorry to hear that.

SELINCOURT: Through no fault of my own, may I add?

HALLAM: No, no!

SELINCOURT: The fact is—

HALLAM: Yes?

SELINCOURT: Shall I come straight to the point?

HALLAM: Please do.

SELINCOURT: Time is short.

HALLAM: Yes, indeed.

SELINCOURT: Very well, then. This that you hear—(*Obligingly, in the distance, there is a roll of drums and a bugle call.*)—this is no elementary exercise in tactics, no mere manoeuvre, but the Real Thing!

HALLAM: You mean—

SELINCOURT: I mean, sir, that Napoleon Bonaparte has landed in England!

There is a suitable pause.

HALLAM: You've seen him?

SELINCOURT: No, not myself. But Mr Brotherhood, here, has seen him in circumstances which—but he might care to explain himself. He is the local Rector, you know. Mr Brotherhood! (BROTHERHOOD *comes forward.*) Tell your story again, Mr Brotherhood.

BROTHERHOOD *proceeds to do so in a commendably military manner.*

BROTHER.: Sir: whilst sitting at a point of vantage on the cliff top and partaking of a small alfresco meal—

SELINCOURT: I provide my men with rations for the field.

HALLAM: Bravo!

SELINCOURT: At my own expense, of course. Proceed, Mr Brotherhood.

BROTHER.: —an alfresco meal which I was interested to note was wrapped in some pages of George Herbert's poems, I was suddenly confronted by what, at first, I took to be an apparition. This fiend seemed to rise from the ground before my eyes. I was about to pronounce an exorcism when the creature shouted: 'Me voici, Monsieur!' The combination of the French tongue and sudden recognition of the uniform worn gave me to understand that I was confronted by none other than the French Emperor, Bonaparte.

HALLAM (*fascinated*): What did you do?

BROTHER.: I ran at once to my superior officer.

SELINCOURT: That's me. We returned to the place together and there was no sign of anyone. But—and I think this important— someone had stolen Mr Brotherhood's bag of biscuits.

HALLAM: Was Bonaparte alone when you saw him, Mr Brotherhood?

SELINCOURT: Ah! That is the confusing point. Bonaparte has landed here, but where are his men?

HALLAM: I can honestly disclaim that I'm concealing them.

SELINCOURT: A confusing point, but I have the solution.

HALLAM: Yes?

SELINCOURT: His men are under the sea.

HALLAM: *Under* the sea!

SELINCOURT: Yes. Bonaparte, intrepid fellow that he is—we must admit that—come, in fairness we must admit it—Bonaparte has come ashore to spy out the lie of the land. His armies wait for his signal and then when it is given they will pour from the tunnel in their thousands.

HALLAM: Tunnel, sir!

SELINCOURT: The tunnel beneath the sea, Mr Matthews. You must have read your newspapers. The method of Bonaparte's arrival has long been a matter for conjecture. Some—and I must admit myself to have once been of their number—some favoured the monster bridge to have been constructed by his engineers. A vast project thrown across the breadth of the Channel, and over which Bonaparte's armies would have marched in their thousands. You may return to your post, Reverend Sir.

BROTHER.: Sir! (*He goes back to the door of the house and takes up a defensive attitude.*)

SELINCOURT: Another school of thought—profoundly unimaginative—took it that he would transport his armies on a series of giant rafts (*He whispers.*) Mr Brotherhood once confided to me that he was of the opinion that by some diabolical power the French would walk to England.

HALLAM: On the water?

SELINCOURT: Yes.

HALLAM: God bless my soul!

SELINCOURT: He's a very good man: he believes in the Devil. The last conjecture—which we can now substantiate as fact—was that Bonaparte would arrive through a vast tunnel bored beneath the sea. This he has done. His armies doubtless wait below for his signal. (*He looks at the ground with some satisfaction.*) Rather like standing on a volcano, isn't it?

HALLAM: Then all, I take it, is lost.

SELINCOURT: Certainly not!

HALLAM: What are you going to do?

BREEZE *has come into the garden from the house.*

BREEZE: Mr Matthews, sir.

HALLAM: Just a moment, Sam. (*To* SELINCOURT.) What you going to do?

SELINCOURT: All that is necessary. I told you that the French armies await a signal from their Emperor.

HALLAM: Yes.

SELINCOURT: That signal will never be given. We shall prevent it. We shall catch him—oh, yes, by heaven!—the hunt is up and we shall catch him. Meantime, I've given instructions for the signal fires to be lighted. There they are, burning well. One, two, three, four—and there goes another—and yet another. (LAMPRETT *runs into the garden. He is properly accoutred, wearing his helmet and carrying another in his hand. He sees* JONATHAN *and, going to him, crams the second helmet on the wretched child's head before snatching him up. He then goes out at a run with the boy literally tucked beneath his arm.* SELINCOURT *has observed this: he shakes his head.*) First sign of panic. (*He turns to* HALLAM.) As for your accepted duties, Mr Matthews, I have your materials here.

HALLAM: I beg your pardon?

SELINCOURT *has taken a large roll of invasion posters from* GIDDY.

SELINCOURT: You will remember—(*He unrolls a poster before* HALLAM.)—and my plea is: run, Mr Matthews, run! Through every town, village and hamlet spread the news with feverish haste. Run, Mr Matthews, run till you drop! Twelve shillings.

HALLAM: What's that?

SELINCOURT: There are one hundred posters. At the authorized reduction, that is twelve shillings. (HALLAM *produces a sovereign.*) I've no change.

HALLAM: Neither have I.

SELINCOURT: I'll owe it to you. (*He takes the sovereign leaving* HALLAM *clasping the bundle of posters.*) We must be off! Squad! (*The* FENCIBLES *assemble in some kind of order.*) Off we go!

And off they go except the Reverend MR BROTHERHOOD, *who lags behind to ask:*

BROTHER.: Are you Hallam Matthews, author of 'A Critical Enquiry into the Nature of Ecclesiastical Cant'?

HALLAM: 'With a Supplementary Dissertation on Lewd Lingo.' Yes, I am.

BROTHER.: You should be ashamed! (*Then he, too, is gone.*)

BREEZE: Can I relieve you of those, sir.

HALLAM: What's that, Sam? Oh, yes, thank you very much. (*He gives the roll of posters to* BREEZE.)

BREEZE: Forgive me if I anticipate, sir, but do you wish me to run through the countryside with a feverish haste?

HALLAM: No, Sam, I don't want you to do anything of the kind.

BREEZE: I overheard your conversation with that gentleman, sir. I was just inside that door. I wasn't going to show myself, but I saw you were getting into difficulties.

HALLAM: God bless you, Sam.

BREEZE: I suppose it's Sir Timothy they've seen, sir, and mistaken him, as is only natural in that get-up, for Boney.

HALLAM: I suppose so. And yet—
They stare at each other.

BREEZE: I know what you're thinking, sir. Suppose it isn't Sir Timothy they've seen. Suppose—

HALLAM: Bonaparte has really landed.

BREEZE: That's what you were thinking, wasn't it, sir?

HALLAM: Of course not! Don't be a fool, Sam! From a tunnel! Do you read the newspapers?

BREEZE: Yes, sir. And they said it was a likelihood.

HALLAM: No, Sam, no! I shall go mad if you put such ideas into my head. We must work on the assumption that it is Sir Timothy these fellows have seen.

BREEZE: Very good, sir.
There is a distant call: Hulloa!

HALLAM: Now, what are we going to do. Have you any suggestions?

BREEZE: Well, sir, it seems to me that the best thing we can do is to get hold of Sir Timothy and keep him quiet until this thing blows over.

HALLAM: I defer to you, Sam. But surely—correct me if I am wrong—surely the point is this: where is Timothy?

BREEZE: That is the point, sir.
Again comes the cry: Hulloa!

HALLAM: I suppose the only thing to do—

BREEZE: Just a minute, sir. Did you hear anything?

HALLAM: No.

BREEZE: I thought I heard—
Again: Hulloa there!

HALLAM: Yes! Yes, indeed.

BREEZE: Oh, what a fool I am! (*He goes to the well, and looking down, calls:*) Hullo, down there! (*He is joined by* HALLAM, *they peer into the well.*)

TIMOTHY: No, no! Hullo, up here, if you please! (*He is above them in the gondola of a gaily painted balloon. He is very happy.*)

HALLAM: Oh, my God!

TIMOTHY: Fortunes of war! Captured from the enemy with amazing astuteness. Do I flatter myself? No, I do not.
HESTER *comes from the house.*

HESTER: Oh, so you're back.

HALLAM: Do you never tread the surface of this earth nowadays, Tim?

TIMOTHY: What an invention! The French have ideas about war. We cannot deny it. Humpage!

HUMPAGE: Sir!

TIMOTHY: May I inform you that in your present position you are completely out of date.

HUMPAGE: Thank you, sir.

TIMOTHY: Hallam, my dear fellow, would you care to come up with me for a while.

HALLAM: Never!

TIMOTHY: You must move with the times. Do you know, I can now literally have my head in the clouds.

HESTER: Where did you get it?

TIMOTHY: From the enemy. Found it in a field being guarded by one French soldier. Typical specimen, unshaven and dirty, armed with a form of bill-hook. Didn't appear to understand his own language. I spoke to him—with kindness, you know—and asked him where he came from. 'C'est à Bordeaux que vous avez été élevé, je crois, n'est-ce-pas?' I said. The fellow just stared at me, his mouth wide open like an idiot, and then ran away. I suppose he'd never seen an Emperor before. Then I jumped in here, released the anchor, and took to the air. But to national affairs. Hallam, come a little closer. I wish to be secret.

> BREEZE *comes forward.*

BREEZE: Now then, sir, don't you think it would be rather nice if you were to get out of that balloon and come and have a lie down for a while? I'm sure things are going very well at the moment, and so you can take a little time off.

TIMOTHY: You're quite right. Things are going exceedingly well. But I must not spare myself. I'm needed in the thick of it.

HESTER: Do be careful, Timothy.

BREEZE: I feel you should conserve your energy, sir, for the last great effort.

TIMOTHY: Which is almost upon us, my dear fellow. No, no! I must go on, weary as I am. I could do with a little refreshment. I've had nothing but a few biscuits since breakfast.

BREEZE: Well, you get down from there, sir, and I'll go into the house and see what I can find.

TIMOTHY: You do that, but I must remain here ready for instant departure.

HALLAM: It's no good, Sam, no good at all.

TIMOTHY: When I have reported I shall be away again.

HALLAM (*suddenly shouting*): Timothy, get out of that balloon at once!

BREEZE: Now, now, sir, that's not going to help.

HALLAM: I'm sorry, Sam.

TIMOTHY: Tell the family that I am well—desperately tired but well and, as yet, unharmed. I have made contact with the enemy troops twice, and a more slovenly, cowardly, uncouth crew I never did see. I don't know why there's been all this fuss about encountering Bonaparte's much-vaunted army.

BREEZE: Probably, sir, because—

TIMOTHY: Oh, we shan't have any difficulty finishing them off by nightfall. Now then, is there anything else? I don't think so. I brought this report back because I didn't want any of you to worry about me. Tell the others, will you, Hallam. Yes, I think that's all. Stand clear! I am about to ascend! (*He begins involved and useless activity about the gondola of the balloon.* HESTER *returns to the house.*)

HALLAM: Well, Sam?

BREEZE: Well, sir?

HALLAM: This is an unexpected development.

BREEZE: Yes, sir.

HALLAM: There can be no harm in it, I suppose.

BREEZE: Not a bit, sir. The old gentleman will be as safe as houses up there. In a couple of days we can send to fetch him from round about Chichester.

HALLAM: Better than the tunnel, do you think.

BREEZE: Oh, much better, sir. I shouldn't let him go down there again, if I were you.

TIMOTHY: Hallam—

HALLAM: My dear fellow?

TIMOTHY: Can you see anything which might control levitation or propulsion?

HALLAM: Throw something out. Yourself, for example.

TIMOTHY *jumps up and down in the gondola. This has no effect. There is a bugle call from the beaches.*

TIMOTHY: They're on the move! The French armies! No time to be lost! (*He stares about the balloon in impotent fury.*) Damned useless object! (*Then.*) Humpage!

HUMPAGE: Sir!

TIMOTHY: Pull that thing there and see what happens. (*He points to a ratline from the balloon swinging dangerously near to* HUMPAGE'S *head.* HUMPAGE *hesitates*.) Well, go on, man—pull it!

HUMPAGE *does so. The balloon begins to descend.* TIMOTHY *in sudden realization of this, turns on* HUMPAGE.

TIMOTHY: You've broken it!

HALLAM (*to* BREEZE): He has, you know.

TIMOTHY: You've let all the—whatever it was filled with—out! (HUMPAGE *gives another tug at the rope*.) Oh, leave it alone. (*He suddenly understands the exact situation. He is descending the well*.) But I don't want to go down here again!

HUMPAGE: We don't want you to go, sir.

TIMOTHY: Then do something!

Nothing is done. TIMOTHY, *in the gondola of the balloon, descends the well.* SELINCOURT *enters*.

SELINCOURT: Some fool is going round putting out all my signal fires!

HALLAM: That must be so awkward.

SELINCOURT: Awkward! It's disastrous! I'm very, very angry.

HALLAM: Oh, dear!

SELINCOURT: Do you know anything about it?

HALLAM: Nothing—nothing.

SELINCOURT: One man and a little boy ruining everything! (*During this the balloon has gently risen from the well, the gondola empty of* TIMOTHY, *and begins to float away.* SELINCOURT *notices this*.) What's that?

HALLAM: A balloon.

SELINCOURT: Yours?

HALLAM: No, yours.

SELINCOURT: Ah, yes. Keep an eye on it. (*He runs from the garden to return immediately*.) I'd better tell you. In a moment we are sealing the entrance to the tunnel.

HALLAM: How?

SELINCOURT: With a ton of explosive. (*He goes out*.)

HALLAM: A ton of explosive! Quickly, Sam! (*They move to the well*.) Come back to us, Timothy!

BREEZE: Don't alarm him, sir.

HALLAM: I thought, perhaps, a word of encouragement—

BREEZE: Not at the moment. (*He calls down the well*.) Sir Timothy!

HALLAM: I'd give half my debts to hear that voice again. Come, Sam, one last great effort.

Together they shout down the well.

BREEZE: I fear it's useless, sir.

HALLAM: You have done me a disservice, Sam.

BREEZE: I'm sorry, sir.

HALLAM: In allowing me to carry the joke too far.

In the distance there is a blast on a trumpet. SELINCOURT *shouts.*

SELINCOURT: Stand back! One-two-three-four-five-six.

There is a tremendous reverberating explosion a short way off: also great pandemonium from the FENCIBLES *which fades in the distance.*

HALLAM: Is there anything we can do, Sam?

BREEZE: It doesn't look like it, sir.

But they go off in the direction of the explosion as the MAIDSERVANT *comes from the house.*

MAID: Oh, you're still there, Mr Humpage.

HUMPAGE: Yes, my dear.

MAID: There was a noise, but if you're still there everything must be all right.

HUMPAGE: From the way things are going I shall be up here until the end of time.

MAID: You're the bravest man I know, Mr Humpage.

HUMPAGE: Thank you, my dear.

HESTER *appears in the doorway of the house, and* EDWARD *and* DORCAS *come in from the orchard.*

EDWARD: Everything still here?

DORCAS: Yes, still here.

HESTER: I thought it was your father.

DORCAS: It may well have been.

HESTER *is regarding a wisp of smoke rising from the well.*

HESTER: What is he doing down there now?

DORCAS: You mustn't go down, Mama!

HESTER: Don't be absurd, child. I've no intention of doing so. Your father is quite capable of managing his own affairs. No one seems to understand that. (*She is about to return to the house when:*) Dorcas—

DORCAS: Mama?

HESTER: You told me earlier—and I was a little sharp with you— that you are in love.

DORCAS: Yes, Mama.

HESTER: I can only presume it to be with you, young man.

EDWARD: Yes.

HESTER: People sometimes smile at the memory of your father and myself, but let me say this to you: remember the first day, my dears. It will mean much to you in the future.

EDWARD: I understand you very well. I'm leaving this evening.

With a cry DORCAS *tears herself from* EDWARD *leaving him standing alone. She runs out to the orchard. Immediately,* HESTER *calls.*

HESTER: Dorcas! Dorcas, come back! At once! Do you hear me—at once! (*After a moment* DORCAS, *silent, reappears at the orchard entrance.* HESTER *takes* DORCAS'S *hand and passes her to* EDWARD.) You need not part for a while, my dears—not for a little while. (DORCAS *and* EDWARD *go out to the orchard.* HESTER *turns to the* MAIDSERVANT.) Don't stand agape, Pippin. Continue with your preparations.

MAID: Yes, ma'am.

As HESTER *and the* MAID *go into the house* HALLAM *and* BREEZE *escorted by* SELINCOURT *and surrounded by the* FENCIBLES *return to the garden.*

HALLAM: Listen, sir—I've no wish to be caught further in your machinations.

SELINCOURT: Not mine, Mr Matthews, but the Devil's. Ask Mr Brotherhood.

BROTHER.: True.

SELINCOURT: For we have unearthed him. He is on the run, among us at this very moment. Everyone alert!

HALLAM *and* BREEZE *merely look mystified.*

HALLAM: Mr—

SELINCOURT: Selincourt.

HALLAM (*with grave patience*): Mr Selincourt. Kindly explain yourself. Once again.

SELINCOURT: Certainly. Our explosion—which you heard—

HALLAM: Yes.

SELINCOURT: —was only partially successful.

HALLAM: Continue.

SELINCOURT: Our proposition was, as I told you—

HALLAM: To seal—

SELINCOURT: Correct. To seal the entrance to the tunnel.

HALLAM: Well?

SELINCOURT: And to stifle the beast in the depths. Well, we set the charge—

HALLAM: A ton of explosive.

SELINCOURT: —and formed about the tunnel entrance in a circle.

HALLAM: Admirable!

SELINCOURT: To prevent, you understand, any possible escape.

HALLAM: In the confusion. Yes, go on.

SELINCOURT: All was prepared—

HALLAM: But—

SELINCOURT: —we had overlooked one thing.

HALLAM: That being?

SELINCOURT: The size of the charge.

HALLAM: It was—

SELINCOURT: Too great; Piggott, here—

HALLAM: Brave fellow.

SELINCOURT: Lit the fuse.

> *A pause.*

HALLAM: Yes?

SELINCOURT: The charge exploded and—here is the error—

HALLAM: Yes?

SELINCOURT: Bonaparte was ejected from the mouth of the tunnel like a bullet from a gun. He flew over our heads—

HALLAM: Amazing sight!

SELINCOURT: —to fall twenty yards beyond the bounds of my cordon.

HALLAM: Unhurt?

SELINCOURT: Apparently. The confusion among my men—understandably—was enormous. And in that confusion Bonaparte made off in this direction. But we shall catch him—never fear!—we shall catch him.

> LAMPRETT *and* JONATHAN, *very dirty, come in from the orchard. They are pleased with themselves.*

LAMPRETT: An excellent day's work! Nine conflagrations totally extinguished.

SELINCOURT: You—you!

LAMPRETT: I cannot recall ever having see you before, sir.

HALLAM (*swiftly*): Mr Selincourt—Mr Lamprett Bellboys.

SELINCOURT: You are the man who has been putting out all my fires.

LAMPRETT: Your fires, sir?

SELINCOURT: Yes.

LAMPRETT: The law holds that a fire, once under way, is public property, sir. Your fires, indeed! But tell me, do you mean you started them?

SELINCOURT: I was responsible.

LAMPRETT: Then you should be ashamed of yourself? A grown man going about the countryside wantonly starting fires.

SELINCOURT: Surely you understand that—

LAMPRETT: If you please, we will discuss the matter no further. They are out.

SELINCOURT: But—

LAMPRETT: Hush! (*He pats* JONATHAN *on the head.*) Good boy!

  BREEZE *has now made his way to the orchard gate. Suddenly he cries out:*

BREEZE: Sir!

HALLAM: Yes?

BREEZE (*pointing through the orchard*): There—there!

HALLAM: What?

BREEZE: There he goes!

HALLAM: Sam!

BREEZE: A small man—

SELINCOURT: Yes?

BREEZE: —in a cocked hat—

SELINCOURT: What?

BREEZE: Breeches.

SELINCOURT: My God!

BREEZE: There—there!

SELINCOURT: Bonaparte! (*He joins* BREEZE *at the orchard gate.*) I can see no one.

BREEZE: Just went down, sir, behind that hedgerow.

SELINCOURT: Fencibles! Follow-follow-follow-follow—

  And so shouting he runs out of the orchard, BROTHERHOOD, GIDDY *and* PIGGOTT *taking after him. There is a pause.*

HALLAM: My dear Sam, what are you doing? Did you see someone?

BREEZE: No, sir.

HALLAM: I thought not. Then why this extraordinary exhibition?

BREEZE: You'll know in a moment, sir.

  It is a fraction of time and then BREEZE *points the way from the cliff-top.* TIMOTHY *has appeared. He is very dirty and his clothes are in a most dilapidated state: he retains his hat and the impersonation is yet very recognizable.* HALLAM *goes to him.*

HALLAM: My dear old friend!

TIMOTHY: Hallam! (*They embrace.*) Tried to blow me up, the devils.

Inefficient fools! Ran into some kind of mine which went off and up I went like a rocket. Amazing sensation! Then, while they stood around gaping, I came to earth. Was rather stunned. Don't quite know what I did. Have they been here?

HALLAM: Yes. But, Tim, they are not—my word, I am pleased to see you!—listen, they are not—

BREEZE: Sir!

HALLAM: What is it, Sam?

BREEZE: Ask him if he's seen anyone like himself.

HALLAM: Why?

BREEZE: Well, sir, we just don't know, do we? Whether Sir Timothy is the one, or whether Boney really is here.

HALLAM: Of course. Listen, Timothy—

TIMOTHY: Um?

HALLAM: This is very important. Have you, in your travels, seen anyone looking like you?

There is a pause.

TIMOTHY: You mean someone has been impersonating me? (*He is suddenly very angry.*) Damned impertinence! Where is he? Before long I shan't be able to call my life my own.

LAMPRETT, *who has been standing by regarding all this, comments—*

LAMPRETT: Well, I'm sure no one else would wish to be credited with it.

—*and leaves the garden taking* JONATHAN *with him.* BREEZE *who is still standing by the orchard gate, calls.*

BREEZE: Look out, sir!

HALLAM: For what?

BREEZE: They are returning, sir.

HALLAM: Heavens! They mustn't see him like this. They'll probably shoot at sight.

BREEZE: They probably will, sir.

HALLAM: In here! (*He begins to bustle* TIMOTHY *towards the alcove.*)

TIMOTHY: My dear Hallam, I'd be very much obliged if you would refrain from jostling me. I'm extremely tired and—

HALLAM: They're here!

TIMOTHY: What's that?

HALLAM *has piloted him into the alcove.*

HALLAMl They're here!

TIMOTHY: Where?

HALLAM: Here!

SELINCOURT, BROTHERHOOD, GIDDY *and* PIGGOTT *march through the garden.* TIMOTHY *speaks to* HALLAM.

TIMOTHY: Pour la famille, mon cher, pour la famille! (*He then steps from the alcove to confront* SELINCOURT *and the* FENCIBLES.) Messieurs! Je suis votre Empereur. Je suis Napoleon Bonaparte. Retirez! Les armées de France sont vaincrent! Retournez à vos domestiques! Allons! Je suis un prisonnier et—

Then the FENCIBLES, *recovered from their amazement, fall upon him. The confusion is indescribable. At last,* TIMOTHY *stands pinioned by the* FENCIBLES *whilst* SELINCOURT *triumphant parades before him.*

SELINCOURT: Aha! Mon petit tyrant! Aha! Mon bête sauvage! (*He tweaks* TIMOTHY'S *nose.*)

TIMOTHY: God damn you!

SELINCOURT: Oh, you speak English.

TIMOTHY: Non.

SELINCOURT: Well, anyway, we've got you, disgusting little pest.

TIMOTHY: Are you English?

SELINCOURT: Of course I'm English.

TIMOTHY: Then what the hell are you doing? Hallam!

SELINCOURT: Are you Napoleon Bonaparte?

TIMOTHY: Oui! Non! No!

SELINCOURT: Of course you deny it. Mr Brotherhood, do you identify this man as the one who stole your biscuits?

BROTHER.: I do.

SELINCOURT: Then, Napoleon Bonaparte, in the King's name I declare you to be my prisoner.

TIMOTHY: Well, if I'm Napoleon Bonaparte who in hell are you?

SELINCOURT: My name is George Selincourt and I am commander of the local forces.

TIMOTHY: Dear God! I'm Bellboys.

SELINCOURT: Who?

TIMOTHY: Timothy Bellboys.

SELINCOURT: So you're Timothy Bellboys, are you? Well, well, well! (*Suddenly very intimidating.*) Impersonation, eh? A knowledge of the local gentry is not going to help you. What have you done with the poor old gentleman—

TIMOTHY: Poor old gentleman!

SELINCOURT: Yes! What have you done with him? Murdered him probably, and stuffed his frail old body into some hole in the ground. What harm had he ever done to you? (TIMOTHY, *in an excess of fury, attempts to break loose from the* FENCIBLES.) Hold him! Hold him!

TIMOTHY: I tell you I am Timothy Bellboys! Ask my friend, Hallam Matthews, there.

SELINCOURT *turns doubtfully to* HALLAM.

SELINCOURT: Can you identify this man, sir?

HALLAM: Certainly, Lord Nelson. (*Then, with* BREEZE, *he retires a little way off.*)

SELINCOURT (*to* BROTHERHOOD): What do you think?

BROTHER.: It is very difficult to know what to think.

TIMOTHY: Or what to think with, apparently.

SELINCOURT: It will not help to be abusive. We are only trying to determine the truth.

TIMOTHY: And whilst you are, as you put it, determining the truth, the French may be preparing to assault the beaches.

SELINCOURT: That is all taken care of. Mr Brotherhood—

TIMOTHY: Taken care of! You do not impress me, sir.

SELINCOURT: Mr Brotherhood— (SELINCOURT *and* BROTHERHOOD *confer in whispers.* TIMOTHY *speaks to* PIGGOTT.)

TIMOTHY: Will you have a care! You are pinching my arm quite unmercifully. I think you take a delight in it, you horrid fellow.

SELINCOURT *and* BROTHERHOOD have reached a decision.

SELINCOURT: Now, sir—

TIMOTHY: Well?

SELINCOURT: Are you willing to answer a few questions to prove your identity?

TIMOTHY: No.

SELINCOURT: Then I'm afraid I must insist. Mr Brotherhood here, is going to help me.

TIMOTHY: Help you with the questions?

SELINCOURT: Yes.

TIMOTHY: Is anyone going to help me with the answers?

SELINCOURT: Certainly not.

TIMOTHY: Well, unless I'm released you'll get nothing from me.

SELINCOURT (*to* GIDDY *and* PIGGOTT): Release him. (*They do so, and* TIMOTHY *comes forward.*) Now, sir, at Mr Brotherhood's suggestion I am going to put to you several questions which only an Englishman could answer. Are you ready?

TIMOTHY: Yes.

SELINCOURT: One. What is a Wykehamist?

TIMOTHY: I am a Wykehamist.

    SELINCOURT *looks at* BROTHERHOOD *who shakes his head.*

BROTHER.: Inconclusive.

TIMOTHY: I can make a guess as to what you are.

SELINCOURT: Two. What was the second question, Mr Brother hood?

BROTHER.: What is a New Leicester?

TIMOTHY: A cow.

BROTHER.: Oh, very good!

SELINCOURT: Is he right?

BROTHER.: Yes.

TIMOTHY: Aha! Go on.

SELINCOURT: Three. Now this requires action. Watch carefully. If I was to do this—(*With an underarm action he bowls an imaginary ball to* TIMOTHY.)—what would you do?

TIMOTHY (*very intent*): Do it again.

    SELINCOURT *repeats the action.*

SELINCOURT: Well, what would you do?

TIMOTHY: This! (*With an imaginary bat* TIMOTHY *strikes the imaginary ball and then proceeds to run madly between two points some ten yards apart touching down at each imaginary wicket.*)

SELINCOURT: Stop! Stop! (TIMOTHY *stops.*) Do you play?

TIMOTHY: Cricket? Of course. Do you?

SELINCOURT: Yes, indeed.

TIMOTHY: God bless my soul! What's your name again?

SELINCOURT: Selincourt.

TIMOTHY: Not Stumper Selincourt?

    At this SELINCOURT *positively simpers.*

SELINCOURT: I must confess that I am sometimes known by that appellation—on the field.

TIMOTHY: But you're famous.

SELINCOURT: Oh, come.

TIMOTHY: Yes, you are. And these brave fellows—(*He indicates* BROTHERHOOD, GIDDY *and* PIGGOTT)—are they some of your team?

SELINCOURT: Yes. We have a side, in its infancy yet, but give us a few weeks. I've been working hard with them since my arrival here from Somerset.

TIMOTHY: Then we must play, Stumper Selincourt. Well, well! Hallam, this is Stumper Selincourt.

HESTER *comes from the house. She is dressed in what appears to be a suit of golden armour and is accompanied by the tiny* MAIDSERVANT *who, dressed for travelling, bears the baggage.*

HESTER: Ah! gentlemen—(*Everyone seeing* HESTER *is momentarily lost in admiration*)—what is this? A congress of war?

TIMOTHY: We were talking about cricket.

HESTER: At a time like this? I feel you must be joking, Timothy.

HALLAM: The immediate danger would appear to have passed, Hester.

HESTER: Nonsense, Hallam! East Anglia is in turmoil. I set off at once. (*She calls.*) Lamprett!

LAMPRETT *comes in and recognizes his wife.*

LAMPRETT: Oh!

HESTER: Don't be afraid. I'm away now.

They embrace.

LAMPRETT: Goodbye. Come back soon.

TIMOTHY: Breeches or not, Hester, you appear to be amply protected.

HESTER: We can but take care. And if one goes down one should go down magnificently. An Englishman's prerogative.

SELINCOURT *comes to attention as* HESTER *and the* MAID *march out.*

TIMOTHY: I say, are you hungry?

SELINCOURT: A little.

TIMOTHY: I am, damnably. Come inside and we'll find some food. Give us a chance to talk. Now that we've met we must arrange something at once. Come along, all of you. (*The* FENCIBLES *go into the house.*) I've quite a fair side, although now my sister-in-law has gone it will be weaker, but I think we can give you a game. In fact, I'm sure we can. (*He takes* SELINCOURT *to the door of the house.*) By the way, this business of my being Bonaparte—

SELINCOURT: Never mind that nonsense!

TIMOTHY: What! (*He roars with laughter.*) Show you my bat. Not bad. Made it myself. (*With* SELINCOURT *he goes into the house.*)

HALLAM: And so, Sam, there is always a basis for understanding however remote it may appear, however dissimilar the two parties, however hopeless the situation.

BREEZE: Yes, sir.

HALLAM: Comforting, isn't it?

BREEZE: Yes, sir.

HALLAM: And what, pray, are you smiling at?

BREEZE: Nothing, sir.

HALLAM: You mustn't have these secret thoughts, you know. Very disturbing.

BREEZE: Sorry, sir.

HALLAM: And you, Lamprett—a good day?

LAMPRETT: Excellent! I'm just cleaning up the engine—oh, it has done magnificently!—and then I shall go to my bed. It has been a somewhat busy day for you, too, I suppose.

HALLAM: Unwittingly, I have sometimes been caught up in the general action.

BREEZE *laughs.*

LAMPRETT: Well, you must enjoy the remainder of your stay with us.

HALLAM: Thank you, Lamprett.

LAMPRETT *goes out.*

BREEZE: Will you come in now, sir?

HALLAM: Not for a while, I think. I propose to revel for a time in this most unaccustomed peace.

BREEZE: Very good, sir. (*He goes into the house.*)

HALLAM: Humpage!

HUMPAGE: Sir!

HALLAM: Anything to report?

HUMPAGE: No, sir.

HALLAM: Thank God. (*He wanders a little way off. From within the house comes a subdued burst of men's laughter. Suddenly, the day is gone, it is evening and from the long shadows come* EDWARD *and* DORCAS.)

DORCAS: But yesterday was just another day—nothing to tell about it.

EDWARD: Nothing?

DORCAS: Nothing at all. The sun shone as it has today, but not so brightly and to no purpose whatever. Yesterday was just—oh, any old day. There are times you remember and times you forget —but your life is made up of the times you remember. Come, let us sit here. (*She draws* EDWARD *towards the alcove.*) We shall be be safe and sound—oh, quite secure and secret. (*They enter the alcove.*)

EDWARD: What is this place?

DORCAS: I used to play here when I was a baby. Yes, it is a good place for us to be together for I have been happy here. It was my world within a world—peopled by folk who were all like me—and that is simple to understand for I was everyone.

EDWARD: I am a stranger.

DORCAS: No, no! We all greet you. (*Lightly, she kisses him.*)

EDWARD: Have you ever been unhappy?

DORCAS: Oh, yes, deeply. Indeed, so very unhappy that I have wept and had to seek comfort.

EDWARD: Which you have always found?

DORCAS: Of course. Oh, look!

EDWARD: I'm looking with all my heart. What is this new wonder you have to show me?

DORCAS: Only my name—Dorcas—scored upon this seat. Oh, that was done many years ago. (*She takes up a stone and begins to mark the seat.*)

EDWARD: What are you doing?

DORCAS: I'm putting your name—Edward—here with mine. Isn't that a clever thing to do?

EDWARD: Indeed it is.

As DORCAS *works, she asks:*

DORCAS: You're going away?

EDWARD: Yes.

DORCAS: Soon?

EDWARD: Yes.

A pause.

DORCAS: Not before I've finished your name?

EDWARD: Not before then, perhaps, but soon—soon.

DORCAS: I shall be a long time. (EDWARD *smiles.*) Perhaps—if I cut very slowly—(*A pause.*)—I cannot come with you?

EDWARD: No.

DORCAS: There! (*She throws down the stone.*)

EDWARD: Finished?

DORCAS *turns to him, her face distraught.*

DORCAS: Yes. Oh, yes. (*She cries out.*) But we all love you—why can't you remain?

EDWARD: Poor Dorcas.

DORCAS: Forgive me. I don't understand.

EDWARD: Then—

DORCAS: Speak in simple words, if you please.

EDWARD: If you tear the words from me, as you are doing now, they are bound to be tattered.

DORCAS: Go on.

EDWARD: For me there is no escape—not even by returning, my darling. There is only a little purpose—the ending of a war to be achieved and then this broken thing I call myself can be discarded, happily relinquished. I am only a scarecrow to frighten away the spirit of hatred. That done I can be left to weather and fall apart in some deserted place.

DORCAS: But do you love me now?

EDWARD: Yes.

DORCAS: For a little while do you love me?

EDWARD: Yes.

DORCAS: Tell me—tell me!

EDWARD: I love you. I love you.

She stares at him.

DORCAS: Then—goodbye.

Out of the falling darkness HALLAM *speaks.*

HALLAM: Circumstances deal with us in a way we cannot approve. As you grow older you will understand that.

EDWARD: Where's the child? (*He calls.*) Jonathan!

LAMPRETT *comes in with* JONATHAN. *The child is dressed as he was on arrival.*

LAMPRETT: I thought you'd be off soon. He's all ready.

EDWARD: Thank you, sir.

LAMPRETT (*to* JONATHAN): Got everything? (*The* BOY *nods.*) Well, thank you very much for your help today. I think we can say we did well. There's only one word of advice I should like to give you and it is this. Out there in the world people will always be telling you not to get caught between two fires. Pay no attention to them. (*Then, very sadly, he adds.*) I'm only joking, you know. Off with you.

HALLAM: Mr Sterne.

EDWARD: Ah! You're there, Mr Matthews.

HALLAM: You're going.

EDWARD: Yes.

HALLAM: I believe you to be wise. Yes, I really believe that. Goodbye. (EDWARD *and* JONATHAN *go, leaving* DORCAS.) You know about them, do you, Lamprett—their journey?

LAMPRETT: Yes, the child told me today.

HALLAM: I reasoned with the man. I gave him the cold fact as to why he must fail—and yet he goes on. And damn it, Lamprett, I'm glad he goes on. This would be hell if we acted always to reason and cold fact. Did you tell the child?

LAMPRETT: That the child of Bethlehem no longer lives? No. It occurred to me to do so—but no, I decided against it.

HALLAM: Why, I wonder?

LAMPRETT: Because our destination is unimportant, Hallam. We journey forward only to discover the reason for our travelling.

HALLAM: Thank you, Lamprett. I feel I should have said that.

TIMOTHY *comes from the house. He has changed from his uniform of impersonation and now wears a dressing robe. He carries a cricket bat.*

TIMOTHY: What are you all doing out here?

HALLAM: Nothing, and it's absolutely delightful.

TIMOTHY: I say, Hallam, this Selincourt is an amazing fellow. Tells me he once stumped Richard Nyren. You know, the captain of Hambledon.

HALLAM: Really!

TIMOTHY: Yes, he did. And he's as modest as milk about it. By the way, we're arranging a match for next Sunday. Think you'll be here then?

HALLAM: I doubt that, Tim.

TIMOTHY: Pity. Now that Hester's gone I've got to find another player and—(*He holds up his bat.*)—I thought you might care to—

HALLAM: No.

TIMOTHY: I could teach you in an afternoon.

HALLAM: No, Timothy.

TIMOTHY: Then Humpage will have to come down.

HUMPAGE: Can I believe my ears?

LAMPRETT: No, you cannot, Humpage. Whatever can you be thinking of, Timothy. Humpage has his duties.

TIMOTHY: Yes, I suppose so. (HUMPAGE *groans.*) Well, Lamprett, I'll have to show you, I suppose. (*He gives the bat to* LAMPRETT.) Try not to make too big a fool of yourself. Oh, God! You're holding it by the wrong end, man.

LAMPRETT: Well, I can't see.

TIMOTHY: Come inside and I'll show you. I hope you're enjoying your stay with us, Hallam.

HALLAM: I am, very much—at the moment.

TIMOTHY: Don't seem to have had a chance to say it before, but

I'll say it now. We're very pleased to see you, Hallam. Aren't we,
Lamprett?

LAMPRETT: Of course.

TIMOTHY: There's some food and drink inside when you're ready
for it.

HALLAM: Bless you, Tim.

TIMOTHY: You're happy, then?

HALLAM: Very happy, thank you.

TIMOTHY: Good. Now, Lamprett, as a beginner you'll have to go
in the outfield.

LAMPRETT: Where's that?

TIMOTHY: You'll find out.

LAMPRETT: Is it a dangerous game?

TIMOTHY: Well, you want to look out for your knuckles, you
know— (*Together* TIMOTHY *and* LAMPRETT *go into the house. The
garden becomes darker. A great branched candlestick, ablaze, is placed in
the window of a ground floor room of the house. From within the house
comes a second burst of laughter and, for a moment, a single voice is raised
in a snatch of song. Distantly, from the beaches, a bugle sounds the Stand
Down.* DORCAS *can be seen against the night sky looking out over the
countryside. After a moment she enters the garden to move to* HALLAM
*and sit beside him. They remain together in silence for a considerable time.
At last* HALLAM *speaks to her.*)

HALLAM: Not tears to end the day.

When DORCAS *speaks her voice is high and clear.*

DORCAS: I'm not crying. Didn't you know, Mr Matthews, that you
do not cry over spilt milk or lost lovers.

HALLAM: I'm sorry.

DORCAS: It's quite all right. (*There is a pause.*) You don't mind if I
sit here with you for a while?

HALLAM: Not at all, darling.

DORCAS: Please don't be kind to me.

HALLAM: I'm sorry.

DORCAS: And please don't continue to be sorry. You have given no
offence. I shall sit here for a while because I don't know where
to go. I've not yet made up my mind, you understand? (*In the
slight pause the sudden rush of an evening breeze seems to disturb the stillness of the garden.*) Can you see me?

HALLAM: Yes.

DORCAS: It is getting dark. Day's end. Nightfall. I suppose there will be a tomorrow. (*A pause.*) I cannot believe that I shall wake to find the sun high. (*A pause.*) Do you know a song beginning 'All my past life is mine no more—'?

HALLAM: 'All my past life is mine no more;
                    The flying hours are gone,
                    Like transitory dreams given o'er,
                    Whose images are kept in store
                    By memory alone.'
Yes, I know that.

DORCAS: I wondered if you did. There is no need to talk if you do not wish.

    BREEZE *comes from the house.*

BREEZE: Mr Matthews—

HALLAM: I'm here, Sam.

BREEZE: That's everything, then, sir.

HALLAM: Thank you, Sam.

BREEZE. Thank you, sir. Goodnight, Miss Bellboys.

DORCAS: Goodnight.

BREEZE: Goodnight, sir.

HALLAM: Goodnight, Sam. God rest you.

    BREEZE *goes out by the orchard. It is now almost dark but for the light of the night sky and the blaze of candles in the window. From within the house a spinet strikes up a tune and men's voices, gay and gentle, begin to sing.* HUMPAGE, *stirs in his sleep and the brass bell sounds once, softly. Then, with an infinite tenderness,* HALLAM *takes up the melody being sung in the house on his pipe. The tune ends.*

    A single star stands in the sky.

CURTAIN

NOTES ON THE REVISED VERSION

THE CHIEF purpose of the revision seems to have been to prune away all the 'charm' from the play and all the generalized philosophizing. Since the play's essential quality rests more on these than on anything else, the changes are extremely damaging. It's hard to be sure whether Whiting had come to think his original play sentimental, or whether he was so depressed by now that he no longer cared enough to resist other people's suggestions.

The new Edward isn't blind and this makes his relationships with both Jonathan and Dorcas a good deal less interesting. To make matters worse, he's militantly radical and obstreperously didactic.

EDWARD: Look, Dorcas, the world's full of people. Yes?

DORCAS: I suppose so.

EDWARD: Believe me, it is. And they live in many different states of power and weakness, wealth and poverty. Right?

DORCAS: Er, yes.

EDWARD: There was a revolution in France, and there's been one in America.

DORCAS: Yes, it was very shocking.

EDWARD: You are a silly girl! It wasn't shocking, it was perfectly splendid. Now, say after me: Revolution is a good thing.

Quiet jokes like having Hallam read Wordsworth as an example of radical thinking are swept away in the flood of Edward's noisy radicalism. Altogether he upsets the filigree equilibrium of the play with his heavy-handed Left Wing rightmindedness. We don't need Edward to tell us how unreal the world is that the Bellboys are living in. The satire was already built into the picture, subtly but strongly enough, and it's a bad mistake to let Edward argue with them, except as he did before, from an equally unrealistic viewpoint. It's also a mistake to put his words into Dorcas's mouth.

He's the kind you meant when you said their passing would be like the melting of snow to show the promise of spring beneath, isn't he?

Much of Hallam's philosophizing is cut in the new version and a lot of Edward's speeches make gestures in the direction of the drama of social consciousness—gestures which simply don't belong to this play:

For the last four years I've been walking about Europe. I've seen such horrible things that it broke my heart. Poverty and disease, love and friendship ruined by war, men and women living like animals in a desperate attempt to stay alive. I was one who sold himself for war so that he could eat, and I've had women sell themselves to me so that their children could eat. Now I may be simple, Matthews, but there's cause for all this. And the cause is laziness and indifference. There are only a handful of tyrants at any one time, but there are millions who don't care. I saw all this, I smelt it, I lay down with it at night, and at last I decided to fight. I carried in my pocket a book which is a weapon. It has a title which will mean nothing to you. It's called *The Rights of Man*.

Both the lovers' scenes and the scenes they share with Hallam are made a lot less lyrical. The new Edward tells Dorcas quite bluntly that he doesn't love her and this has a bad effect on her self-consciousness:

DORCAS: After all, I'm still young enough to talk about a very common experience as if it were the most original thing in the world. . . . Pooh, nobody understands how awful it is to be a child. All that loneliness and muddle. All that anger. Well, it's over now. Thank you very much. . . .

It also makes it too easy for him to leave her, but there is a nice, new, very brief quarrel scene when she fails to dissuade him from going to London.

EDWARD: What's this? A quarrel?
DORCAS: Yes, it is. Goodbye. (*She stares into the distance.*)
EDWARD: Goodbye.
 (*Neither of them move: silence.*)
DORCAS: Forgive me.
EDWARD: All forgotten.

Not being blind, Edward emerges less as a victim of war than as a veteran, cynically expert in the techniques of survival. In the flurry of confusion which ends Act One when the others all think Napoleon has landed, he gives them the benefit of his experience:

Don't stand under a flag, stay far away from anybody in a fine bright uniform, take a look at the sun so that you'll always know which way you're running, if there's a loaf of bread about put it in your pocket, and if there's a hole in the ground sit in it. Ignore all cries for help, stay deaf to all exhortations, and keep your trousers tied tight about your waist. In any difficulty, look stupid, and at the first opportunity go to sleep.

In the lovers' scene with Hallam in Act Two (p. 219) the speeches about the 'infrangible burden' of self-knowledge and fighting our love 'from a catena of unprepared positions' are all cut and we lose the scene in which Hallam takes Edward on one side to warn him that the King is mad but encouragingly pretends to believe that there may still be some point in going to see him. Instead they argue fairly explicitly and a lot less dramatically:

HALLAM: How are you going to change the world, Mr Sterne?
EDWARD: By conviction.
HALLAM: And who are you going to convince?
EDWARD: Everybody.
HALLAM: Starting where? Top or bottom? That's something which has always confused me about reform. Where to begin.
EDWARD: Start with the people.
HALLAM (*doubtfully*): Yes. But they're always a little slow to follow on.
EDWARD: All right, then. Start at the top, with the heads of state.
HALLAM: My dear boy, do you know what you're saying? Here we are on the brink of war, and the head of the state is a dear, silly man. At the moment we call him eccentric. In a few years we shall be forced to call him something else.
EDWARD: Well, there's your hereditary monarchy for you.
HALLAM: And what has your democracy thrown up on the other side? This frightful little Bonaparte person, who's just had himself crowned with considerably more splendour than Westminster Abbey has ever seen. He has that awful wife, and the bottoms of his family cover almost every throne in Europe. No, no, my dear Sterne, men of good will, such as ourselves, will have to find a third course.
EDWARD: If you're suggesting what I think you're suggesting the answer is—never!
HALLAM: I was afraid you'd say that. No compromise, eh?
EDWARD: Radicalism has a purity, Matthews, which is probably beyond your comprehension.
HALLAM: All right, my dear fellow, keep your political virginity, but don't be upset if others get on with governing the world. Let's not quarrel.
DORCAS: No. I won't allow it.
HALLAM: Take her away, Sterne. She'll never be my sweetheart, but give me another half-hour with her and she'd be voting for me, if she could, in an election. She's a woman, you see. Off you go.

Good though the end to this sequence is, it's no replacement for what's lost.

Hallam's scene with Jonathan (p. 221) is also sacrificed and replaced by a passage which is less whimsical but totally lacking in magic. The chief joke in it is that Jonathan, who is now French, fails to understand Hallam until he quotes de la Rochefoucauld.

Lovely day. Yes. (*A pause.*) You must learn to talk about the weather. (*A pause.*) Very boring, this war, don't you think? I came down here to get away from it, you know. But it's with us, like other things one would like to escape from. Love, for example. I don't suppose it bothers you at the moment. But there's your friend in front of my eyes: I'm reminded of the past. They're happy, those two. What are you? What am I? Never mind, we must cheer up. As has been said, *On n'est jamais si heureux ni si malheureux qu'on s'imagine.*

The small BOY *finds this very funny indeed.* HALLAM *stares at him.*
I can't make you laugh, but de la Rochefoucauld can.

There is a bugle call from not far off.
And there's all this talk about the equality of man. That worries me very much. What ground do you and I meet on? It's a problem, isn't it? Forty years must separate us. We know nothing about each other, and seem quite incapable of telling. (*A pause.*) Those eyes of yours have seen more than they should. I don't know why I feel that, but somehow I understand why you reject the weather, the war and other trivial matters, such as love and justice, as subjects for conversation.

In the final scene between Edward and Dorcas, he takes over the line which she spoke in 1951.

There are times you remember and times you forget, but your life is made up of the times you remember.

The line is rooted far more meaningfully into its context when Dorcas speaks it because she's comparing the memorable day today has been with yesterday, which *looked* very similar.

The 1962 version cuts the lines in which she shows him the alcove she played in as a child (pp. 240-1) and she no longer carves his name on the seat.

The new scene uses fewer words but it's comparatively prosaic.

DORCAS: What are you going to do in London?
EDWARD: I shall find people who think as I do, and work with them.
DORCAS: Do any women think as you do?
EDWARD: There are some.
DORCAS: Are they beautiful?

EDWARD: Well, it's sad. Nearly all girls with the right ideas—my ideas —seem to have the plainest faces.

DORCAS: I'm glad. I don't think it's sad at all. (*She looks round the garden.*) There hasn't been enough time, Edward. Not enough time to tell each other all that needs to be told.

EDWARD: There never is. When you're properly in love a lifetime isn't long enough.

DORCAS: There has to be a lot of parting in the world.

EDWARD: Yes. Men are cursed with ideas, and ideas aren't much use unless they're put into practice. This means travelling far, going to war, parting from people you love. But there'll come a day, if I have my way, when women will be able to go with men, equally.

DORCAS: Even the beautiful ones?

EDWARD: Even the beautiful ones. Like you. (*Pause.*) I must go now.

DORCAS: Yes. It's all right, I'm not going to cry.

EDWARD: Of course not. Try to believe that what I believe is important.

DORCAS: I do!

EDWARD: People of my kind get laughed at a lot, you know. There is something comic about the very serious. But, all the same, these questions I ask *are* serious. Mr Matthews is the kind of man who laughs to stop himself from crying. That takes a lot of courage. I've never been able to do it.

DORCAS: You mustn't ever do that. You must never change.

EDWARD: I've never cared what people think of me. Somehow I care what you think. (*Pause.*) I must go.

And so they part. And the play ends, as before, with only Hallam's philosophizing to console the abandoned Dorcas as they sit together in the garden. But in the austerity version of the play, he no longer has a recorder to pick up the spinet tune when it starts inside the house.

MARCHING SONG

INTRODUCTORY NOTE

THE PLAY takes its title from one of Yeats's *Marching Songs,* which contains pointers to many of its themes.

> The soldier takes pride in saluting his Captain,
> The devotee proffers a knee to his Lord,
> Some back a mare thrown from a thoroughbred,
> Troy backed its Helen; Troy died and adored;
> Great nations blossom above;
> A slave bows down to a slave. . . .
>
> What if there's nothing up there at the top?
> Where are the captains that govern mankind?
> What tears down a tree that has nothing within it?
> A blast of the wind, O a marching wind,
> March wind, and any old tune,
> March, march, and how does it run?
>
> *What marches down the mountain pass?*
> *No, no, my son, not yet;*
> *That is an airy spot,*
> *And no man knows what treads the grass.*

Whiting started on it in 1951 and finished it the next year. Two years passed before it was put on. After a provincial tour, it opened at the St Martin's Theatre on 8 April 1954 and closed after forty-three performances on 15 May. Frith Banbury directed with Robert Flemyng as Rupert, Diana Wynyard as Catherine, Penelope Munday as Dido, Hartley Power as Harry, Ernest Thesiger as Cadmus and Michael David as Bruno. Here are the reactions of the main critics.

The Times:

It is refreshingly sincere, it deals with a contemporary dilemma intelligently and interestingly, and though it swerves in the end into an otiose sentimentalism it creates for the greater part of the evening a genuine tension.

If this tension is more intellectual than dramatic, that is because Mr Whiting appears more interested in ideas than in people.

W. A. Darlington in the *Daily Telegraph*:

> With only a slight concession to the ancient theatrical virtue of clarity
> he could have the audience following him with excitement and delight.
> Instead of that, he makes everything as difficult as possible for the
> public and wins from them no tribute higher than a lively respect.

Alan Dent in the *News Chronicle*:

> It's all, pretty obviously, an allegory about the state of mankind in the
> modern world. Man is the general who has been imprisoned for seven
> years after the war, and returns to the house of his helpmate only to be
> offered poison or retrial.

Milton Shulman in the *Evening Standard*:

> Mr Whiting is a playwright who will never be obvious when he has a
> chance of being obscure.

Derek Grainger in the *Financial Times*:

> Any masterpiece of the theatre, however much its thought may rever-
> berate afterwards, should also be immediately explicit in clear-cut
> dramatic terms.

Ivor Brown in the *Observer*:

> What exactly is the significance of the title, 'Marching Song'? 'Funeral
> March' would seem more accurate . . . the unnamed country with the
> unnamed capital must surely be Symbolia. Accordingly you can sit and
> make your own guesses to the twenty or so questions raised by quiz-
> master Whiting. Some of the characters, presumably of set purpose, do
> not so much act as intone their parts; Forster's lines are given a metallic
> monotone by Robert Flemyng, and this confirms the impression that the
> general is to be regarded as an obstruction rather than as a human being.

Harold Hobson in the *Sunday Times*:

> He has a troubled and uneasy poetry whose shadowy tides never wash
> against the shores of our own land of cricket bats and football pools, of
> bells in the old school chapel, and the Welfare State. This, perhaps, is
> only another way of saying that the play extends the boundaries of
> English drama.

Anthony Hartley in the *Spectator*:

> Its failure is the author's failure to work out his position either in
> adequately human or adequately philosophical terms.

In September 1954 it was produced at the Haagse Comedie, Amsterdam, by Paul Steenbergen and it was broadcast in November by the BBC with Sebastian Shaw and Googie Withers.

In January 1955, Gustaf Gründgens directed it at the Düsseldorfer Schauspielhaus, playing Rupert himself.

In 1956 the BBC televised it with Patrick Barr and Faith Brook.

In 1964 it was televised by Rediffusion with Derek Godfrey, Maxine Audley and Judi Dench.

PERSONS

HARRY LANCASTER
DIDO MORGEN
MATTHEW SANGOSSE
FATHER ANSELM
CATHERINE DE TROYES
RUPERT FORSTER
JOHN CADMUS
BRUNO HURST

*The action of the play takes place in a room of
Catherine de Troyes's house set on the heights
above a capital city in Europe.*

ACT I.   Late evening, moving to night.
ACT II.   The next day. Night.
ACT III. Later the same night, moving to dawn.

ACT ONE

The scene is a room in CATHERINE DE TROYES'S *house set on the heights above a capital city in Europe.*

The time is the present: it is late evening moving to night.

The house, of which the room is representative, was designed by a great German architect of the nineteen-thirties. Built into the hillside which ranges high above the city lying to the south, it transcends the mere purpose of a dwelling-place.

The room is a shell caught within a web of glass and steel. It is dominated by the sky.

Entrances to the room: a wide circular stairway leading down to the main door of the house.

A second entrance: a gallery leading to an apartment of rooms above which stand alone. This is the highest point of the house.

A third entrance: from a balcony of considerable size—a main feature of the room and of the house—projecting like a finger towards the city (or an arrow, perhaps, set within the bow of the room).

The house is built of stone, glass and steel. Within the room there is an impression of air and space—an impression of delicacy, almost fragility, yet the place is a fortress in strength and position. A warmth is given to the room by the use of wood and fabrics in the decoration and furnishing.

In the spare decoration of the room there is a plinth surmounted by an antique bronze helmet.

It is the late evening of a spring day. The great expanse of sky above the room retains a savage brilliance, but within the room shadows have begun to form. The lights have not yet been put up.

HARRY LANCASTER *stands in the centre of the room. He is in the act of getting out of a heavy sheepskin coat which is half-off his shoulders.*

HARRY: You! (*He is shouting to a man who is standing on the balcony with his back to the room.*) I'm speaking to you! (*The man does not turn.*) All right, then. To hell with you! (*The man is motionless, silent.*) To hell, sweetheart, with you. (HARRY *throws the coat over a*

chair and speaks to another person.) I said just now that my youth
must be considered past—done with. Know why? Because— (*He
turns to find himself alone in the room. After a moment he goes to the
circular stairway and calls down.*) Come on up! Don't be scared.
Come on up! (*He backs from the stairway keeping in sight and speaking
to the ascending person.*) My youth—done with. For why? Because
I want you for my workmate, believe me. And believe me truly
last Fall I'd have wanted you for my playmate. Last Fall—six
months ago—I was young and loving. Now, I can only say—
welcome. (DIDO MORGEN, *a young girl, has come up the stairway and
now stands within the room.*) Welcome! Look—but look kindly—on
these grey hairs. Trust this ancient head. Will you?

DIDO: Yes.

HARRY: That's the girl.

DIDO: Who's in this place?

HARRY: Relax. They're friends here. (DIDO *silently points to the man
on the balcony.*) You're right. A stranger. Tourist, maybe. (*He
shouts again to the man.*) Have a drink! (*The man is silent.*) Not an
American, anyway.

DIDO: You are.

HARRY: I was made unhappy there so I came over to Europe. I'm
unhappy here too—so I guess it's the condition of the man. Let's
not blame places, shall we?

DIDO: A long way to come just to stay unhappy.

HARRY: And let's not talk around the point. My misery is my
dearest possession—for God's sake leave me that. You're not one
of those women who think men should be made happy, are you?

DIDO: No. But if you don't want to be made happy why did you
pick me up and bring me here?

HARRY: I want to give you a job. Why do you clip your hair?

DIDO: Keep it clean. Cleanliness before wantonness, you know.
What sort of job?

HARRY: How long have you lived down in the city?

DIDO: All my life. Nearly twenty years.

HARRY: The day you were born there was music and laughter—
and maybe they let off fireworks.

DIDO: It was a very obscure birth.

HARRY: But twenty years ago there was music and laughter every
day. I know. I was there.

DIDO: Laughing with the best of them.

HARRY: Sure. I was young and the place was—well—(*he sings and pantomimes an old waltz song*)—but you won't remember.

DIDO: No, I don't remember. What were you doing here then—besides laughing and letting off fireworks?

HARRY: I was making a film—a movie—something I've done all my life. That's what's known as my job. I was young then—do I talk too much about my age? I had money and people said I was —well, they said I was all right. They said Harry Lancaster was all right.

DIDO: That's you.

HARRY: That's me. I'm back again.

DIDO: Welcome!

HARRY: But I'm not young—I've no money—nobody remembers me and the old songs have all gone, but here I am and I'm making a new picture. Twenty years ago I made the picture of my youth. I'll show it to you. Only one copy left. I keep it with me against the dead days. Like an old actor's yellow press-clippings. Baby, look up to me—I once did this!

DIDO: And the new picture?

HARRY: The magazines'll call it the film of my maturity. Let's leave it at that.

DIDO: What do I do?

HARRY: I don't know yet.

DIDO: What sort of picture is this, for God's sake?

HARRY: You'll see.

DIDO: Where do you make it?

HARRY: On the streets—around. I can't pay you. I know! I said I could—well, I can't. Want to go? I can feed you, keep you happy by telling you stories of the old days, give you somewhere to sleep, maybe make you laugh. That's all. But it's better, surely, than sitting on bar stools and drinking beer and eating broken biscuits out of your pocket.

DIDO: Where? All this eating and sleeping, I mean.

HARRY: Here. Kate won't mind.

DIDO: Kate? Let's play fair.

HARRY: Catherine de Troyes. This is her house. I knew her 'way back. When I came over some six months ago I sort of moved in here. Kate's putting up the money for this new picture—enough for the truck, the cameras and film, and a half-witted assistant.

DIDO: Can she afford it?

HARRY: Look around you and ask that again.

DIDO: I like money.

HARRY: She was born to it.

DIDO: What's more, she's kept it. I couldn't live here. I'd get lost.

HARRY: That was the idea.

DIDO: To get lost?

HARRY: Kate was in love. The house was built for Kate to get lost in with her man.

DIDO: And they were happy. Say they were happy.

HARRY: For a time. Then he went away. Kate stayed on.

DIDO: In this place? What's that? (*She points to the bronze helmet.*)

HARRY: It belonged to a man called Forster. A soldier. It's an old helmet.

DIDO: Rupert Forster. He fought this last war.

HARRY: It's he who has left Kate alone. He was a terrible man. I mean that. He—I don't know.

DIDO: Well, never mind. He's dead.

HARRY: What?

DIDO: I said, never mind. He's dead.

HARRY: No, no, he's not that. But they caught up with him. They shut him up in prison. There's still something you know, that catches up with men like that. Even now, in this world, there's something says, No! this is enough. That's what happened to Forster. He got his arse kicked so hard in that last fight they daren't even bring him back. I guess they'll let him die up there in the camp in the mountains.

DIDO: You're glad.

HARRY: I'm not sorry. I knew him back in the old days with Kate. When I was making the first picture the Government lent me some soldiers for a couple of scenes. He was the young officer commanding them. I liked him then. But in the preliminaries for war, in the war itself—I don't know what happened to him. Men should be humble, I guess.

DIDO: And that helmet's all that's left for Kate. What's she like?

HARRY: You'll see her. She's beautiful. Rupert was beautiful too. They were both beautiful—in the old days.

DIDO: So was the first picture.

HARRY: So was the first picture. So was the world.

DIDO: In the old days.

They laugh. From the well of the circular stairway FATHER ANSELM *calls.*

ANSELM: May we come up?

DIDO: Who's that?

HARRY: It's all right. Mustn't be scared. Look, I'll show you. (*He leads her to the stairway, and together they look down.*) See! Nothing to frighten you, is there? (*He calls.*) Come on up, boys. (HARRY *and* DIDO *move from the stairs.*) Be nice to them.

DIDO: Who are they?

HARRY: Ssh! (FATHER ANSELM, *an elderly priest, and* MATTHEW SANGOSSE *come up the stairway and into the room. They wear coats and carry hats.*) Hullo, Father. Hullo, Doc.

ANSELM: Are we disturbing you, Harry?

HARRY: I'm doing nothing. (*To* DIDO.) This is Father Anselm, and this is the Doctor.

MATTHEW: My name is Sangosse.

HARRY: Have you got another name?

DIDO: Morgen.

HARRY: This is Dido Morgen. Where've you boys been?

ANSELM: For a walk.

MATTHEW: It's a strange feeling walking down there now that all the foreign soldiers have gone. You can miss something you dislike, I suppose.

HARRY: Do you know, it hadn't struck me they'd gone. But then you're a native. I'm not. Anyway, you had a good walk.

MATTHEW: We went as far as the monument and back.

HARRY: That must've taken you quite a time.

MATTHEW: Two hours.

ANSELM: Catherine sent us.

HARRY: Sent you? I've only just got back. Been out all day in the truck. So I don't know about things. Tell me, boys, what goes on?

ANSELM: Goes on, Harry?

HARRY: Yes. You were sent out for a walk. Sent out. And look— (*He points to the man on the balcony.*)

MATTHEW: Who is it?

HARRY: You don't know, either.

MATTHEW (*to the man*): Excuse me, what are you doing out there? *The man does not answer.*

HARRY: Was he there when you went out?

MATTHEW: No.

HARRY: Hell! Where's Kate? What is all this? Go find her. Tell her somebody's trying to break up the happy home.

ANSELM: Coming, Matthew?

HARRY: That's my boys. (FATHER ANSELM *and* MATTHEW *go out.*) Question is: good or bad?

DIDO: News?

HARRY: I don't want my quiet life disturbed. I'm happy. Looked after.

DIDO: Are there servants here?

HARRY: Plenty. Kate keeps them under cover. Like kids of an earlier generation—but better!—they're neither seen nor heard.

DIDO: But we kids of this generation—say me!—when do we eat?

HARRY: Hungry?

DIDO: Yes.

HARRY: Keep going. (*From his breast pocket he takes a bar of chocolate, which he throws to* DIDO, *who catches it.*)

DIDO: It's soft.

HARRY: From the warmth of my heart. You're too young to know —but that's the last part of you to die. The coldness creeps around your more private parts, but that public organ, your heart, just won't go out. (*He attempts to kiss her but she pushes him away and laughs with her mouth full of chocolate.*) You'll make yourself sick.

DIDO: I don't care.

CATHERINE DE TROYES *comes from the upper room. She wears a dressing robe.*

HARRY: Don't care, eh?

DIDO: No. Don't care.

HARRY: Give him—(*the man*)—a bit.

DIDO: No.

HARRY: Gi'me a bit.

DIDO: No!

HARRY: Poor Harry! Gi'm li'l bit choc'late.

DIDO: No. No choc'late f'Harry. Eat't all m'self. (*She has stuffed the remaining chocolate into her mouth.* HARRY *appeals to the man on the balcony.*)

HARRY: She's ate up—right up. Now, an't that nasty—plain nasty? No choc'late f'you'n'me—s'none f'working men like you'n'me. Though what in hell your work is—standing there!—God knows.

CATHERINE: He's my new guardian angel, Harry. Don't abuse

him. And how very interesting to hear that you look upon your-self as a working man.

HARRY: Why not? I've been out on the truck since early morning.

CATHERINE (*to* DIDO): He gives himself away every time. Have you found that?

HARRY: Sleeping! You should be ashamed.

CATHERINE *has come down into the room, and again speaks to* DIDO.

CATHERINE: He'll manage to put you in the wrong, too, when you come to play your part. I take it you are one of his troupe, or whatever it is he makes his pictures with.

DIDO *wipes her mouth with the back of her hand.*

HARRY: This, incidentally—indeed, quite by the way—is Dido Morgen.

CATHERINE: I'm Catherine de Troyes. How do you do.

HARRY: Miss Morgen will be staying here. (*There is silence.*) For a few days. She's temporarily part of my troupe, as you'll have it. Just for a few days.

CATHERINE (*to* DIDO): Americans possess two endearing qualities. Their innocence, which delights me—and their feeling for hospitality which often inconveniences me. But of course you must stay, Miss Morgen. For tonight, at least. Did you come up those stairs on your way here? (DIDO *nods her head.*) Well, now go down them, and instead of turning through the main door—which will take you out into the world—turn the other way. There you'll find someone to attend you. Have you any night things with you?

HARRY: No, she hasn't.

CATHERINE: It can be arranged. (*There is silence.* DIDO *has not moved.*) Have you understood what I've said?

HARRY: Go on, honey. I'll be around to see you soon. We'll talk about the picture.

DIDO *wanders to the stairway and begins to go down. Before she is out of sight or hearing* CATHERINE *speaks.*

CATHERINE: Like a puppy. Where did you find it?

HARRY: In a bar.

CATHERINE: What do you want it for?

DIDO *has gone.*

HARRY: I've told you. For the picture. She's fine. Right out of that stinking city.

CATHERINE: Like the filthy old man we had up last month. What

was he? Christ down on his luck, wasn't he? He came out of that
stinking city. But he wasn't right after all.

HARRY: There was nothing back of his eyes. That's what I'm looking for to photograph. The something back of their eyes.

CATHERINE: And this girl has it?

HARRY: Maybe. I don't know yet.

CATHERINE: When will you know? When you've tried to sleep
with her?

HARRY: That's not fair, Kate.

CATHERINE: What is fair, Harry? You, living here on my weakness
and indulging your notions at my expense. Is that fair? I don't
think it is.

HARRY: Go on—give. I'm expecting the worst.

CATHERINE: Here it comes. I'm afraid there'll be no more money
for the film.

HARRY: No more money. What've I done?

CATHERINE: Nothing. That's the point. You should have made up
your poor muddled mind before this, and finished the picture.
Finished it while I was prepared to pay for your ridiculous antics.

HARRY: My ridiculous antics.

CATHERINE: I've gone beyond such amusements, Harry. I don't
want—I shan't need you about any more.

HARRY: Suddenly seen sense, you have.

CATHERINE: You admit it? That however much money and time
I give you, the film will never be made? You know, don't you,
that all the business of getting the faces, finding the places—the
right faces and the right places to photograph at the right time—
it was nothing more than a putting off because you've nothing to
say any more. You see and you feel the misery—say down there
in the city—but you can't do anything about it. You can't even
represent it by your old love, the camera, on a screen. You're not
big enough, Harry.

HARRY: Maybe not. But you knew what I wanted to do.

CATHERINE: Yes, I knew.

HARRY: That I wanted to go back of their faces.

CATHERINE: Yes.

HARRY: Back of their faces—those godawful masks—and get whatever it is.

CATHERINE: Yes, that.

HARRY: And keep it on film. That hope, that something—

CATHERINE: At the back of their eyes. But it's in everyone, Harry. You don't have to look for it. It's in me. But the failure to see is in you.

HARRY: Sure. So—no more money.

CATHERINE: No.

HARRY: No money—no picture. What about Poppa and the Doc?

CATHERINE: They must go too.

HARRY: No picture, no sweetness from the little white pills, no God any more. You've found something.

CATHERINE: Yes. You talk about it. You talk about love an awful lot, Harry. But do you understand what you say, I wonder?

HARRY: I talk to myself in a language I understand, if that's what you mean.

CATHERINE: I was a young woman when Rupert left to fight nine years ago, and through the two years' absence at war and the seven years of his imprisonment I've had to live on my kind of love. You don't understand, do you?

HARRY: I've never understood.

CATHERINE: You like me, Harry, because you're sorry for me. That's safe, isn't it? Because I'm one of your old tramps or funny little girls with my heart in the wrong place. Because I'm alone. But, Harry, you can stop being sorry for me. I'm not alone any longer.

HARRY: He's back.

CATHERINE: Yes. Rupert's back.

HARRY: Up there? (*He points to the upper room.*)

CATHERINE: He's sleeping. Very tired. Long journey.

HARRY: You've been up there with him.

CATHERINE: Yes. With him.

HARRY: You knew he was coming back today.

CATHERINE: This morning. They sent me a message.

HARRY: That's why you sent Poppa and Doc out for a walk.

CATHERINE: I wanted to meet him alone.

HARRY: You've muddled them. They don't know what goes on. I didn't either for that matter.

CATHERINE: I'll explain to them. Soon enough.

HARRY: And show them the door.

CATHERINE: Well, am I expected to have you three old things around my neck for the rest of my life?

HARRY: So Forster's back.

CATHERINE: Yes. And Harry—Harry, he's going to be free!

HARRY: Are they unlocking all the cages at the zoo today as well? Free. My, my! (*He points suddenly to the man on the balcony. It is darker and the man is barely visible.*)

CATHERINE: That man? He was sent with Rupert to guard him. There are two more below. They'll only be with us for a little while. Just so long as the country needs to get used to the idea of Rupert being free. All great men must be guarded in these days.

HARRY: Sure, sure.

CATHERINE: Well, got everything straight now?

HARRY: I guess so. Was there a need to be quite so harsh? I suppose there was. I'd never get out of anywhere nowadays without being pushed out. There's one thing I'd like you to know—not important to you but important to me. It's in you, Kate, that my lamented youth resides. You're the person who represents all that I wanted to be and believed I could be when we first knew each other in the old days. I translated everything—ambition, talent, all values—into your person. I suppose—in my own way, a way you despise—I love you. Don't put up the lights for a minute!

   It is very dark within the room.

CATHERINE: Dry your tears. I'm not looking.

HARRY: It's just that I hate saying goodbye.

CATHERINE: The party's over, Harry.

   FATHER ANSELM *and* MATTHEW SANGOSSE *have come into the room.*

MATTHEW: Catherine?

CATHERINE: Yes, my dears. I'm here.

MATTHEW: May I put on the light?

CATHERINE: Not for a moment. We must allow Harry to recover himself.

HARRY: Also, I'd imagine, we must give you time to think of something you can say to these boys.

ANSELM: Are you upset about something, Harry?

HARRY: Poppa, we're all three of us going to be upset together in a minute. Go ahead, Kate.

CATHERINE: You tell them, Harry.

HARRY: Well, I'm damned!

CATHERINE: Go on. Tell them.

HARRY: Poppa, Doc—we're fired. We're out, boys. On our ears.

MATTHEW: Out?

HARRY: The life we've had here, bringing in our several ways comfort to this lady, is finished. An incident has occurred.

ANSELM: Have you quarrelled with Harry, Catherine?

HARRY: No, no. It's all quite friendly. Just this: we're being told to leave, boys. Find other quarters. As simple as that. Go fasten your suckers, you suckers, on somebody else. But don't forget we have done her some small service. That's why the light's out; to spare her blushes. (CATHERINE *does not speak.* HARRY *continues, very softly.*) If you listen very hard both of you, you'll hear the sounds of war. Coriolan—Coriolan. You'll hear the soft stumbling tread of returning men. Men out of order and out of heart. There's no trumpet left will call them to attention. There's no drum can fit the broken rhythm of their march. But they are come back—they have come home.

RUPERT FOSTER *calls quietly from the gallery before the door of the upper room.*

RUPERT: Catherine! (*The lights go up in the room.* CATHERINE—*she has her hand on the light switch—and the three men look up at* RUPERT. *He speaks to* CATHERINE.) You left me alone. You promised not to do that.

CATHERINE: I was coming back.

RUPERT: Shall I come down? I'm quite awake now. (*He comes down into the room.*) Good evening, gentlemen. I overheard—forgive me!—the lament spoken by one of you. Coriolan, may I remind you, was a tyrant. But yes, I've come back.

CATHERINE: Have you had a good rest?

RUPERT: How long have I been asleep?

CATHERINE: Only two hours or so.

RUPERT: It must have been the darkness that woke me. It can, you know.

CATHERINE: Are those the only clothes you have?

RUPERT: I borrowed them from my servant. I'm no longer allowed to wear uniform.

HARRY: Too bad!

CATHERINE *speaks to* MATTHEW *and* FATHER ANSELM.

CATHERINE: This is Rupert Forster, Father Anselm and Doctor Matthew Sangosse.

They shake hands as CATHERINE *turns to* HARRY, *who speaks.*

HARRY: Remember me, sir?

RUPERT *stares at him without recognition.*

CATHERINE: It's Harry Lancaster, darling.

HARRY: Well, if my face doesn't mean anything to him it's scarcely likely my name will.

RUPERT: You must forgive me. I've been away.

HARRY: I know.

RUPERT: Away for a long time. I can't recall—

HARRY: Ever having seen me before in your life. I know.

RUPERT: Won't you help me?

HARRY: It was a long time ago. And it doesn't matter.

CATHERINE: You met Harry when he was making a film here. Remember?

HARRY: Years ago.

RUPERT: God! Yes, of course. I'm so sorry. What are you doing here now?

HARRY: I was making another picture of your beautiful city. It was to be a sequel to the first picture you remember so well. It was to show how all the pretty little girls of the first picture have become cellar drabs. How the dirty finger of time has pushed in all their sweet little cheeks. It was to show how all the fine young men in their uniforms of the first picture have—well, it was to show that they aren't around any longer.

RUPERT: It sounds most entertaining.

HARRY: Yes, it's the sort of thing would make you laugh a lot.

RUPERT: And you were going to film it in the city.

HARRY: Yes. There—or in somebody's armpit.

CATHERINE: Harry, do you think you should so neglect your girl?

HARRY: My girl? You want us to get out at once?

CATHERINE: Of course not. Stay, at least, tonight.

HARRY: Many, many thanks. (*He has moved to the stairway. He looks down.*) I promised her lots.

CATHERINE: Fulfil your promises.

HARRY: For one thing I told her she was among friends. (HARRY *goes down the stairs.*)

CATHERINE: I thought we'd have dinner later.

RUPERT: Yes, I'm a little—

CATHERINE: What?

RUPERT: I'm a little confused. What is it? Early evening?

CATHERINE (*laughing*): Yes, darling. Later, then.

RUPERT: Remember I've been on a prison diet.

CATHERINE: What was it like?

RUPERT: Not bad. Everything had onions in it.

CATHERINE: Everything?

RUPERT: Even the shaving water.

FATHER ANSELM *and* MATTHEW *have been speaking together.*
FATHER ANSELM *now comes forward.*

ANSELM: I'm speaking for myself and Matthew.

CATHERINE: What's that?

ANSELM: When do you want us to leave, Catherine?

MATTHEW: No arrangements have been made, of course.

CATHERINE: Have you anywhere to go?

ANSELM. We shall stay together. Matthew has a sister living in the country. He thinks it probable she'd welcome us.

MATTHEW: I'll telephone her tomorrow.

CATHERINE: Very well.

MATTHEW: For tonight we'll go to our rooms. Unless you need us for anything.

CATHERINE: No, I shan't need you.

ANSELM: Your prayers, later.

CATHERINE: Not tonight.

FATHER ANSELM *and* MATTHEW *go out.*

RUPERT: Why are they here?

CATHERINE: To look after me. To keep me well and safe until you came back.

RUPERT: But why those men? So shabby, so at odds with the world.

CATHERINE: Are they shabby? I suppose they are. I've never noticed. They needed somewhere to live after the war. And I needed friends.

RUPERT: Friends?

CATHERINE: No, that's not the word, is it? I needed someone to notice that I was here and that I was human. You've been away a long time, Rupert.

RUPERT: They're not what I'd have expected to find with you. And the American—I don't remember him at all. I said I did, but it's not true. Faces and names, you know, they just disappear. Not one thing about him remains.

CATHERINE: He's changed since the old days. He was amusing then, I think. But he's been home and seems to have picked up the national failing: he sees everyone as a distorted reflection of himself. He feels he should straighten out the image. So he questions strangers on their misfortune. It doesn't amuse him to have a woman now unless she's down on her luck. There's a girl in this house at the moment. Brought her back this afternoon. She's to be in the film, he says, Ach! he's pathetic. He doesn't even take them into his bed any more—only into his great big American heart. He came over six months ago, penniless, and asked me to put him up.

RUPERT: You took them all in because you were sorry for them.

CATHERINE: Not exactly. Darling, you make the place sound like a charity lodging house. They're none of them quite as bad as that, you know. Father and the Doctor do their jobs professionally, and Harry once made very good films.

RUPERT: So they've filled your life for the past seven years in place of the others I remember.

CATHERINE: The others?

RUPERT: The men who dressed your hair and painted your face, designed your clothes and fitted your shoes. Those are the people I remember with you.

CATHERINE: When they sent you away to prison and I was left alone I did a very natural thing—I got down on my knees. But the words that had been there since childhood weren't there any longer. I just couldn't say them. It was Father Anselm who in his own muddled way gave me back the words. We started from the beginning—it was 'say after me' all over again. As for the Doctor, he's easy to explain. I was not able to sleep—not for a long time —and he had magic in his boxes and bottles.

RUPERT: Now you've told them they must go. You feel you can do without them.

CATHERINE: Of course. You're back, Rupert. Why should I need anything more?

RUPERT: Catherine—(*in silence he measures, in a number of paces, a certain distance across the room*)—that, square, was the exact measurement of my room at the camp. I was sent to that place direct from the freedom of a battlefield. I occupied it for seven years. That little space could have been my childhood nursery, my cadet's room at the military academy, my old battlefields, this room in this house with you—indeed, it could have been any of my particular heavens or hells. Imagination could have made it so. And I could have been any man I wished to be. A free man, if I liked. I chose that the room should be a brick and steel cell in a prison camp in the mountains and that I should be its occupant. A man called Forster.

CATHERINE: You're accusing me. I don't understand why.

RUPERT: I'm not accusing you. You told me of your life during my absence. I'm telling you of my life at that time. Nothing more. There's no accusation.

CATHERINE: I've got into the habit of imagining things.

RUPERT: Yes.

CATHERINE: You're trying to tell me something.

RUPERT: How I lived at the camp. My room was entered twice a day by my servant—the first time to clean the room, the second time to attend me, the prisoner. I left the room once a day for exercise—alone. I was permitted to walk to the boundary of the compound and return at once. I was allowed to look at the sky. The camp commandant visited me once a week, but as a gesture of faith didn't enter the room. That procedure was followed exactly for the first two years. Now, tell me from that description, Catherine, is that the man you remember?

CATHERINE: Of course not. Never imprisoned—never! No, I think of you as—

RUPERT: Let me go on. In the third year the conditions in the camp altered. I was given more food and a change of bedding. The comforts multiplied. One day I was sent a message saying that if I wanted a woman a young girl could be obtained from the village below the camp. The message came by a junior officer, who assured me that the child would be bathed and deloused before being sent to my room. I refused the offer.

CATHERINE: Because you loved me.

RUPERT: It had nothing to do with love.

CATHERINE: Because you remembered me.

RUPERT: You don't understand, Catherine. I didn't think of you in that place. I didn't think of you at all. If I'd done so, it would have become a place of freedom. In fact, it was a prison.

CATHERINE: Some men would have tried to get out if only by imagination—by memory—

RUPERT: Some men dream away their lives without having to be put behind bars. I'm not one of them.

CATHERINE: You talk like this because we made love only a little while ago. You were always cruel afterwards.

RUPERT: That demand hasn't changed, certainly. I refused the girl at the camp—but not you.

CATHERINE: There is a difference. Take a risk and think back for a moment. You'll remember, I love you.

RUPERT: You love the man your loneliness has created, perhaps.

CATHERINE: Then tell me: what are you now?

RUPERT: A defeated soldier who is allowed to live only to further his disgrace.

CATHERINE: All right! I'll accept that.

Then, from all the speakers of a public address system which covers the city, a man's voice speaks.

ANNOUNCER: The time is twenty hours. The time is twenty hours. It is now—officially—night.

A bell is struck.

RUPERT: What is it?

CATHERINE: It comes from the public address system all over the city.

RUPERT: What are they—amplifiers?

CATHERINE: Yes. Rupert, kill your pride—kill it!

RUPERT: Who put up those things?

CATHERINE: John Cadmus. To speak to the people. There are speakers in every street—even all over the hillside in the trees. They make announcements.

RUPERT: Has John Cadmus been here?

CATHERINE: Yes. Very often.

RUPERT: Why?

CATHERINE: I asked him to come the first time. It was a few days after your arrest when he was recalled as Chancellor at the time of the defeat. I asked him to use his authority to have you released. He said it was impossible. The second time he came here without invitation. We sat in this room and talked. I can't remember what about—not about you. After that he came here at irregular intervals but very frequently.

RUPERT: What you're saying, in effect, is that you formed some kind of friendship with him after that first meeting.

CATHERINE: He was kind and often amusing. Sometimes he gave me small gifts. For instance, the last time he brought a string quartet which played Beethoven for three hours. I went to sleep in front of them.

RUPERT: Why didn't you ask him about me? He got a weekly report on my behaviour.

CATHERINE: I didn't want a weekly report on you—to hear of you growing older and sadder and more and more hopeless.

RUPERT: Why not? If it was true.

CATHERINE: I want to know you as you were! If they've changed you I don't know what I shall do. O God! I remember you, Rupert. But do you remember me—do you remember me?

HARRY LANCASTER *has come a little way up the stairs.*

HARRY: Forgive.

CATHERINE: What is it?

HARRY: There's been a message.

CATHERINE: Well?

HARRY: Over the telephone.

CATHERINE: Yes?

HARRY: The Chancellor is on his way here to see General Forster. His arrival is imminent. Poppa's waiting to receive him at the door.

CATHERINE: All right, Harry. Thank you. What does he want, Rupert?

HARRY: Affairs of State, maybe. Ssh!

CATHERINE: Go away, Harry. (*He remains.*) Tonight. Why must he come tonight? (*She begins to move to the upper room.*)

RUPERT: Where are you going?

CATHERINE: I must dress. Were you expecting him tonight?

RUPERT: No. Were you?

HARRY: There's one you're going to have to tell yourself, Katie. Tell him he's like the rest of us boys—just not welcome here any more. All right! I didn't speak—I'm not here. (CATHERINE *goes into the upper room.*) This can hardly be the return you imagined in your youth, General.

RUPERT: What's that?

HARRY: I say, when you were a young man you must've thought the return from war to your native city would be very different.

RUPERT: In what way?

HARRY: Oh, come now. Where is the triumphal drive through the streets, the heroic music, the garland of war? Where is the howling mob upping its sweaty nightcaps? Where are the young virgins casting themselves in front of your jeep?

RUPERT: You're a romantic, Mr Lancaster. I suppose all entertainers are that.

HARRY: I wonder what it is the world finds so unfunny about you? In my part of professional entertainer you interest me. Suppose I put you in a cage like a wild beast, would they pay their pennies to come and look at you? I doubt that. I doubt it very much.

RUPERT: Please leave me alone.

HARRY: Tell me, sir, is your release unconditional? If so, who is our constant companion?

RUPERT: I'm told he's to protect me from annoyance.

HARRY: Then he's not doing his job, is he? Why don't you call him to order?

RUPERT: I've no authority to do that.

HARRY: Authority. That's an interesting word. Are you sure you don't mean power?

RUPERT: No, Mr Lancaster, I mean authority. I have power. Power to throw you down those stairs, for instance. That remains.

HARRY: Would you resort to violence, General?

RUPERT: You're a small man.

HARRY: Has that anything to do with it?

RUPERT: The use of power? Of course, you fool! (*From below the stairs* DIDO *calls:* Harry!) You're being called.

HARRY: All right, honey. I'm talking to what looks like a man. They tell me he's something more, but he looks like a man. I guess the failure to see is in me. Eh, Kate?

CATHERINE *has come from the upper room. She is dressed. She does not answer* HARRY.

CATHERINE: Is this an amusing dress, Rupert?

HARRY: Even if you think it is, General, you're not supposed to laugh. I once made that mistake. (HARRY *goes down the stair.*)

CATHERINE: There's one good thing about this visit of John Cadmus. We shall know your exact position. What have they told you?

RUPERT: Nothing. What have they told you?

CATHERINE: There was a message this morning giving me the time of your arrival.

RUPERT: Is that all?

CATHERINE: What do you mean?

RUPERT: I thought you must know something more.

CATHERINE: It was enough. To know you were coming back was enough. (FATHER ANSELM *appears on the stairway.*) Yes?

ANSELM: The Chancellor is here.

CATHERINE: All right. Bring him up. (FATHER ANSELM *goes down the stairway.*) When did you see him last?

RUPERT: Seven years ago. On my way to the camp. Catherine, we really know nothing of what's happening.

CATHERINE: He'll tell us. We'll just let him talk himself out of the house. We'll be alone together soon, and then we can find our way. We've wandered off the road for a while, that's all. It's only to be expected.

> JOHN CADMUS, *assisted by* FATHER ANSELM, *comes up the stairs. He is a man of great age, physically and spiritually wasted by many years spent in the exercise of power.*

CADMUS: After such a climb as that I always expect to find myself in heaven. (*To* CATHERINE.) Angel! (*He kisses her.*) Somewhere to sit. (CATHERINE *takes him to a chair, and he sits.*) Hullo, Forster.

CATHERINE: Would you like something to drink?

CADMUS: Yes, I would. I'd like my usual warm milk.

CATHERINE (*to* FATHER ANSELM): Get it.

> FATHER ANSELM *goes down the stairs.*

CADMUS: As a temporal power, Catherine, you speak with unusual authority to the spiritual. You must attend one of the tea parties I give for my princes of the church.

CATHERINE: They'd eat out of my hand.

CADMUS: As long as there was something in it. Otherwise they'd bite. A good journey, Forster?

RUPERT: Yes, sir.

CADMUS: Did we provide transport suitable to your position?

RUPERT: Three cars, six guards and an aide.

CADMUS: Excellent. And they brought you safely to this place.

RUPERT: They did. The guards are still here. I say, the guards have stayed on. I was told they are for my protection.

CADMUS: Forster, we all go in mortal danger. Can we even trust the guards? The whisper of ambition is in their hearts without a doubt. Who is to guard the guards? That's an old question which has never been answered.

RUPERT: What am I to understand by it?

CATHERINE: Wait. He never asks questions he can't answer.

CADMUS: Ah! it's possible to breathe up here. Down in the city the smell of corruption becomes insufferable. The stench of the spilt guts of the world is always in the nose. D'you know, Forster, twice in a lifetime I've been brought from retreat to stand over the murdered body of our country. They turn to me. The misfortune of being the father image. I'm known as Daddy Cadmus now. Did I say I'd like some hot milk?

CATHERINE: It's coming.

CADMUS: You'd imagine the aftermath of war to be depressing, wouldn't you? Not a bit of it. Defeat has resulted in a splendid get-together. At least, socially. The difficulty is to keep them apart. The birthrate is astounding. Politically we are split exactly down the middle, and however I play the submissive female part we remain distressingly infertile. A few weeks ago it was thought the body-politic might produce a tiny policy, but it was only wind. Seven years married too. But my problems of administration don't interest you.

RUPERT: They might, but I'm out of touch.

CADMUS: Has my gadget spoken to you yet? The amplifiers, I mean.

RUPERT: They announced the time.

CADMUS: They can do better than that. When I'm faced with excitement in the city—they riot, you know—those things pour out music and it works like a charm. The angry fellows have their grievances washed away by the memory of what has been or the thought of what might be. The way to prevent revolt is to stop men living in the present time. Given a sad song they drift off with their wives and sweethearts and resolve their misery in quite the oldest way. That, of course, gives rise to another problem already mentioned. But the human milk supply luckily remains constant. (FATHER ANSELM *comes up the stairway. He carries a tray on which there is a flask of milk, a drinking glass and a bowl of sugar.*) From the cow, I hope.

ANSELM: Quite fresh, sir.

CADMUS: Pour it out. Three spoons of sugar. (FATHER ANSELM *serves the milk.*) I find a grave distaste for all food now. For instance, this innocent looking liquid on which I'm compelled to live is actually the glandular secretion of a dying animal. But then, if we were to look too closely at any of our main supports, we'd— (*He stops speaking for a moment and tastes the milk.*) What would happen, Forster? You've had plenty of time to think about such things. Let's have your opinion.

RUPERT: I'm afraid I can't share your obvious horror of material existence.

CADMUS: You can't? That's a pity.

RUPERT: Why a pity?

CADMUS: I'll tell you. (*To* FATHER ANSELM.) Thank you. (FATHER ANSELM *goes down the stairs.*) Catherine, would you like to leave us?

CATHERINE: No.

CADMUS: Very well. First of all, Forster, I can take no credit for fetching you out of prison today. If I had my way you'd remain shut up for the rest of your life.

RUPERT: That's very interesting. Who am I to thank for this— freedom.

CADMUS: Freedom? You're back here for a purpose. It's three shots a penny at you now, Forster. But I'm confusing you. You may or may not know that modern government is based not on theory or even practical policy but on emotion. This country has been compelled to accept that system of government from the conquerors. It is known as democratic. It means that I have an opposition party. This, of course, is a great novelty. My opposition party is liberal minded, and they have all the savagery possessed by good men. They say it is love but they bare their teeth when pronouncing the word. It is these men who have brought you back.

RUPERT: Why?

CADMUS: We're now an autonomous state again. The occupying forces were withdrawn some weeks ago. For seven years we've been able to refer our major problems to foreigners. Now, once again, as in the war, we're on our own. We have to make up our minds about bigger things than the city drainage. One of these bigger things, my opposition tells me, is to find out who was responsible for this country losing the war. There has to be a man, Forster. Something they can stretch out and touch, which breathes and reasons and answers questions. They can't put Bad Luck in the dock, Forster, but they can put you there.

RUPERT: I'm to stand some kind of trial?

CADMUS: That's the intention. It's to be a big show. It'll take place in the Parliament House. Your accuser is the State and its People. The charge will be treason arising from cowardice in the face of the enemy. Your behaviour during that last battle in the East appears to give certain grounds for such an accusation.

RUPERT: Do you expect me to defend myself—to you, here and now?

CADMUS: No.

RUPERT: You said—I think—that you would not have brought me back.

CADMUS: I did say that. But these men who've asked for your return have the country behind them. So, you see, I can't refuse to have you brought to trial. It would look, you must admit, as if I defended your behaviour. And I can't do that. It seems on the face of it a reasonable request.

RUPERT: My section of the Eastern front was comparatively small. Too small, I should've thought to have merited consideration as a factor of absolute defeat.

CADMUS: That has nothing to do with it. You're a man. More, you're Rupert Forster. These good men must give the country something worth having. Something the butcher, the baker and the candlestick maker—in their guilty sickness—can recognize as the cause of defeat and disgrace. Those ordinary people want to go out into the world and say, I wasn't responsible for the war starting or for the war ending in defeat: it was that man Forster. He was tried, you know, and found guilty. That's why the people of this country will back the group of men who oppose me. You are about to be taken into the great mouth of that modern monster, the Demagogue.

RUPERT: The result of the trial is a foregone conclusion, then.

CADMUS: Not at all. If it takes place I shall do everything to ensure that it's fairly conducted.

RUPERT: What do you mean, if it takes place?

CADMUS: Catherine, a social fact of some importance to you. I can allow no one to leave this house for thirty-six hours or so. No one, that is, except myself. And I must go straightaway. (*He rises.*) I had luncheon with the actor, Constant, today. I asked him how he would go about telling a man that it was necessary, indeed imperative, that he should kill himself.

RUPERT: What did he say?

CADMUS: He said drama was, of course, inherent in such a situation for the essence of drama is the dilemma of the central heroic figure. He was very interesting about that.

RUPERT: Did he advise you further?

CADMUS: Yes,

RUPERT: May we not be told?

CADMUS: Certainly. Constant went on to say that if he was to play such a scene in the theatre the prosaic details would be sufficient.

RUPERT: Will you not tell me those details?

CADMUS: I was about to do so. The time: within thirty-six hours. That is, by dawn of the day after tomorrow.

RUPERT: The place?

CADMUS: Within this house, secretly. The means— (*He has taken a jewelled box from his pocket.*) I have removed the dismal original package. Look upon this box as a gift, Forster. The substance within, I'm told, is also used for extracting gold from its ore. A factor which, applied philosophically, may be of comfort to you.

RUPERT *takes the box.*

CATHERINE: You don't take it seriously. You're smiling.

RUPERT: Am I? Why didn't you get her out of the room, Cadmus?

CADMUS: He takes it seriously, Catherine, and you must bring yourself to believe it is right.

CATHERINE: Right!

CADMUS: The thing to do. You must bring yourself to believe it is necessary.

CATHERINE: But why, John, why?

CADMUS: Because I cannot allow this trial to take place. I love this country, Catherine, and I believe that given a few years I can make it again seem worthy of a place in Europe. But not if I have this trial forced on me. The mud that is thrown won't only hit Forster. It will stick to every man, woman and child of this nation. That is why I will not allow the trial to take place. That is why Forster must kill himself.

CATHERINE: You've no authority to give such an order.

CADMUS: It wasn't an order. It was a request. I thought that was understood.

RUPERT: Perfectly.

CATHERINE: A request. Is that all? Can we do anything else for you?

CADMUS: Nothing. Will someone help me down? I've a horror of falling nowadays.

CATHERINE: You're not to touch him, Rupert! You've done the wrong thing, John. He's safe with me.

CADMUS: Any complete protection—even one of love, Catherine— is also an effective prison. Yes, he's safe with you. (*He takes*

RUPERT'S *arm and they go down the stairs.* CATHERINE *remains alone until* RUPERT *returns.*)

CATHERINE: Can you ask for a man's life as simply as you'd ask for his advice?

RUPERT: Yes, you can. I've done it. With many lives.

CATHERINE: You were their commander.

RUPERT: Yet the final decision remained with each man. We never really command. We only—like Cadmus—request.

CATHERINE: And you were obeyed. Why is John so sure that you'll obey him?

RUPERT (*he is standing beside the bronze helmet*): I found this helmet beneath the tracks of my carrier in battle. I picked it up and a skull rattled inside. After hundreds of years he'd come to the surface, and we were still fighting over the same ground. Nothing had been gained since the day he'd fallen. I was attempting with my armoured vehicle only to do what he'd tried to do with his armoured head and his antique sword. His end on that field was death, mine was disgrace. But I was left as surely and eternally in that clay-cold earth as was this comrade-in-arms of mine. Our intentions must now be effected by another man in another time: it no longer rests in us. They've taken away the means of achievement, my soldiers. I can't stretch out to the future because I've nothing to use. Cadmus knows that. When I was young I could see far into the future and that makes a man alive. When he cannot see—as at this moment—then a man may as well grant such a request. Cadmus knows I'll do what he asks because there is no future action for me. He knows there is nothing here—nothing anywhere to detain me.

CATHERINE: I am here.

RUPERT: I'm no longer in love with you, Catherine. Such things need to be said. When they are true and the time has come, such things need to be said.

CATHERINE: You have a great regard for the truth. I knew the truth all through today—but I pretended that you still loved me. Couldn't you have done that? Truth of your kind is for the very young—not for me.

RUPERT: Did you want me to lie?

CATHERINE: It would've been for such a short time. John said within thirty-six hours.

RUPERT: I gave you the truth in the past,

CATHERINE: Now you give it to John Cadmus.

RUPERT: I loved you, Catherine.

CATHERINE: In the past. What do you want? (*She speaks to* DIDO, *who has come a little way up the stairs.*)

DIDO: Can I come up here? My honour is imperilled.

CATHERINE: What does that mean? Harry?

DIDO: Yes. He talked about God, social injustice—he cried a little there—war and love of mankind. What he meant, of course, was love of his own kind. I want to go home.

CATHERINE: And they won't let you out.

DIDO: The men at the door said I stay. So here I am.

RUPERT: I'm sorry. It's my fault.

DIDO: You're General Forster, aren't you? My experiences with soldiers have so far been unfortunate. (*She holds out the palm of her hand.*) That scar was a mortar shell fragment in the street fighting when I was a baby. (*She touches her face.*) This, a broken bottle in bar-room fighting when I was somewhat older.

RUPERT: I hope our acquaintance—however short—will be more peaceful.

DIDO: I thought you were dead, but Harry said you were up here. You know, he doesn't like you.

RUPERT: I know. What's your name?

DIDO: It doesn't matter.

CATHERINE: Yes, it does. She's called Dido.

DIDO: Please don't laugh. Blame my father. He was an archaeologist. Always grubbing in the past. Disgusting occupation. I say, am I bothering you?

CATHERINE: No.

DIDO: Well, with those men on the door it looks as if I'll be here for a time.

CURTAIN

ACT TWO

The scene is the same.
The time: the following day. It is night.
The room is in darkness. A small film projector has been set up, and is in action with a film showing on the screen.
Before the screen in the darkness sit RUPERT, CATHERINE, DIDO,
FATHER ANSELM *and* MATTHEW SANGOSSE.
HARRY *is standing by the projector as operator.*
The film is in its final sequence. It ends.

HARRY: Will somebody put up the lights? (*The lights of the room are put on by* MATTHEW. RUPERT *and* DIDO *are shown to be sitting together—*DIDO *on the floor with her head resting against* RUPERT'S *knees.* CATHERINE, *turned away from the screen, is observing them as she must have been in the darkness.*) That's all, everybody.

ANSELM: Thank you, Harry. It was most enjoyable.

HARRY: It's all right, Poppa. Anything I can do to make our enforced stay in this house tolerable—just call on me.

ANSELM: I thought the girl was rather like you, Miss Morgen.

HARRY: You're being spoken to, honey.

RUPERT: She's asleep.

HARRY: Well, I'm damned!

FATHER ANSELM *laughs.*

CATHERINE: Wake her, Rupert.

RUPERT *ruffles* DIDO'S *hair.*

RUPERT: Wake up.

DIDO: What?

RUPERT: Wake up! The show's over. Do you want to be locked in?

DIDO: God! Sorry, everybody. Sorry, Harry.

HARRY: It's all right.

DIDO: Did I miss much of it?

HARRY: I don't know. Did you?

DIDO: From what I saw of it I'd say it was funny and old. The women! Did they ever look like that? Did they ever behave like that?

HARRY: They did. Just twenty years ago.

DIDO: The young ones look sort of muddy—and don't they grin a lot? Was there so much to laugh about in those days? (*She suddenly looks round at the others.*) I suppose all of you were young at that time.

HARRY: Yes. Yes, we were. Around that time.

DIDO: So that's your masterpiece, Harry.

HARRY: It is. You must see it sometime.

CATHERINE: Shall we go down to supper? It's ready.

HARRY: Let's do that. There's always eating left for us. I must clear up this junk first.

CATHERINE: Come along, Father—and Matthew.

RUPERT (*to* HARRY): I'll help you with this.

HARRY: I can manage. All right, pack up the screen, please. (CATHERINE, *with* MATTHEW *and* FATHER ANSELM, *goes below.* HARRY *begins to dismantle the projector and* RUPERT *the screen.* DIDO *stands beside* RUPERT.) I'll not bother to rewind.

RUPERT: What's that?

HARRY: The film. I'm not bothering—oh, forget it. From all the sense it made tonight I might just as well run it backwards next time. Not that there'll be a next time.

DIDO: How long since you last showed it?

HARRY: Long time. Maybe ten years. I don't know.

DIDO: Why did you show it tonight?

HARRY: I thought—wrongly, of course—that it might relax the tension for a couple of hours. I thought it'd give Kate something to look at beside you two. You'll forgive me asking this: what the hell are you up to?

RUPERT: Where do you want this? (*He refers to the cinema screen.*)

HARRY: I'll take it down with me. For God's sake, Forster, couldn't you have kept this sort of thing until we were all let out of this place? I know you've been shut up for seven years, but you could surely have waited a while longer. Until you could have got this —this girl out of here. Away from Kate.

RUPERT: Anything else I can do? With this stuff, I mean.

HARRY: Not a thing. Do you think since you came back last night you've been playing fair?

RUPERT: Fair?

HARRY: Look. I'll try to explain. Don't you think it would have been better to pretend for a while? Pretend with Kate that everything is just as it has been. Christ, man, you're breaking her heart! Is that simple enough for you?

RUPERT: There! Everything packed. You can go down.

HARRY: All right. But just tell me this: how much longer are we going to be shut up here?

RUPERT: Not much longer.

HARRY: What's the reason for it anyway? I suppose we're the only people to know you're back and they don't want the news to leak. What are they going to do—suddenly release you into an unsuspecting world as the latest saviour? If so, I take cover. Who's the enemy going to be this time? Or haven't you decided yet?

RUPERT: I have to act on my decisions, Lancaster. Unlike you I don't make up my mind and regard it as an end in itself.

HARRY: Me! I'm just an old dreamy-eyes. But I don't murder.

RUPERT: When you have you'll find it simpler to tell the innocent from the guilty.

HARRY: You'll go to hell, Forster.

RUPERT: That, too? You go to supper.

DIDO: Harry, I'm sorry—sincerely sorry—that I went to sleep during your picture.

HARRY: The difficulty with you, sweetheart—and with him—is that you're honest about yourself. I'm sorry, but I've lost the talent for doing that sort of thing.

RUPERT: Can you carry all that?

HARRY *is laden with cinema equipment.*

HARRY: Sure. I'll tell Kate you're on your way. (*He goes down the stairs.*)

RUPERT: It's sad.

DIDO: Harry?

RUPERT: He has an affectionate nature which overrules his moral judgement. Because of what he believes he must censure me for being what I am—and you for accepting me—but he comes near to liking us. That conflict can upset a man.

DIDO: Surely that was a damned bad film.

RUPERT: I thought so.

DIDO: He told me you commanded the soldiers in it.

RUPERT: I believe I did. It was in my comic-opera days. We'd no other use for the army then.

DIDO: You found a better use for it later.

RUPERT: It was put to its proper use.

DIDO: All right. I don't need convincing.

RUPERT: I'm sorry. Anyway, that's all over.

DIDO: So what are you going to do? Live in retirement? Say, a house in the country, your feet up of an evening, early to bed. You'll be healthy all right, but I've doubts as to your wealth and wisdom. What else? You'll be able to walk round your estate in the morning and again in the evening. If you get very bored perhaps you could shoot a small animal ever so often. Do I make the prospect sound attractive?

RUPERT: No.

DIDO: I wasn't trying to. As an alternative you might make it up with Catherine, stay on here, and—as Harry suggested—pretend.

RUPERT: I'm not good at that.

DIDO: No good at pretending! Then I'd say your future is about as bright as a blind man's holiday.

RUPERT: You're very encouraging. What about you?

DIDO: People like me don't think about the future. We don't matter you see. If we survive—that's good. If we go out—well, there's not much harm done. Mind, if somebody tries to put us out before we think it's time we fight. What for? Just to stay alive to see one more day end, have one more hot bath, be made love to once more, hear one more tune we've heard before and got fond of. This is apt to make us a nuisance about the place, but you people are getting better at making bigger gadgets to end all that.

RUPERT: In a little while they'll let you out of here. What will you do?

DIDO: Go back where I came from. Pick up where I left off. You're the problem. You can't pick up where you left off. Have you got any friends who might start a nice new war for you to fight?

RUPERT: There seems to be difficulty in financing such a project at the moment.

DIDO: We might start a subscription fund.

RUPERT: Do you think Harry would give something?

DIDO: You know, he might—just to get you out of here. That man's got principles, but he can sometimes step over them. Ought we to go down?

RUPERT: Not yet.

DIDO: I don't want to go down. I'm out of my depth with Catherine. I suppose I should be out of my depth with you.

RUPERT: Aren't you?

DIDO: No. And it's obvious to everybody. But Catherine—she's in a hell of a position. Do you know, we've talked to each other all day. Couldn't you try talking to her for a while? It's not easy, I suppose, but surely there's something left between you. There must be. It'd be too horrible if there wasn't even kindness left. Won't you try?

RUPERT: Why do you think I've spent my time with you today?

DIDO: Well, Harry's not your sort—nor are the boys. Catherine—difficult. That leaves me. You had no choice.

RUPERT: I could've shut myself up—alone.

DIDO: Yes, you could have done that. Look! I know I'm young but may I give you a bit of advice?

RUPERT: If you want to.

DIDO: You're about to make some kind of confession to me. Well, don't do it. I don't want to hear.

RUPERT: Very well.

DIDO: I don't want to get mixed up. I don't want to have any influence on what you think or do or say. I'm free, and I want to stay like that. It's been very nice and interesting talking to you, but now I must be getting back.

RUPERT: To what? Somebody down in the city? Are you in love?

DIDO: That's the point. I'm not. I've told you, I'm free and I want to stay free.

RUPERT: What's the danger here?

DIDO: Oh, don't be such a bloody fool! You are. (RUPERT *laughs*.) It's not funny! Think of Catherine. For seven years she's been shut up in her love for you. Everything she has done—everything she has thought and believed has been decided by that love. Was it worth it? I don't think so. She may get free again in time—she's brave, you can see that—but life's too short, too damned short for these stretches of hard labour.

RUPERT: I'm convinced.

DIDO: You are? Good. Start work to get me out of here.

    CATHERINE *comes up the stairway.*

CATHERINE: Aren't you coming down to have some food?

RUPERT: I'm not hungry.

CATHERINE: Can't you persuade him, Miss Morgen?
     DIDO *shakes her head.*

RUPERT: Is the telephone down there?

CATHERINE: Yes.

RUPERT: I want to speak to Cadmus. There's no reason to keep
     this girl here another night. I'm going to ask Cadmus to let her
     go home. (RUPERT *goes down the stairs.*)

CATHERINE: Do you want to go?

DIDO: Yes, please.

CATHERINE: Where will you make for?

DIDO: Back to my room.

CATHERINE: What's it like?

DIDO: My room? Oh, it's fine. It belongs just to me. I don't have
     to share it as you share this place.

CATHERINE: Where is it?

DIDO: In a part you wouldn't know. The house looks over—or
     rather, leans over, the river. I couldn't be more strange to you
     if I came from the moon, could I?

CATHERINE (*she smiles*): No. My manner towards you last night
     when you arrived with Harry wasn't welcoming. I'm sorry.

DIDO: I understand.

CATHERINE: I suppose you do. Harry tell you about Rupert and
     me?

DIDO: In a way.

CATHERINE: Rupert's had a very bad time and he's desperately
     uncertain of the future. We mustn't blame him for what he does.
     You won't do that, will you?

DIDO: No, I won't blame him.

CATHERINE: He likes you very much so won't you stay on?

DIDO: No.

CATHERINE: For tonight, at least.

DIDO: No. I want to go home.

CATHERINE: Is there something urgent calling you back?

DIDO: No. I just want to get out of here.

CATHERINE: Please stay. For my sake.

DIDO: For you?

CATHERINE: Yes.

DIDO: I'll stay for you.

CATHERINE: You funny girl. Do you make a habit of the

unexpected? Anyway, thank you. Would you like a change of clothes? You've been in those since you arrived.

DIDO: I haven't got any others.

CATHERINE: Well, you didn't come prepared to stay. What can we do? I know. My maid has some very pretty things. Run along and see her. I'm sure she'll help us.

DIDO: I don't want to.

CATHERINE: Now don't be silly. She dresses very well.

DIDO: Where do I find her?

CATHERINE: She'll be in her room. (HARRY *has come from below. He has a glass of wine in his hand.*) And whilst you're there get her to comb your hair.

HARRY: Excuse me, Miss, but you're beautiful. You should be in pictures. (DIDO *passes* HARRY *and goes down the stairs.*) Is Forster calling off the watch-dogs?

CATHERINE: What do you mean?

HARRY: He's on the telephone down there. He asked me to get the number. Didn't want to give his sacred name.

CATHERINE: He's speaking to Cadmus about something. Harry, why did you tell that girl about the break between Rupert and me?

HARRY: Dear Kate, I didn't tell her. Not in so many words. It's been pretty obvious to everybody that—well, that—

CATHERINE: That he's not come home to me. Yes, I suppose so.

HARRY: You're putting up a good fight, Kate. I'm proud of you.

CATHERINE: It's not that he doesn't want to love me any more. It's really that in losing everything he lost me.

HARRY: Yes, that's the way it is. Kate, answer me two questions.

CATHERINE: What are they?

HARRY: One—why did Cadmus come here last night?

CATHERINE: To welcome Rupert back.

HARRY: Two—what big fish are you expecting to catch with my little girl friend as bait? You're not going to answer that, are you?

CATHERINE: No.

HARRY: Here's an alternative. What are you fighting to keep?

CATHERINE: Nothing for myself. That surprises you, doesn't it? You've always thought me possessive. It's not altogether true. I don't like waste. There are some things worth keeping because they're rare and fine. Not for yourself. I suppose it's like having children. They're never yours—as a possession—but they're worth

having and sending out to be themselves. That's me at this
moment. I'm not fighting to keep something, Harry, but I am
fighting to save something.

HARRY: To save something from going to waste?

CATHERINE: Just that.

    HARRY *looks into his wine glass.*

HARRY: Empty. Yet if I bring this and the bottle below into union
it will breed kindness in me. So down I go.

CATHERINE: Don't get too kind, Harry.

HARRY: Oh, Poppa and Doc asked me to say that they've gone to
bed. (HARRY *and* RUPERT *meet on the stairs.*) If you don't want to
keep on meeting me like this, Forster, you'd better do something
about getting us all out of here.

RUPERT: Are you coming down?

HARRY: I am. (HARRY *goes down the stair.* RUPERT *comes up into the
room.*)

CATHERINE: Did you speak to Cadmus?

RUPERT: He's not at the Chancellery, but he's expected back within
an hour. I left a message.

CATHERINE: The girl's staying.

RUPERT: What?

CATHERINE: I asked her to stay. For a little longer. That's what
you wanted, isn't it? Rupert, it's not a sign of weakness to have
someone with you through these hours. Why be afraid of showing
that you're human? It's a failing the rest of us admit. Why not
you? There have been times in the past when I've been able to
comfort you. I don't remember them as moments of weakness.

RUPERT: Catherine, I didn't want it to end like this with you.
Believe that. But I had to tell you.

CATHERINE: I know that, now.

RUPERT: I hate lying. Anyway, I'm no good at it.

CATHERINE: I wanted you to love me—not merely be faithful to
me. That was before. Now I only want you to live.

RUPERT: Why try to save me? I'm useless now. I've been tamed
by long captivity.

CATHERINE: That's not true. You've just forgotten how to fight,
I think. And you're mistaking the enemy.

RUPERT: I don't think so.

CATHERINE: The real enemy is the darkness you hope to bring on
yourself tomorrow morning.

RUPERT: There's a word for it.

CATHERINE: I know. I know from the past seven years. There was the early morning when I didn't want to wake, the sound of my footsteps going about this house, the end of each year. At those times I longed to stop fighting. But I believed it would be wrong to give in. Sinful, if you like.

RUPERT: In my profession death can never be a moral problem. You were always brave, Catherine.

CATHERINE: You've never thought of your absence in that way, have you?

RUPERT: No. No, I've not.

CATHERINE: Don't let it influence you. Live for yourself. Face this trial. How can they condemn you?

RUPERT: Very easily. I failed in what I set out to do.

CATHERINE: They'll not sentence you.

RUPERT: Perhaps not. Then I'll have to live. Where's the girl?

CATHERINE: Have you told her? About John's visit last night and the trial.

RUPERT: Of course not. Why should she be involved?

CATHERINE: Yet you want her to stay. You watch her. You wait for her to speak. What do you hope to hear?

RUPERT: I don't know.

CATHERINE: Something that can never come from me. So I asked her to stay. She may casually—without any thought at all—help you.

RUPERT: I think it's unlikely.

CATHERINE: You have to trust someone at this time. I'll leave it to the girl.

DIDO *has come up the stairs and into the room. She is now in a simple dress and her hair has recently been brushed and combed.*

DIDO: Be careful. I'm here.

CATHERINE: So you are. (*To* RUPERT.) What did you arrange on the telephone?

RUPERT: That Cadmus should call me when he got back.

DIDO: Is that about me?

RUPERT: For permission to leave this place.

DIDO: I always came and went as I pleased before I met you people. Anyway, I thought you wanted me to stay.

CATHERINE: I do.

DIDO: Well, I'm still here, so what's the fuss about? Are you going?

(CATHERINE *has moved to the stairs.*) Do you want me to come with you?

CATHERINE: No. Stay. (CATHERINE *goes down the stairs.*)

DIDO: Well, I'm back. Looking different, but don't let that put you off. What were we talking about?

RUPERT: I can't remember. What have you done to yourself?

DIDO: She thought I was looking grubby. I probably was. No pride, that's what's wrong with me.

RUPERT: It's very late. Don't you want to go to bed?

DIDO: No. If I do, I'll have just got in when there'll be a very small knock on the door, and then a very small American voice will ask to come in. Whatever I say, in it will come. It'll want to know if I'm all right and it'll move about the room for a while—somehow getting near to the bed. When I feel its breath I'll say, Go to hell! and off it will go—hurt. At least, that's what happened last night. I'll stay up. What's going to be left to me? By Catherine. I overheard. 'I'll leave it to the girl.' That's what she said.

RUPERT: You mustn't bother your head about it.

DIDO: It's not my head that's bothered—it's my heart. I like her, you see. I'm sorry for her too.

RUPERT: Save your pity.

DIDO: What did you say?

RUPERT: I said, save your pity.

DIDO: For you?

RUPERT: I don't need it.

DIDO: Who is there left? Harry. He'd love it. But not tonight. What's the matter?

RUPERT: A little while ago you said it would be horrible if there was nothing left between Catherine and me. Well, there is that. I don't care to hear her pitied.

DIDO: Sorry. Forgive me asking this, but I've a conventional mind: why didn't you marry her?

RUPERT: Because of my job. I was always away. She's not the sort of person who could've lived the life.

DIDO: That's not the reason. That's an excuse. Tell me the reason, please.

RUPERT: Very well. It was unwise to commit myself to another. Not from a sense of independence. Nothing so simple. One of my predecessors in war, an Irishman, once said: 'All the business of war, and indeed all the business of life, is to endeavour to find out what you don't know by what you do.' And he went on: 'That's what I called "guessing what was at the other side of the hill".' That's how he put it, and that has been my job—to guess what was at the far side of the hill. Towards the end my sense for doing that was highly developed, but only because I kept myself free. Were I committed I saw the other side of the hill with eyes not entirely my own. Do you understand?

DIDO: Let me tell you something before you go on. I'm not frightened of you.

RUPERT: Why did you decide to stay?

DIDO: Because of Catherine. I don't have to help or comfort many of my friends, you know, because none of us have much to lose. But people like Catherine, who've had a lot and lost it—well, that's new to me. And she was so damned proud when she asked me to stay. People are too often humble. She was fighting like hell at that moment. Suddenly I felt—well, this is as good a point as any for me to stop running away. I'm on the edge of a trap, but it can't be helped.

RUPERT: A trap? Do you mean a conspiracy?

DIDO: No, I mean a trap. The thing you catch wild animals in. Look! Now, look here. You kept yourself free because of your job. Well, I kept myself free because I'm not strong enough, good enough or wise enough to have another living, loving person with me. But the trap's always there. You—I've only to discover something about you—you've only to tell me something and I'm caught.

RUPERT: Tell you what?

DIDO: How do I know until I hear it? What was it shut the trap on Catherine all these years?

RUPERT: You think I'm preparing the same for you?

DIDO: Nobody—not even the proudest person—knows when their cry for help goes out. It may not even be spoken by you. When I was a kid there was a boy and he went to the war. He came back from the fighting earlier than was expected. I went to meet him at the East Railway Station, and it was there the trap was sprung. He'd come back without his eyes. I cut myself loose from that one easily enough, but as I get older it's more difficult. Everywhere I go there are the unhappy and the aimless waiting for me to put out my hand and walk into that trap made of human arms. Ach! this loving business.

HARRY *has appeared on the stairs. He carries a glass of whisky which he is careful not to spill.*

DIDO: What do you want?

HARRY: Just to know if you're all right.

DIDO: How do I look?

HARRY: Different. You tired?

DIDO: So I look tired.

HARRY: I didn't say so. You going to bed?

DIDO: Not yet.

HARRY: You're all right.

DIDO: Yes.

HARRY: Sorry about this, but I feel responsible—bringing you here.

DIDO: Don't get that on your conscience as well, Harry.

HARRY: You're all right, then.

DIDO: I'm all right. (*In silence she stares at* HARRY. *He goes down the stairs.*) Why do I do it? He means it kindly. Always has. He picked me up last night in that bar because he thought I was down on my luck. But he was really looking for somebody to do him a good turn. And you, Rupert. Catherine kept herself and this place for you in all kindness. You refused it. What's the matter with us? What are we afraid of losing? You know, we must think very highly of ourselves to keep ourselves so free.

RUPERT: You're young. You won't be free for long. You'll have to commit yourself and love because you're a woman.

DIDO: It's an easy excuse for weakness. You kept free for years. What's the secret? Being a man?

RUPERT: That and having an objective.

DIDO: Something you fought for in that war of yours.

RUPERT: Yes.

DIDO: They said it was for your country and for people like me.

RUPERT: It was for myself. Not for Cadmus or country or you, but myself. To impose myself.

DIDO: They say that's wrong. They say we should live, suffer and finally die for others.

RUPERT: Yes, that's what they say.

DIDO: You don't believe it's true. Well, what do you believe?

RUPERT: The night before that last battle I still believed that I could reach a point of achievement never before known to a man. The way I chose was conquest by war. Some men need an art to fulfil themselves. Saints need a religion. I had to pursue a triumph of arms. The greatest the world has ever known. By that I believed I could become myself, the man I was intended to be.

DIDO: But whatever you believed, you were caught like everybody. You were caught in that battle.

RUPERT: Not by man. No man could have trapped me at that time.

DIDO: You were caught. I heard about it, don't forget. The papers were full of it. The radio chattered day after day.

RUPERT: Did anyone defend me?

DIDO: Not that I remember. But I was young—seven years ago I was about fourteen.

RUPERT: Just the age to have been there. It might have been you.

DIDO: Seven years ago.

RUPERT: It was a fine morning. The action was a small one along the main route of advance. It would never have found its way into the history books. The town lay in the bend of a river. I intended to take the place by a *coup de main*. The main enemy forces had evacuated the town and were in prepared positions on the far side of the river. My intention was to go in at dawn and take the town at my leisure through the day, but at dusk, with the full weight of my force, to establish two bridgeheads over the river and attempt a crossing that night: on the supposition that the enemy would expect a break between the attack on the town and the river crossing. You understand? It was to be a very beautiful battle, having an elegance difficult to achieve with the use of armoured forces. I was satisfied with the preparations, and at dawn the attack went in. I led in my command tank. We were not delayed by infantry movements as the infantrymen were on the flanks moving with us and not intended to engage, but to save themselves for the river crossing at night. On reaching the town I halted my force preparatory to its dispersal for street by street occupation. My own tank was halted beside a small church. I got down and walked the length of the street ahead alone. The place was deserted and there was no indication of the roads being mined. It seemed safe to proceed. I went back to my tank and climbed in. I had picked up the microphone of my transmitting set—I was using open communication—and I was about to give the order to continue the advance when the church door opened. I was shocked by the noise in the silence, and I turned. A little boy had come from the church and was standing on the steps. He put his hand to his mouth—oh, as if to put in a sweet—but it was a whistle he held. He blew the whistle and at once the children were upon us. Hundreds of them. They came from the church, from the houses in the street and from far off down the street itself. They rolled like a wave towards us, screaming and shouting, some armed with sticks, some carrying flags. Reaching us they beat themselves against the sides of our tanks. I saw my commanders and their crews laughing at them, cheering them on, encouraging them in their attempts to scramble over the armour. We might have been liberators and not an attacking force. Was I the only man to see the danger? We were virtually immobilized, for they were everywhere, even beneath our tracks. The laughter of my men became louder. Our concentration was broken. The attack—timed by seconds to co-ordination—was flinging itself to pieces. My central armoured force was the governing factor of movement. Delay it and the two infantry groups became as ineffective as naked men. The boy who had come first from the church had clambered on to my tank. He was black-haired and black-eyed and he carried a wooden sword which he swung above his head. He shouted something which I didn't understand, and then spat at me. That was no provocation for what I did: I had already decided, I stretched out and drew his head to my shoulder like a lover, and shot him in the mouth. I took him by the hair of his shattered head and held him up for my men to see. They understood. The shooting began. They also used knives to cut them free from the armour. The note of the children's cry changed and was in mercy drowned as the motors started up and we moved forward.

DIDO: They say four hundred were found dead.

RUPERT: Four hundred. Do they say that? I'd no idea.

DIDO: What was the place?

RUPERT: It was a children's colony, I was told later. They were of all nationalities. Some of the enemy, some of our own, herded together by the shuttle of armies. You always get such things in modern war. Nobody's discovered what they were about that morning. Was it a reckless imitation of their fathers and older brothers? Were they put up to it by unscrupulous commanders? Or had those children reached a point from which there is no further retreat and a stand—against whatever odds—must at last be made?

DIDO: They say you're a coward, you know.

RUPERT: I know.

DIDO: It's not true. What is true, then?

CATHERINE *and* JOHN CADMUS *come into the room by way of the stairs.* CADMUS *is in evening dress.*

CADMUS: I got your message, Forster. Forgive the fancy dress but I didn't wait to change.

RUPERT: I was prepared to speak to you on the telephone.

CADMUS: Impossible. I never hold two-way conversations on that instrument. It allows for great ambiguity of meaning. Who is this?

CATHERINE: Miss Morgen. A friend of Harry Lancaster.

CADMUS: How do you do. What have you been talking to Forster about, Miss Morgen, until this late hour? Has he been telling you stories of his battles? He's a great fellow. We shan't see his like again. But we must thank the Lord we're not a couple of his soldiers. They tell me he has them drilled until the blood boils in their tails.

DIDO: Has he got any soldiers now?

CADMUS: Not at the moment. But he will have—he will have. Glorious legions at his command fighting for a nobler cause than we can give him.

DIDO: You mean when he's dead.

CADMUS: Yes, I did mean that. Who are you?

DIDO: Dido Morgen. Don't bother! I know who you are.

CADMUS: There is an old-fashioned idea that extreme youth and, if I may say so, beauty—

DIDO: I'm not beautiful.

CADMUS: No, you're not. I'm so sorry. Never mind. Perhaps you're clever instead. Are you?

DIDO: No.

CADMUS: Oh, dear! Neither beautiful nor clever. You're kind-hearted, that's what it is. That's the gift God gave you. To understand your fellow beings.

DIDO: That's it.

CADMUS: Catherine—Forster, will one of you disengage me from this conversation, please.

DIDO: I'll go.

CADMUS: No, don't go. Catherine, would you do a little errand for me?

CATHERINE: What is it you want?

CADMUS: You haven't forgiven me, I see.

CATHERINE: What do you want me to do for you?

CADMUS: Go to the car, outside at the door, and ask the driver for my benzedrine tablets. I shall want to take one in about five minutes.

CATHERINE: Very well. In about five minutes.

CADMUS: It's very good of you. (CATHERINE *goes down the stairs*.) Even at my age we play the game. She sees through that device to get her away for a while, and from the first I know she'll see through it. Yet we observe the convention. You, Miss Morgen, wouldn't do that, would you?

DIDO: No.

CADMUS: Then you're made of the same stuff as revolutionaries. Unlike poor Catherine. So intensely vulnerable by her love of life. I detest vulnerable people, don't you?

DIDO: I like her very much.

CADMUS: Oh, you've mistaken me. I was speaking generally. I love Catherine. Surely everyone does. I mean, rather, that I find it difficult to like people for whom I feel pity.

DIDO: Yes, that's true. So do I.

CADMUS: Good! A point of agreement. I am pleased!

DIDO: Are you?

CADMUS: Do you like Forster?

DIDO: Kind of.

CADMUS: Then you can't be sorry for him.

DIDO: Should I be? Look! I don't know anything. All right? I'm the girl you see on the edge of the crowd at a street accident. It's got nothing to do with me. I just happened to be there. I don't want to be a witness. All right?

CADMUS: What did you want to speak to me about, Forster?

RUPERT: Miss Morgen. Is it necessary for her to be shut up here? She came with Lancaster and it seems senseless for her to be virtually imprisoned. She can have no influence on your plans.

CADMUS: No influence. She can have no influence, you say.

RUPERT: None. May she go home?

CADMUS: Certainly.

DIDO: Thank you very much.

CADMUS: At once, if she wishes.

DIDO: We just wanted your permission. Liberty consists of doing what you want to do when you want to do it. That's in the books. I don't want to go yet. But it's good to know I can leave when I wish.

CADMUS: My car will take you back. Don't you think it would be wise to go at once?

DIDO: No, I don't.

CADMUS: Go away! I want to speak to Forster alone.

DIDO (*she laughs*): No conventional excuses for me. Go away, he says.

CADMUS: And I mean it. Also keep Catherine below for a time. I'm sure you've something in common to talk about.

DIDO: Yes, we have. (DIDO *goes down the stairs*.)

CADMUS: Who is she?

RUPERT: Lancaster picked her up yesterday and brought her here.

CADMUS: Yes, but who is she?

RUPERT: One of the people you govern.

CADMUS: Forgive my astonishment. Are there many like that, I wonder? Is it a volcano I'm sitting on and not, as I'd supposed, a dung-hill?

RUPERT: It might be wise to reconsider your position in such a light.

CADMUS: What does that mean? Can it mean your own position?

RUPERT: Certainly it can mean that.

CADMUS: That's very interesting. But there's not much time, Forster, for a detailed reconsideration. When I saw you last night you were content with my proposal. You're not content now?

RUPERT: No, sir.

CADMUS: Why not, damn you?

RUPERT: What are you going to do if I don't use this stuff? (*He has taken the jewelled box from his pocket.*)

CADMUS: What can I do?

RUPERT: There's always assassination.

CADMUS: Don't be so tiresome. From the facts I gave you last night you must know that's impossible. There's only one course I can take: to produce you for trial. I'm asking you to make yourself unavailable. Something's occurred which makes you unwilling to do that, if I understand you correctly, but I'm now only asking you to make up your mind, Forster.

RUPERT: Where do I go if I'm still alive and kicking after dawn this morning?

CADMUS: You'll be taken to the military prison in the city. The place the soldiers laughingly call Arcady. I shall make a statement that you are there and that you are to be tried. The process of law will be set in motion. As the trial proceeds you'll be forgotten, and all we shall be aware of will be the rotting corpse of the country covered by the ordure of our recent history.

RUPERT: You're appealing to me as a patriot. I find that odd.

CADMUS: I'm doing nothing of the kind. I'm asking you to make up your mind. Decide.

RUPERT: My last positive action—by my decision—was the murder of that child seven years ago. From that moment I not only relinquished command of my army, but also of myself. For the seven years in prison I lived by other men's decisions regarding my habits, my actions and my thoughts. I did what I was told. Nothing more. I was content it should be like that. Soldiers, you know, are forced to action by their decisions. There's no getting out of it for men in my job. No going back and saying I didn't mean it, when in my hand I'm holding the casualty list for thousands. You'll forgive my contempt for men who think they've fulfilled their obligations by expressing an opinion.

CADMUS: My God, Forster, you're talking like the romantic 'man of action' which all the intellectuals are in love with nowadays.

RUPERT: I'm talking as myself, not as any man's conception of me.

CADMUS: Go on.

RUPERT: I found freedom only in the years of fighting. I waited for that war, Cadmus. I wanted it with physical desire. It came, and I was released into action. In the years of preparation before the war—ach! my life was a formality. Because a man is seen in a crowd it must never be thought that he is of the crowd.

CADMUS: What you're telling me is that solitariness—aloneness, if you like—cannot be imposed. In your case imprisonment was never a punishment. Have I got that straight?

RUPERT: Do you believe absolute imprisonment to exist?

CADMUS: Yours seemed very efficient. At least, it was intended to be so.

RUPERT: Absolute. With no line of communication.

CADMUS: Put it that way if you like.

RUPERT: An army's line of communication is both its strength and its weakness. It stretches back sometimes broad and firm, sometimes fine and worn to base. It is not a steady supply. It pulses like a human vein according to need. Yet it must always be kept open. It must always be kept alive. In war I have struck so far forward that the line back has been stretched until it is in invisible to all eyes but mine. For it is not always a thing you can mark on a map—you can't neatly signpost it for everyone to follow. You can only feel it in your belly like homesickness. It is what makes an isolated group fight its way out of an apparently impossible situation. Faith that there's a way back.

CADMUS: Yes. I understand you.

RUPERT: A man is an army, a striking offensive force. Each one of us has the line of communication stretching out. With some of us it is weak and with some of us it is strong according to our courage. The line goes back to other people, places and ideas. From you and Catherine back into the past: from myself and the girl out to the immediate happening. But we all call it by the same name, don't we, Cadmus? Love. And as long as that line remains open we have to live.

CADMUS: How did you manage to keep contact in prison? There are classic examples, of course. Did you adopt a mouse?

RUPERT: No, it was not a mouse. It was a human voice. On the hills behind the camp there was a goat-herd. At dusk he greeted the night and at dawn the day with song. I've no idea what he sang—some prayer, I suppose. I tried to take it down phonetically but I failed. It must have been in some local dialect. I don't know. Early on I tried to resist it. I felt it was an intrusion. However, I was compelled to accept him. I came to be fond of him—like a man with a plain wife—and I ended by understanding that you can't shut out the human voice—especially when it's expressing itself in an act of faith. The pulse became stronger. I continued to live.

CADMUS: I thought I knew exactly who would be in this house today. Catherine, the doctor, the priest and that clown of an American. I was safe with them. Not one of them would touch the sensibilities of a man such as yourself. But this girl—I'd not counted on her being here. She is now the sentimental singer of your goat-song, I suppose.

RUPERT: Yes.

CADMUS: Very well. You'll be taken down within six hours. I shall send for you.

RUPERT: What are my chances?

CADMUS: Reasonable. Of getting away with your life. You won't save anything else.

RUPERT: I go within six hours, you say.

CADMUS: At daybreak.

HARRY *comes up the stairs.*

HARRY: Where are the girls, Forster?

RUPERT: Below.

HARRY: Well, what are they doing?

RUPERT: I've no idea.

CADMUS: You're drunk.

HARRY: No, sir. Not yet. But I'm on the way. And when I am I'll have me to talk to, see? That'll be fine because myself and me will have some very interesting things to say to each other. But until that happy time I want someone to hold my hand. You'd look silly doing that so it'd better be one of the girls. Where are they? (*He shouts.*) Dido!

CADMUS: I'm told she's a friend of yours, Mr Lancaster.

HARRY: Dido? Well, I don't know about being a friend, but she'll hold my hand when the horror's on me, and I can only see the past and never the future. She's that sort of girl. A kind kind of girl, you know.

CADMUS: And you need her at this moment?

HARRY: Sure do. (*He shouts.*) Dido!

CADMUS: Would she hold Forster's hand if he needed her?

HARRY: She's been doing that all day, so now I move up for a bit of comfort.

CADMUS: She must be a very extraordinary girl.

HARRY: She is. Dido!

CADMUS: Pay attention, Mr Lancaster. Why should Forster need the comfort this girl's given him today?

HARRY: Because he's a man, I guess. Beneath the splendour, you know—(*he is beside the bronze helmet: he taps it with his fist*)—empty. Hollow. Nothing. Nothing but a man signalling to be let out of the trappings of war. Asking to be taken back into the herd.

CADMUS: Is that so, Forster?

RUPERT: Lancaster has a liberal mind. To him no man is entirely evil. Not even me. And so he is compelled to mistake my gestures of defiance for signals of distress.

CADMUS: But Mr Lancaster says this girl has been with you all day.

HARRY: Holding his hand.

CADMUS: Where is she leading you, Forster?

RUPERT: Didn't we agree on that just before Lancaster came up?

HARRY: Excuse me. Were you two talking important when I broke in?

CADMUS: We were speaking of Forster's future.

HARRY: Oh, that. Well, I'm sorry for Kate, and in a little while I suppose I'll have to be sorry for Dido.

CADMUS: Couldn't you find a little sorrow for me, Mr Lancaster?

HARRY: Why? Is he breaking your heart, too?

CADMUS: He certainly is.

HARRY: Don't let him do it. That kind break more than hearts. They're not often caught as you've caught this one, and you don't often see the naked face out of its idiot covering. Don't let it go free.

CADMUS: But we're not, Mr Lancaster. Let me tell you: Forster is back here to be put on trial.

HARRY: Ah!

CADMUS: That makes you happy, I see.

HARRY: So they've finally caught up with you, Forster. What a chance for us all—all us little people—to take a smack at you.

CADMUS: Yes, Mr Lancaster, it'll give you all a splendid opportunity, won't it?

HARRY: Do I believe this? Are we moving into an age of enlightenment?

CADMUS: We can only hope so, Mr Lancaster.

HARRY: How y'going t'take it, Forster? You'll have to find the words to defend yourself now, not the actions. No more legend, Forster, hidden in the midst of any army or up in a camp in the mountains—just a man like any other. You're going to have to stand up and answer for what you did.

CADMUS: Yes, indeed, he'll have to be very truthful in the cross-examinations.

HARRY: I can't wait. I can't wait for the day when the whole world'll know what you are. How there was nothing back of those bloody murders but your lusting ambition. We only needed the opportunity, Forster—we just needed this to bring you down to our own level. That's all.

CADMUS: And when you've proved him your equal—what then?

HARRY: He may go off and live the best way he can. We'd be playing his game if we killed him. Mr Cadmus, I'd like to shake you by the hand. You're doing a fine job. Thank you, sir.

CADMUS: Thank you, Mr Lancaster. Well, Forster, he's given you a hint of the feelings of the ordinary people. I hope you'll respect those feelings. (CATHERINE *and* DIDO *come up the stairs.*) May I appeal to your good sense once more? Let go, give up and do what I ask.

CATHERINE: He says you have them with you, John.

CADMUS: Who says I have what with me?

CATHERINE: Your driver: the benzedrine tablets.

CADMUS: Have I? Probably. Well, Forster? (RUPERT *does not answer.*) Miss Morgen, will you help me down those stairs to the car?

DIDO: Of course. Aren't you afraid I might push you?

CADMUS: Why should you?

DIDO: I might be tired of the Government.

CADMUS: Who isn't? (CADMUS *and* DIDO *go below.*)

HARRY: Kate, sweetheart, I seem to have run out of drink. I mean the immediate supply below.

CATHERINE: Haven't you had enough?

HARRY: No, Kate, I've not had enough.

CATHERINE: Then you'll have to go to the kitchen. Ask for some. Take it to your room.

HARRY: I'll do that. Kate, how did you feel about the picture?

CATHERINE: Picture?

HARRY: The picture I showed tonight. My picture.

CATHERINE: It was very good, I think. Of course, it's old. Out of date now.

HARRY: That's right. Not much use now. It lacks the drama of these times. I should've put in a trial scene, eh, Forster? My, the news-reel boys'll have a hell of a time with you the next few weeks. Those cameras don't miss a thing—they pick it all up, you know, every bit of it. Wish I was going to be behind one. (HARRY *goes down the stairs.*)

CATHERINE: What did all that mean?

RUPERT: That Lancaster thinks it a good thing I should be put on trial.

CATHERINE: How does he know about it?

RUPERT: Cadmus told him. And raised the rabble in him. It was done to frighten me, to make me understand what I must face when the time comes. As it seems it has.

CATHERINE: You've decided. It's terrible, you know, to watch a man going coldly along the edge of decision. You were beyond my reach. I was afraid to cry out and make you look back. Couldn't trust myself. I had to leave it to the girl. She could speak in a matter-of-fact way which you'd understand.

DIDO *has come up the stairs into the room.*

DIDO: That man—that old Cadmus man—he says there's going to be some sort of trial. Are you going to let them do that to you?

CATHERINE: There's only one other way out. Because of you he's not going to take that way.

DIDO: Because of me. What've I done?

CATHERINE: Enough. Thank you.

DIDO: I don't want thanks. Thank you, you say and smile. So, all right. I've made you happy. Rupert's come to a decision because of something I've said or done. Fine for you—yes!—but for me—? Try to catch some of my bloody misery when that old man said—

RUPERT: What did he say?

DIDO: He said, 'You shouldn't have held him back. He had a chance to finish clean. Now, because of you, he's going to finish dirty and old and lonely and angry. Because of you.' That's what he said.

CATHERINE: John Cadmus thinks that. We know better.

DIDO: I don't know anything. I don't want to know anything!

CATHERINE: Then why did you stay?

DIDO: Oh, leave me alone!

CATHERINE: Alone? Is that what you want? Yet you're not happy. You're not even free.

DIDO: It'll do for me. As I am.

CATHERINE: For how long? It is the middle of the night. No time for envy or pain. Quite soon now the day will come when you'll have to admit that the anger and despair you feel is not because of other people. It is for them. (*To* RUPERT.) I suppose they'll send for you.

RUPERT: Yes.

CATHERINE: Call me. I'll be in my room below. (*She has moved to the stairs.*)

DIDO: Catherine!

CATHERINE *has gone from the room.*

RUPERT: First of all I must tell you—that old Cadmus man is an honest man. He believed what he said.

DIDO: You've been brought back for this trial.

RUPERT: Yes. John Cadmus doesn't want it to be. He wants me to take Catherine's 'other way out'. He wants me to die clean. That's what he meant when he spoke to you.

DIDO: And he thinks I'm stopping you.

RUPERT: Yes, but don't worry. The decision is entirely mine.

DIDO: It is, isn't it, Rupert?

RUPERT: Do you want me to live, Dido?

DIDO: I want you to do what is right for a man like you. Life's not everything, I know, for men of your sort. But you must decide.

RUPERT: I've told Cadmus I'll stand the trial. They're coming at daybreak to take me to the military prison in the city.

DIDO: You'll be in Arcady. It's just across the river from my place.

RUPERT: The questioning will begin there. The investigation of the past.

DIDO: Will you tell them the truth?

RUPERT: Yes, but they won't be interested.

DIDO: And when it's all over?

RUPERT: They'll let me go.

DIDO: To be old and angry and lonely. No!

RUPERT: You mustn't concern yourself. Keep free.

DIDO: All right. I love you, if that's what you want to hear me say. I love you. You seem to me a very good man.

RUPERT: I'd like you to stay with me through the rest of the night. Only a few hours.

DIDO: You will say exactly what you mean, won't you?

RUPERT: I mean only that. Stay with me until first light. Until they come for me.

DIDO: Long time since I saw the dawn come up. I was walking back alone from a party. I'd danced all night and I was a bit drunk because I thought I was in love again. I was going home the long way—making it last out. Restless, you know, because his arms had been around me as we danced. And I'd got a tune in my head and it wouldn't get out. (*She sings:*)

> 'Don't shut your eyes to,
> You must get wise to
> The fact that we're in love.'

I was singing it as I walked in the comfortable darkness when the dawn came up and smacked me in the face so hard I nearly fell on my back. Another day. They always take me by surprise.

RUPERT: I've always prepared for the day. I could never let myself be taken by surprise. The dawn's a time of great danger, you know. I remember how cold it was, summer and winter, and how still. The men about me whispered and a cough sounded like a shot. I would stand staring into the darkness towards the enemy and he would be looking into my eyes. Then, at the appointed time, the darkness would dissolve. Towards the end of the campaign I almost came to believe that it was the intensity of my vision which dispelled the night and the strength of my faith which lifted the sun into the sky.

DIDO: I'm not surprised they shut you up when you talk like that. You're dangerous.

RUPERT: I'm sane, you know.

DIDO: Yes, and they know it. That's the danger. You're safe with me. Here, with me. The Doctor and the Father are in bed, Harry's getting drunk in the kitchen, and Catherine's at prayer. You and me—here. That's fine. My singing in the streets and you staring into the East—that's the past. You going to Arcady and me going back to my room—well, that's in the future. But you and me, here. That's now.

RUPERT: Yes, we're safe.

DIDO: Of course we are. Safe.

RUPERT: How will you remember the time you've spent in this house? When you're free of it. Will you remember?

DIDO: I suppose so. Something'll bring it to mind. (*She is crying.*) Sorry. Doesn't mean a thing. For instance, always happens when somebody gives me a present. Stupid!

RUPERT: I've nothing to give.

DIDO: I don't want anything from you. Did your soldiers—those men who waited with you for those other daybreaks—did they expect you to reward them? That night seven years ago—after the fight with the children—were your men against you then?

RUPERT: They were with me.

DIDO: Well, then. So am I. What happened. (*A pause.*) I'm not just curious.

RUPERT: I didn't go on. I waited. On the wrong side of the river.

DIDO: Yes? (RUPERT *does not speak*.) Would like to roll up and sleep for a while? I'll watch. Oh, come on. I'm not such a fool. You've trusted people before me. Rest. I'll watch. Sleep.

RUPERT: Yes, you have to trust someone. That's the comradeship of soldiering. The knowledge that you're a man. And need to be watched over in the last hours of the night. Protected. From hurt. and death.

DIDO: Rest.

RUPERT: Watch.

CURTAIN

ACT THREE

The scene is the same.
The time is later the same night moving to dawn.
RUPERT *and* DIDO *are within the room.*

RUPERT: If you stand there I shan't be able to see the sun rise.

DIDO: Ah! that's cheating. I thought you were asleep. You haven't spoken for ages.

RUPERT: Do you like dancing?

DIDO: Oh, yes. Two things I like best of all are dancing and going to the Lido and lying in the sun. I'll do that all through this summer. I've been saving my pennies.

RUPERT: There was a lot of music for dancing in the old days, I remember.

DIDO You remember. That's why you've been so quiet. Were those days good—so good?

RUPERT: No better than others.

DIDO: But you—did you have a good time, then?

RUPERT: I was a very serious young man deep in the study of war. But I loved Catherine very much and she liked the things you like and so, of course, I did them. I was stricken by the time they took from my studies, but yes, I enjoyed myself. I think I danced very well—especially waltzes. Do they waltz much now?

DIDO: Not very much. We dance to a lot of American music.

RUPERT: Catherine was beautiful when she danced. She's always been most beautiful when happy. You know, I wasn't in love with her when we first met. She was travelling in this country. She gave up everything she had at that time in her own country and settled down here. She seemed to find what she needed in me.

DIDO: It must've hurt you to tell her that it was over. Yesterday, I mean. Why did you do it?

RUPERT: I found her love for me remained, but it was the love of her young days.

308

DIDO: She thought you were going to be free.

RUPERT: Yes. She meant to take advantage of that and drag me back into the past. I was to live what should have been in the last few years if the war hadn't taken me away. But I want the present time as offered to me by John Cadmus. And I want it alone. I have to take it alone to make what I wish of it.

DIDO: What do you want to make of the present?

RUPERT: A triumph.

DIDO: Haven't you ever—in all your life—loved a small thing? Something I could share with you?

RUPERT: I've a great fondness for natural things. Flowers and things of young growth, of brief life. Through the war I collected wild plants. I kept little boxes for the purpose in my command wagon. The men knew this, and I think they laughed at me. But even though they laughed they'd bring me unknown flowers taken from the roadside and stand by whilst I identified them. My pride and happiness, Dido, has been that the soldiers loved me. Did someone call?

DIDO: Yes. Catherine.

CATHERINE *comes up the stairway.*

CATHERINE: Miss Morgen, will you come down? Harry's asking for you. There's been an accident.

DIDO: What's happened?

CATHERINE: Harry's burnt his hands very badly. So stupid. He put those rolls of film into the electric furnace in the kitchen. They flared up and caught his hands. I've got the doctor out of bed, and he's dressing the burns now, but Harry is asking for you. Will you go down? I'm afraid he's very drunk.

DIDO *goes down the stairs.*

RUPERT: Why did he do it? A quixotic gesture, surely. I mean, there must be more than one copy of a thing like a film.

CATHERINE: Apparently not. Everyone's forgotten it except Harry. That was the last copy. A personal possession.

RUPERT: It didn't remotely resemble life before the war. It was a fiction, a fairy-tale with everyone in love and happy ever after.

CATHERINE: Perhaps it's unfortunate that life's longer than six reels of celluloid.

RUPERT: It's as well he hasn't the talent to make this new film. It's entertaining to misrepresent happiness, but there's nothing funny in lying about misery.

CATHERINE: He's not lying. That's the way he sees it. Why should you say it's wrong for him to take the world he knows and try to make something beautiful and tragic? Why should you say that?

RUPERT: I don't. I say it's unwise and dangerous to distort the world around you to satisfy your longing.

CATHERINE: There's more danger, you know, in trying to destroy it to satisfy your ambition. You made me say that. I don't want to drag up the past any more. The damnable part of it is that men of your kind shatter the ordinary, everyday human pride of people like me.

RUPERT: By that you're at last seeing me as I am.

CATHERINE: I believe so. Let me look at you.

RUPERT: It will be easier for you—in the future—if you understand me. At this time.

CATHERINE: If I understand you, see you for what you are—I'll not be in love with you. Is that what you hope? There's your true weakness. Believing love can be recognized, evaluated, made to fit into the situation of the moment. It's not so. Not so at all. Even at the height of your power you could never control that. Never.

MATTHEW SANGOSSE *comes up the stairs.*

MATTHEW: Catherine, I think you should know that the Chancellor's car has just driven up.

CATHERINE: Thank you, Matthew. (*To* RUPERT.) Did he say he was coming back?

RUPERT: No. I thought he'd just send the guard. I've nothing more to say to him.

CATHERINE: How's Harry, Matthew?

MATTHEW: Miss Morgen's with him. He's quieter now. His hands are badly burnt. I've done what I can in the way of dressing them, but until I can get out for more stuff he'll have to do. He's scorched one side of his face which makes him look rather comic, but that's not serious. He'll be better when he's sober.

CATHERINE: Thank you for all you've done.

MATTHEW: It's many years since I've been got from my bed to attend a case. Makes me feel quite a youngster.

JOHN CADMUS *and* BRUNO HURST *come up the stairway.* BRUNO *is a young man of twenty-two years.*

CADMUS: You look as if you might be attending someone in a professional capacity, Doctor.

MATTHEW: I have been. Harry Lancaster's burnt himself about the hands.

CADMUS: Combustion by righteous indignation, I suppose. Otherwise everyone is well. Forster?

RUPERT: Perfectly. Spare me your bedside manner.

CADMUS: I'm not trying to be kind.

RUPERT: Then shall we get this visit over?

CADMUS: Certainly. This is Captain Hurst who is now responsible for you. He is the guard commander and had better tell you of the arrangements himself. Shall we go down, Catherine? Forster is now a state secret and we mustn't listen. Come along.

CATHERINE: I shall see him before he goes?

CADMUS: Of course. This'll only take a moment.

CATHERINE, CADMUS *and* MATTHEW *go down the stairs.*

RUPERT: Well, Captain Hurst?

BRUNO: Do you want to know the particulars of the escort, sir?

RUPERT: Is there anything out of the ordinary about them?

BRUNO: Nothing, sir.

RUPERT: Then I'll take them as read. Why aren't you in uniform?

BRUNO: My orders were to report in civilian clothes, sir.

RUPERT: You're very young to have reached your captaincy.

BRUNO: We are very young now, sir. Because of the reformation of the army.

RUPERT: Is this a routine detail or have you special qualifications?

BRUNO: I've been on guard duty at the Chancellery.

RUPERT: And Cadmus took you from there today.

BRUNO: Yes, sir.

RUPERT: I'll try to give you my co-operation.

BRUNO: Thank you, sir. I'm to start thirty minutes after daybreak.

RUPERT: The details are not important.

BRUNO: Will you please take leave of your friends before that time?

RUPERT: Yes, Captain Hurst, I will. Is there anything else?

BRUNO: No, sir.

RUPERT: Very well.

BRUNO: I've orders not to leave you, sir.

RUPERT: I see. Then sit down, Captain Hurst. How long is it to sunrise?

BRUNO: Twelve minutes.

RUPERT: It will be light now over the mountain camp.

BRUNO: Yes. I found night duty out there worse than anywhere.

RUPERT: You know the place?

BRUNO: I was stationed in the Eastern Provinces last year.

RUPERT: Ah! Then you, too, have heard the goat-singers.

BRUNO: Yes, sir. (*He laughs.*) Those songs.

RUPERT: You know what they are?

BRUNO: The goat songs? Of course.

RUPERT: Well?

BRUNO: They are obscene.

RUPERT: Obscene?

BRUNO: It's the goat-herd's expression of love—to his goats. The songs don't make sense.

RUPERT: Go on.

BRUNO: They're just filth. That's all. Did you hear them at the camp, sir?

RUPERT: What? Yes, I heard them there. (*He is silent.*)

BRUNO: Talk to me if it helps you.

RUPERT: What did you say?

BRUNO: I said, Please talk to me if you want to.

RUPERT: Thank you. Have you ever put your faith in love songs, Captain Hurst? Believing them to be something more. How did it go? 'Don't shut your eyes to, you must get wise to the fact—' And do you like dancing and going to the Lido and lying in the sun? And being in love? Do you like being in love? (BRUNO *does not answer: he does not move.*) Forgive me, I'm in a privileged position. Yet I was a young soldier once, you know. Twenty years ago, I might very well have been you.

BRUNO: I have been you, sir.

RUPERT: What?

BRUNO: I have been you. I've been Rupert Forster.

RUPERT: Tell me what you mean.

BRUNO: I fought that last battle of yours several times. I fought it in the streets of this city. I was fifteen. I wanted to be a soldier. My command truck was an old bicycle, my troop of tanks were toys, my battle ground was the waste around the railway yards. But my enemy, sir, was the same. All the howling children of the neighbourhood.

RUPERT: I hope you conducted the affair with more success than I did.

BRUNO: Every evening for weeks the shout would go up: Let's play Forster's game! They'd all run away and hide. Then, with six others, I'd pedal my way to the head of the street, dismount, and walk the length of the street. I'd hear them laughing in their hiding places—they knew they wouldn't properly die. I'd go back to my machine, mount it, and be about to give the signal when they would be upon us. That was all very simple. You had set me an example. I'd only to follow it.

RUPERT: Not absolutely, I hope.

BRUNO: There were broken heads, nothing more. Perhaps a few pinched fingers. But after that I was lost. You had disposed of the children. The forward movement was poised. I wanted to go on, but I couldn't because it was not your course. May I ask you something?

RUPERT: Yes.

BRUNO: Why did you wait for twelve hours before continuing the advance? The attack over the river which failed. Why did you wait?

RUPERT: Would you have gone on?

BRUNO: Yes. Every time I played the game and got to that point it was agony to hold back. The forward impetus was overwhelming.

RUPERT: I wasn't playing a game, Hurst.

BRUNO: Neither was I at the end. I was planning for the future. I don't want to be caught in the way you were caught. Think back. Why did you wait?

RUPERT: The armour moved on over the children and through the town.

BRUNO: Yes?

RUPERT: There was no more opposition. I had occupied the town by late afternoon.

BRUNO: You set up headquarters?

RUPERT: My staff had done so. In a deserted schoolroom. It was a convenient place.

BRUNO: You waited.

RUPERT: Until night. It had begun to rain. A little. Nothing much. They'd put my maps on a long trestle table. The situation was there. Clearly marked.

BRUNO: You waited.

RUPERT: Reports began to come in. The room was very noisy. The footsteps of men were deafening as they came to me across the wooden floor. Someone put a meal in front of me.

BRUNO: You say reports were coming in. What did they show?

RUPERT: That everything was exactly as I'd planned.

BRUNO: Then why didn't you act?

RUPERT: I was trapped. Trapped by the memory of the child. I couldn't free myself from that moment. The moment when I stood alone, sad, lost, childless, with the child in my arms. And looking down saw that it was a human being. Warm, as the bitter smell of its body struck up at me: dirty, fearful, brave and—living. It was then the secret was forced on me. I'd shut it out until that morning by making my own prison, Hurst, years before they sent me to the camp in the mountains. A prison of pride and ambition. Then, when I caught the child to me, the secret was revealed. I suddenly understood what a man is. For I held it close.

BRUNO: If you felt this why did you shoot?

RUPERT: I had no choice. The way I'd chosen to live led to that encounter, which was in itself a challenge. Are you so great? Then fire! I fired, and the secret flew up leaving only blood on my sleeve. I became human. So I waited.

BRUNO: For twelve hours.

RUPERT: For twelve hours. It was my second-in-command who took the pencil from my hand and wrote the order for the attack across the river. It was too late.

BRUNO: You went over with them?

RUPERT: Yes. And lived.

BRUNO: Have you admitted this before?

RUPERT: Never.

BRUNO: You must consider yourself guilty.

RUPERT: I do.

BRUNO: Are you prepared to go on trial for this, to admit your error as you have to me, to be found guilty and to be sentenced? You'll serve the rest of time at the camp in the mountains. And your comfort will be the goat-songs.

RUPERT: You're exceeding your authority!

BRUNO: You did more. You misused yours. You had as your responsibility a part in a great conquest and you lost faith. I shall fight over that ground again in future years and next time the attack will go on.

RUPERT: I'm content to leave it in your hands. I'll fight no more.

    DIDO *comes up the stairs.*

DIDO: I'm sorry I had to leave you. He's disgustingly drunk, and he's burnt his hands very badly.

RUPERT: What have you done with him?

DIDO: He's sitting down there talking to himself. He doesn't need me. He doesn't need anybody. They've come for you, have they?

RUPERT: Yes. This is Captain Hurst of the escort.

BRUNO: How do you do.

DIDO: Hullo. Is the old man here, too?

RUPERT: He's down with Catherine.

DIDO: Going to make sure they get you away, aren't they? How many soldiers?

BRUNO: Eight.

DIDO: Certainly making sure. Enough to carry you away if necessary with full military honours.

BRUNO: We're an escort, ma'am, not a bearer party.

DIDO (*she laughs*): Did you hear what he called me? He called me 'Ma'am'! (*To* BRUNO.) Are you doing the right thing?

BRUNO: That doesn't concern me.

DIDO: Not concern you. You just do what you're told.

BRUNO: Yes.

DIDO: Leave the room! Well, go on.

BRUNO: Don't be a fool.

RUPERT: You mustn't make fun of him. He's an unenviable job in front of him.

DIDO: Can't he wait downstairs. Oh, hell? (HARRY *has come up the stairway. His hands are bandaged and the burns on his face have been treated with a vivid dye.*) Go 'way, Harry.

HARRY: Peace, honey. Forster, I want to say something t'you. I want t'say something t'you. Listen—now listen. It's this. You're wrong, see. The whole way you've gone is'n insult to what y'could be. Don't ask me why it's wrong. I d'know why. But I feel it—here! Is that g'enough for you? I'm a man. All right, too, I'm a drunk. I've no pretty pictures left in me no more, I was born in a barn and my mammy knew my daddy just five minutes one hot afternoon—but I'm a man, Forster. And the way I've lived has been right, Forster, and the way you've lived has been wrong. You know something? You're wicked. That's it! You're just wicked. (*He sways at the head of the stairs.*)

DIDO: For Godsake, Harry!

HARRY: That's all, sweetheart. I've said it. That's all.

DIDO: Well, if you've said it just go off to bed.

HARRY: You want me to go to bed. That's funny. It's no remedy now, Dideeodo. No remedy at all. Can't draw the blanket of love over our heads now. Why can't? Because it's too late. Look, it's morning. Time to get up!

DIDO: Oh, you're—

HARRY: Drunk, I know. These damned stairs! They look to go so far down—they look they might go to hell.

DIDO: Try them.

HARRY: Hullo. (*He speaks to* CATHERINE, *who has come up the stairs.*)

CATHERINE: There you are.

HARRY: Here I am. You want me?

CATHERINE: No, I don't want you. What are you doing up here?

HARRY: Just looked up to tell Forster something.

CATHERINE: The doctor said you were to lie down. Try to sleep.

HARRY: Sleep it off? My hands hurt like hell, Kate. My hands.

CATHERINE: Well, what do you expect? It was a very silly thing to do.

HARRY: It was the only thing to do, surely. I just wanted you to feel something for me. Just anything—pity, or whatever you've left over. (HARRY *goes down the stairs.*)

CATHERINE: Captain Hurst, the Chancellor wants to speak to you.

BRUNO: I've orders not to leave General Forster.

CATHERINE: Who gave you those orders?

BRUNO: The Chancellor.

CATHERINE: Well, then—

BRUNO: Where is he?

CATHERINE: Immediately below. (BRUNO *goes down the stairs.*) Are you ready to go?

RUPERT: I'm ready when they are. They said daylight.

The first light has come to the eastern sky. DIDO *has put on* HARRY'S *sheepskin coat and gone on to the balcony. She stands beside a man who can now be seen beyond the window.*

CATHERINE: Will you need anything? Anything I can get for you.

RUPERT: I've everything I want. Did Cadmus really ask to see the boy, or did you invent that?

CATHERINE: No, he asked for him.

RUPERT: Why?

CATHERINE: I don't know. Now I'm trying to think of something to say that will keep you with me for a little longer. This seeing people off.

RUPERT: Walk away. Just let me go.

CATHERINE: I've always done that. First to war and then to prison. All in all, I've been a good soldier's woman, haven't I? And yet I wish I could have come a little nearer to you in the past few hours. I've failed. It's not a pleasant feeling. Have I been too concerned with myself? I wouldn't like to leave you with the thought that I've intruded my own unhappiness. Haven't you anything to say to me?

RUPERT: I don't think so.

CATHERINE: My God, couldn't you make up something for this moment? Dear, dear Rupert, there's nothing of the harlot player about you, is there? If you've nothing to say then you keep quiet. This is goodbye, Robert—goodbye. When the trial's over you'll not come back here. I know that. We'll never see each other again. Never. I'm sorry. I'm behaving like this because I don't understand. I've tried. There are some things that are right to me and there are some things that are wrong. I can't tell you why they are right or wrong because I don't know. I suppose like most women I feel—I don't reason. And it is the feeling for rightness which made me take you and will make me love you for ever. There. Now I just want to say goodbye.

RUPERT: Goodbye, Catherine.

CATHERINE: Goodbye. (RUPERT *has moved to* CATHERINE. *He puts his arms about her for a moment. She whispers.*) No, don't say you love me. (CATHERINE *goes down the stairs.* RUPERT *stands watching her. Then, he calls.*)

RUPERT: Time to go home, Dido.

DIDO *comes into the room.*

DIDO: I know. Funny—this morning didn't take me by surprise.

RUPERT: You were watching for it.

DIDO: I suppose so. Would you like this coat? We could steal it from Harry. He'd never know. It's warm. Keep you warm in Arcady, it would.

RUPERT: No.

DIDO: Can I send you things? Will they let me do that? Cigarettes and things.

RUPERT: I don't smoke.

DIDO: Of course you don't. Well, books and—oh, you know— cakes. I cook sometimes.

RUPERT: They won't allow anything to be sent.

DIDO: Letters?

RUPERT: No. Save your pennies.

DIDO: All right. You want to finish here and now.

RUPERT: Here and now. I want to give you this, that's all. (*He takes the jewelled box which was given to him by* CADMUS *from a pocket and holds it out to* DIDO.) Take it.

DIDO: Thank you:

RUPERT: There's nothing in it, I'm afraid. Just a box. Do to keep your powder dry.

DIDO: Did it belong to Catherine?

RUPERT: No.

DIDO: Then I'll take it. Thank you very much.

RUPERT: I want you to go now. I want you to leave at once. Don't wait about. On your way give a message to Captain Hurst from me. You know, the young soldier.

DIDO: What is it?

RUPERT: Tell him he's mistaken if he thinks he has learnt or will learn anything from my behaviour. I faced the same problems over the same ground as that man—(*the wearer of the helmet*)—and young Hurst will face them in the future. They are unchanging but the time and place of decision is personal.

DIDO: I'll try to remember that. To tell him, I mean. Have you anything to tell me?

RUPERT: Only this. Don't stay caught in the memory of the past day. Escape. Get out.

DIDO: I will. (*She holds out her hand.* RUPERT *takes it with his left hand. Leaving* DIDO *he goes to the upper room.*)

RUPERT: Goodbye, Dido.

DIDO: Goodbye.

RUPERT *enters the upper room. An Announcer on the public address system of the city speaks.*

ANNOUNCER: The time is zero four one five hours. The time is zero four one five hours. It is now—officially—Day. (*A bell is struck. The man on the balcony enters the room, crosses, and goes down the stairs. The* ANNOUNCER *speaks again.*) Attention! Here is a statement. General Rupert Forster is dead. General Rupert Forster is dead. Further reports follow later.

A bell is struck. DIDO *is staring towards the upper room.* CATHERINE *comes from below.*

CATHERINE: Where? (DIDO *points to the upper room.*) Is it true?

DIDO: I don't know.

CATHERINE: Go up. Go up there. (DIDO *moves slowly to the upper room.* CATHERINE *calls.*) Rupert! Rupert! (DIDO, *at the door of the room, looks back.*) Go on. Please! (DIDO *enters the room.* CADMUS, *alone, comes up the stairs.* CATHERINE *speaks to him.*) You're lying! I don't trust you.

   DIDO *returns.*

DIDO: It's true. There's a little stain at the corner of his mouth.

CADMUS: He'd only to break the glass before his face. He knew well enough.

CATHERINE: And you knew he'd do it.

CADMUS: Yes.

CATHERINE: Surely enough to tell them to say that over the speakers while he was still alive?

CADMUS: Yes. I gave instructions for the guard to be withdrawn and for that announcement to be made at daybreak. I gave those instructions some hours ago. (DIDO *has come down into the room and now goes down the stairs.*) The news of his return was beginning to get out. The morning papers might have got it. I couldn't allow it to happen that way. I could never have controlled the demand for him. They won't want a dead man. Also that was the only method by which I could tell the opposition of their failure. To tell them I was forced to tell everyone—even you—in that way.

CATHERINE: You were so sure? You can't have been! It was a gamble.

CADMUS: It was a certainty. I knew the man and I knew the situation. That was all I needed.

CATHERINE: Did you know him so well? You must have known him better than I did for I believed he would live.

CADMUS: I knew him as a man to be very much like myself. But he'd something I've had to put away whilst I'm in office. Honour. So I knew what the end would be.

CATHERINE: Honour. That means nothing. A word.

CADMUS: You're thinking of these last hours as a struggle between you and myself for his life. It was nothing of the kind. He was quite free to choose.

CATHERINE: Why do you say that? You wanted him to do it for a purpose.

CADMUS: I don't deny it. But I'm an old man, Catherine, and apart from the smallest things I don't do much to please myself. All I said of the situation in the country at the moment is true.

CATHERINE: You murdered him.

CADMUS: No. We're all victims of injustice, Catherine, every moment of our lives. We can shut ourselves up in the day and lie awake at night dreaming of revenge. But revenge against whom? Against each other? Why? Forster had great cause to dream in that way. It was an injustice that we had to imprison him, and he had reason to sit in that camp in the hills thinking up ways of reckoning. But he didn't do that. All he wanted was to be taken back into the service of the world. The world wouldn't have him and so he turned away. In acceptance. There was no hatred in him. He was a great soldier. Learn from him.

CATHERINE: Will you learn?

CADMUS: I can't allow myself to do so. At ten o'clock this morning I shall make a statement to the House and tell them the lies they want to hear. I shall belittle Forster's past achievements and say that he died under a burden of conscience. The sooner forgotten the better. That's the great thing. That he should be forgotten.

CATHERINE: Go, now. Go down and tell your lies.

CADMUS: Very well. Do I need to say how much your friendship has meant to me. In the past.

CATHERINE: Are you trying to tell me that you, too, have made a sacrifice?

CADMUS: I suppose I am.

BRUNO *comes from below.*

BRUNO: The guard is dismissed, sir.

CADMUS: Thank you, Captain Hurst.

BRUNO: You called me away from him, sir.

CADMUS: What's that?

BRUNO: You called me away. If you'd not done so this wouldn't have happened.

CADMUS: Wouldn't it?

BRUNO: I shall deny dereliction of duty.

CADMUS: It won't be necessary, Captain Hurst. What are you afraid of?

BRUNO: The incident was unavoidable, sir. I didn't want to leave him.

CADMUS: I called you away. The responsibility is mine.

BRUNO: Thank you, sir.

CADMUS: But sometime—when you've nothing better to do—reflect on the consequences to yourself if I'd refused to admit it.

Catherine, you'd better have someone here for a day or two. Hurst can make all arrangements for this and that.

CATHERINE: Very well.

CADMUS: May I call on you once again?

CATHERINE: I think not.

JOHN CADMUS *goes down the stairs.*

BRUNO: The house is no longer under guard, ma'am. You're free to go where you wish.

CATHERINE: Where do you suggest?

BRUNO: There's no need to concern yourself any longer with General Forster. All arrangements will be made.

CATHERINE: Then I'll forget him at once, Captain Hurst. At once.

DIDO *comes up the stairs. She has changed into her own clothes.*

DIDO: The old Cadmus man has gone, and now I must be going. I suppose that's all right.

BRUNO: Everyone in the house is quite free now.

DIDO: Well, I've come up to say goodbye.

CATHERINE: Did Rupert tell you what he was going to do?

DIDO: No. He just said goodbye and walked up there.

CATHERINE: You don't seem touched by what's happened.

DIDO: There was nothing else for him to do, was there? (BRUNO *turns to go from the room.*) I've got a message for you.

BRUNO: For me?

DIDO: From Rupert. Let me get it right. You're not to think that you learnt anything from him. You'll face the same problems— same place, perhaps—but you've got to find your own way out. All right?

BRUNO: Yes. (BRUNO *goes down the stairs.*)

CATHERINE: Did Rupert give you a message for me?

DIDO: No. He said he loved you.

CATHERINE: I'd like you to stay here.

DIDO: I can't do that. The life I live isn't much, I know, but it's the way I want it.

CATHERINE: And you think I'd take that from you.

DIDO: Well, I'd not have it in this place. Why do you want me to stay now? Good turn?

CATHERINE: Oh, no—it's for my sake, not yours. I'd like to try to live again. Help me.

DIDO: Please let me go now.

CATHERINE: Wait! I'm not offering the things I'd have offered before. Money, clothes and amusement. I've learnt enough from you to know they won't keep you. I'm not offering you anything. Listen! You are the only person in nine years who has broken into my life against my wish. I've chosen others—people who wouldn't lead me away from Rupert. So, you see, they can't help me, but you can. Just for a little while, Dido.

DIDO: No! You'll eat me right up. Then you'll be fine, but where shall I be?

CATHERINE: You can have absolute freedom, I promise. Just live here.

DIDO: I like you, Catherine—always have. And you're good and strong, really. You can do it all without me.

CATHERINE: I'm not. Rupert's dead.

DIDO: Well, then, it's too bad. You'll just have to go downhill. Look, the sun's shining. It's going to be a fine day. (HARRY *comes up the stairs.*) Perhaps I'll walk out into the country and sleep through the day in the open. Who knows?

HARRY: You going? Hey! you can talk to me. I'm sober.

DIDO: I'd talk to you if there was anything to say, but there isn't. Goodbye. (DIDO *goes down the stairs.*)

HARRY: I've been thinking, Kate. Let's sell up—sell out. You settled here because of him, that's all. Nothing to keep you now. Let's get away.

CATHERINE: No.

HARRY: All right. We stay. Kate, he wasn't any good. He wasn't worth waiting for. It wasn't what he was but what he did. You made a mistake anybody might've made and I'm sorry for you. Truly, I'm sorry for you. He walked out on you, Kate. I'm staying with you. Surely that's in my favour. And I'll get on with the picture. Honest. (FATHER ANSELM *and* MATTHEW SANGOSSE *come up the stairs.* CATHERINE *has moved to stand looking through the windows over the city.*) Hullo, boys. So here we are. Let's start the day. I'll do that with a bath. God! I'm filthy. Kate, can I go and freshen up?

CATHERINE: Do as you like. There's no need to ask me. Please go on as you've done in the past. There's all the time in the world now for us to be kind, for us to do good. Let me look at you. Come here. How shall we spend the time? All the time that's left. What shall we do with it? This fortune to be rid of. Shall we be charitable? Give me your part and I'll give you mine. But we have equal portions which makes it absurd. We shall end up where we began with no more and no less. There'll be no loss, no gain, but it will pass the time—the time we have to spend—it will pass the time, this give and take—it will pass the time. O dear Christ, I'm cold!

   HARRY *takes up the sheepskin coat and puts it over* CATHERINE'S *shoulders. Then, with his arm about her, he leads her back into the room. The morning light catches* CATHERINE'S *face: it shows her as an aged woman.*

HARRY: Not to worry, Kate. We're here. We won't let anybody hurt you—not any more we won't. (DIDO *comes up the stairs.*) What do you want? Well, what d'you want? You back for something?

DIDO (*whispers*): Go 'way, Harry.

HARRY: What're you back for?

DIDO: Changed my mind.

HARRY: So, all right, you've changed your mind. From what to what?

DIDO: Go 'way, Harry, go 'way. (*She moves towards* CATHERINE.) Catherine. What I know. Can it be taught? I'll try.

                    CURTAIN